[...] tener en la [...]
Pres. Muy bien en lo [posible...] [...] en
[...]
Esp. [...] en una forma [...]
[...]miento y concentración.
Pres. Muy bien.
Esp. Es todo.
Pres. Da cuenta de la inauguración del centro "Isis" de Don Pablo que es dejada
20 del entrante, sea el 23 de este mes, pues nos comprenderán que el [...]
[...]tendrá igual éxito, todos estigan [sentados?] por las fiestas de las P[...]
y hubo cambio de miembros en la Directiva.
Esp. ¿Por que?
Pres. Por renuncia de algunos socios.
Pres. [...] vendremos estará aquí, pues los actos no lo haran [...] y la lectura de las
[...] de los hermanos del centro "Isis."
Esp. ¿Iremos nosotros y [...]?
Pres. Yo, [...] y el Presidente del centro el Progreso y alguna que otro
hermano que quieran seguir.
Esp. [...] ¿que mas?
Pres. ¿Está aprobada esta inauguración?
Esp. [Si...]
Pres. Da cuenta que una hermana fijó una propaganda en la calle Valencia
distrito de Sanpedro.
Esp. Si.
Pres. Pide la resolución sobre las visiones que se vienen manifestando en las
[...]siones, que no redunda mas que en amenazas, que llegarán el [...]
[...] nuestros de visionario.
Esp. ¿Cuando?
Pres. [Sesión] en plena sesión, obligando a los mediums videntes a que vean
Esp. Bien cuantas sesiones [...]
Pres. Todos los jueves y los sábados estudios.
Esp. Bien, en cada sesión debeis de tener programas anunciado con dos se
manas de anticipación y en cada sesión los videntes, deberán procura-
no recibir visiones que no necesiten transmisión al público, en lo suce
sivo debéis preparar los programas de cada sesión o conferencia

What Others are saying about *The Secret Teachings of the Espiritistas*

In the Book of Solomon we are told that "Wisdom builds her temple." Harvey Martin has shown that "Wisdom builds her temple" in the poor and broken bodies of the people of the Philippines as a witness to the world. Harvey Martin's remarkable book cuts far deeper than the psychic surgeon's knife, for it cuts through many veils of religious history and the outer garments of ritual...examines the long-hidden relationship of biblical texts and the realization of 'healing power' that opens the eyes and ears of the reader. In the rainy atmosphere and small halls of the remote jungles and in the dusty urban centers of the Philippines, the 'small, still voice speaks' – and we encounter the powerful force behind the Espiritistas...the 'Holy Spirit.'

- **J.J. Hurtak Ph.D.**
Researcher and Director of the Academy of Future Science
Author of *The Keys of Enoch*

In The Secret Teachings of the Espiritistas, Harvey Martin has presented a lucid, provocative account of Filipino Christian Spiritism. This book makes a valuable contribution to the literature on folk healing, its adherants, and its practitioners.

-Stanley Krippner Ph.D.
Professor of Psychology
Saybrook Graduate School
Co-author of *The Mythic Path*
and *Realms of Healing*

Harvey Martin's book is a probing search into the mysteries of healing. It is a venture into a world too long ignored by orthodox medicine. This book should be taken seriously by anyone interested in the relationship between spirituality and healing.

-Larry Dossey MD
Author of *Be Careful What You Pray For,*
Prayer Is Good Medicine, and
Healing Words
Executive editor, *Alternative Therapies in Health and Medicine*

The Secret Teachings Of The Espiritistas

Harvey Martin

Harvey Martin

Published by:
Metamind Publications
Post Office Box 15548
Savannah, GA 31416

THE SECRET TEACHINGS OF THE ESPIRITISTAS
Copyright 1998 by Harvey J. Martin III
All rights reserved.
No part of this book may be reproduced
or transmitted in any form or by any means, electronic
or mechanical, including photocopying, recording or
by any information storage and retrieval system
without written permission from the author,
except for the inclusion of brief quotations
in critical articles and reviews.

Endpapers are a reproduction of the original
Minutes of the Union Espiritista, November 9, 1919.
See page 93 for the English translation.

Copyright 1998 by Harvey J. Martin III

Library of Congress Catalog Number 97-092715

ISBN: 0-9660843-8-1

Printed in the United States of America

Printed on recycled paper

TM

Acknowledgements

Words cannot express the thanks I wish to extend to Kitty, the love of my life, for the patience, loving support, and editorial skills she has contributed to this sometimes long and arduous project.

I also want to thank my grandmother for her sage advice and my mother for instilling in me a deep and lasting love of the written word. A special thanks to Ann Fisher for her insight and skillful editing of my book.

My deepest gratitude to my friends in Hawaii and elsewhere who have lived through this amazing saga at my side. This includes of course my many Filipino friends and mentors, including Alex and Marcos Orbito, Froilan Christi, Lino Guinsad, Lita Castellano, and Ester Bacani whom I consider to be members of my very special extended family. A deep and sincere aloha to my friend Donn DeShayne for his typesetting skills and graphic design wizardry evident in the cover design and layout of this book.

To my dear friend and teacher Reverend Benjamin Pajarillo, my eternal gratitude for your love and guidance in the mysteries of the Spirit of Truth. I couldn't have done it without you.

A special thanks to Brother Cypriano Ramos, the archivist of the Union Espiritista Christiana de Filipinas for his invaluable assistance in my research.

Last but not least, I want to offer my thanks to William Henry Belk Jr. for the years of support and encouragement he has extended to me in writing this book. I first met Henry in Manila at the Second International Healing Conference sponsored by the Philippine Healer's Circle in 1985. He had returned to Manila to produce a video documentary on the developments in the work of the Filipino psychic surgeons. Henry had been among the first to seriously study the Filipino psychic surgeons. In 1965, while doing research in the Philippines, he met a charismatic young psychic surgeon named Antonio Agpaoa. Henry was so impressed with Agpaoa's paranormal abilities that he decided to offer financial assistance to the then struggling Agpaoa. With the stipend Agpaoa received from the Belk Foundation, he was able to devote all his time to healing.

In 1967, Henry commissioned the author Harold Sherman to write the book *Wonder Healers of the Philippines* which drew worldwide attention to the psychic surgeons. During a period of our history where challenging the status quo was equivalent to condemning oneself to derision and scorn, Henry pressed forward, funding not only parapsychological research in the Philippines, but Brazil as well. Henry funded Andrija Puharich's study of Arigo, the gifted Brazilian psychic surgeon. It was my good fortune that Henry kept meticulous records of the amazing research he conducted.

In writing this book, as the true nature of the enigma of psychic surgery has unfolded, so too has the enigma of Henry Belk. Henry has had the courage and faith to persevere against tremendous odds so that the hidden purposes of God could be brought to light. Thank you.

Philippine Healers' Circle, Inc.

No. 9 Maryland St., Cubao, Quezon City
Philippines • Tel. 98-59-30
S.E.C. Reg. No. 118187

February 10, 1986

TO WHOM THIS MAY CONCERN:

    This is to certify that MR. HARVEY MARTIN III is a bona fide member of the Philippine Healers' Circle, Inc. and is therefore entitled to all rights and privileges appurtenant thereto.

    This is to certify further that in the annual conference and election of the Philippine Healers' Circle, Inc. held on January 29, 1986 at the Manila Midtown Hotel, MR. HARVEY MARTIN III was duly elected by the general membership to the 15-man Board of Directors and was subsequently appointed as Vice President for the U.S.A.

    As member of the Philippine Healers' Circle, Inc., more specifically as Director and Regional Vice President of the P. H. C., MR. HARVEY MARTIN III is expected to fulfill his duties and obligations to the Circle, among them the promotion of the goals and objectives of this organization.

    MR. HARVEY MARTIN III is therefore commissioned to undertake membership and fund campaigns in his region for and in behalf of the Philippine Healers' Circle, Inc. and his official acts shall be deemed as extensions of presidential prerogatives. It shall be understood, however, that such acts must be for and in the best interests of the Philippine Healers' Circle, Inc.

    For reference and authentication, the specimen signature of MR. HARVEY MARTIN III is being affixed in this document.

HARVEY MARTIN III

Thank you for your kind attention and cooperation.

MELVIN S. ADVIOR   REV. ALEX L. ORBITO
Secretary-General   President

:msa
2/10/86

Contents

Copyright Page	iv
Acknowledgements	v
Foreward	viii
Introduction	xi

Chapters

1.	Miracles on the Big Island	1
2.	Into the Realm of Espiritu Santo	21
3.	From Shaman to Christian	49
4.	The Union Espiritista Christiana de Filipinas	65
5.	The Spiritual Messengers of Christ	83
6.	Christian Mediumship Training	111
7.	The Enigma of Psychic Surgery	145
8.	Psychic Surgery and Placebo Research	163
9.	Spirit-Directed Psychic Surgery	181
10.	The Coming of the Holy Spirit	203

Glossary	243
Index	250
Permissions	256
Bibliography	257
Illustrations Credits	264

FOREWORD

"The Secret Teachings of the Espiritistas" provides never before published details of obscure religious sects in the Philippines and Brazil and brings to light a spiritual legacy that has remained enshrouded in mystery for centuries. Poised, as we are, at the dawning of a new millennium, our understanding of this spiritual legacy takes on an urgent importance. The teachings that Harvey received from the Filipino Espiritistas are nothing less than the hidden history of the Holy Spirit. In this remarkable account, the ecclesiastical facade is stripped away to reveal the living essence of a Christian tradition that evolved independently in the obscurity and isolation of the rural areas of both the Philippines and Brazil.

Harvey applies the teachings of the Espiritistas, and projects this spiritual legacy into the present to establish himself as one of the prominant philosophers of a new spiritual dispensation; still in its infancy. As we examine the work of the Holy Spirit from a historical perspective we discover the common ground that links the spiritual consciousness that emerged during the Civil Rights Movement, the Counterculture, and the worldwide emergence of Charismatic Christianity both within and outside the orthodox Catholic and Protestant Churches. The links between these seemingly unconnected events lead us to conclude that that the Spirit of God is setting the stage for the spiritualization of humanity and ultimately the emergence of a divine civilization here on earth. The "Kingdom of Heaven," the "New Age," the "Millennium," and "Fifth World" are among the names used to describe this coming civilization. What you choose to call this awakened civilization, however, is less important than understanding how this spiritual paradigm shift is emerging.

Seoul, Korea - December 1986: Standing at the curb at a busy intersection at the front end of a crowd of pedestrians waiting impatiently to cross the main thoroughfare-the traffic light turns to indicate "Walk" and in a great hurry the man beside me steps off the curb and I instinctively follow suit, but something stops me. My foot stays as if frozen to the curb while a car, speeding to run the light, smashes this man just a few feet in front of me, immediately taking his life. My heartbeat goes through the roof and I become weak-kneed with the realization that I have just narrowly escaped death. What stopped me? What held me back from stepping off the curb? Details of the street, the crowd, the man, have faded from my memory, but the unforgettable experience of "something" having intervened to save my life is as clear to me today as the moment it happened.

Divine intervention is a fact of life that a great many of us have encountered and set aside because there is no place for this experience in our belief structure. That is about to change if you are able to read ahead with an open mind. Among the Espiritistas, the experience of divine intervention has evolved within their mediumistic culture to the extent that trained Christian mediums regularly confer with the Holy Spirit. This dialogue with the Holy Spirit is the source not only of their spiritual insight, but the paranormal abilities of their healers as well. The Espiritistas have long recognized that the spiritual nature that lives within each and every human being is the common thread that links humanity to the divine as well as to each other. Within this inner sanctuary, the Spirit of God embraces every individual, every race and culture. The Holy Spirit is available to all humanity regardless of religious beliefs.

I have closely followed the works of Harvey Martin for the past twenty-seven years, during which time his life has been dedicated to healing as part and parcel of spiritual development. His hands-on research on the dynamics of mind/body healing and the spiritual context of healing has been a life-long pursuit that has taken him to the far corners of the Earth. Though he has consistently taken the intellectual, theoretical, and academic points of view into consideration, Harvey has never hesitated to test conventional wisdom against the pragmatic results of the broad range of healing practices he has researched. It is the conflict between conventional wisdom and his own well documented research that has led to this book.

If a particular healing technique produces compelling results that diverge from what conventional wisdom would lead us to expect, Harvey applies the scientific method and perseveres until he has found a plausible explanation. He not only studies, but lives his subject matter whether it be New Age healing techniques in Hawaii, acupuncture in Sri Lanka, or psychic surgery in the Philippines. His study of the much maligned and controversial practice of psychic surgery epitomizes the eclectic research methods with which he has unraveled one enigma after the next.

Over the past twenty-seven years, due to my association with the author I have been chiropractically adjusted, cupped, and shiatsued. I have been successfully treated with magnets, diagnosed with pendulums and received psychic surgery from the Espiritist Reverend Alex Orbito. My tastebuds have been assaulted by herbal remedies and I have spent hours wearing light-emitting goggles and stereo headphones for the latest in biofeedback relaxation and healing. And I'm just a run-of-the-mill kind of guy. Joking aside, I feel honored and priviledged to have travelled some of the many paths that have led the author to become one of the most knowledgeable and well respected leaders in the world-wide non-conventional healing community. The pursuit of alternative healing practices that led Harvey to research Filipino Espiritism as it relates to psychic surgery has served to resurrect the heart of Christianity as well as other religions by disclosing a parallel spiritual dimension in which we exist and which we have the capacity to perceive. Read on with an open mind, enjoy, and grow.

Daniel Foxman
Honolulu, Hawaii

x

THE CHRISTIAN SPIRITIST OF THE PHILIPPINES, INC.
HEAD OFFICE: 94 Roxas St., Trancoville
Baguio City
S.E.C. Reg. No. 29382

№ 141

CERTIFICATE OF AUTHORITY

TO ALL MEN THIS PRESENT MAY COME GREETINGS:
This is to certify that

REVEREND HARVEY J. MARTIN III

of legal age, and resident of P.O. BOX 1342 PAHOA, HAWAII 96778 whose picture and signature appearing is hereby named by the General Membership and through the inspiration of the Holy Spirit as the **MEDIUM HEALER** and concurrently **MINISTER** of the above mentioned religious organization. And by virtue of which he/she is empowered by the constitution and by laws to exercise and propagate the noble aims and purposes duly embodied thereon.

All presents and future members of the Christian Spiritists are hereby enjoined to give respect and honor to the subject **MINISTER**.

Done at Baguio City Philippines this 30th day of March in the year of our Lord one thousand nine hundred and eighty eight.

Affix with dry seal of the said religious organization.

APPROVED:

REV. PRUDENCIO C. HIPOL
General Secretary

REV. BENJAMIN A. PAJARILLO
Bishop

ATTESTED:

Rev. Harvey J. Martin III
Signature of Holder

MONSIGNOR DIONISIO GASPAR
General Minister

INTRODUCTION

*T*he longing for proof of God's existence is among the most persistent and unquenchable thirsts of the human spirit. This longing exists not only among followers of organized religions but throughout the great majority of the human race. Of all the phenomena that demonstrate the miraculous intervention of God, none is more personal or credible than the spontaneous restoration of health. From a scientific perspective, the restoration of health is an empirical fact that can be measured in a number of ways. On a personal level, the restoration of health may lead to a deep and lasting transformation in one's own appreciation of and reverence for life. Beginning with the works of Jesus and the Apostles in the biblical narrative, spiritual healing has demonstrated the manifest power of God for centuries and continues to do so. In 1972, I moved to Hawaii. A bona fide member of the counterculture, I, like many others was disillusioned with mainstream American society. In the islands, I discovered lots of people who, like myself, were ready to explore the evolutionary possibilities of a world that had never before existed. The dawning information age gave us access, for the first time in history, to the collective knowledge of the entire human race. Access to this collective knowledge suggested that we were destined to discover new, if not ultimate, horizons of both temporal and spiritual knowledge. As we learned of the accomplishments of other cultures, we discovered much that we believed would benefit American culture. In Eastern religion, we found precise systems of physical culture, dietary models, and methods of breathing, all designed to enhance and facilitate the higher evolution of human beings towards the eventual emergence of a spiritualized world. Western religions, which espoused salvation for the few, markedly contrasted with the Eastern concept of enlightenment for all.

The intricate and all-inclusive systems of spiritual philosophy that we discovered in the Orient, such as Hinduism and Buddhism, made the religious teachings of Western society seem incomplete at best.

After years of living in a virtual clearing house of unconventional healing practices, I thought that I had heard and seen it all. Nothing, however, could have prepared me for "psychic surgery." Psychic surgery was so far beyond my imaginings that, after many years of research and healing practice, I felt I was starting all over. This controversial alternative healing method was introduced to me through a dear friend who had sustained a serious injury which had refused to heal. He learned of the work of Filipino psychic surgeons and went to the Philippines for treatment. Subsequently, he returned with his injury much improved and photographs of his operation. He explained that during his 'operation,' the psychic surgeon had opened his shoulder with his bare hands and removed a piece of tissue from the shoulder socket, which the psychic surgeon identified as scar tissue. Once the operation was complete, the psychic surgeon removed his hands from within his shoulder and, with a simple gesture, closed the opening in his shoulder with no scar or sign of entry. As he told me of his experience, he showed me the series of photographs that had been taken during the operation. As for the results, his shoulder was much better but still not fully healed.

Seeing the photographic record of my friend's psychic surgery convinced me that it was worthy of further research. Soon, I would get a chance to observe psychic surgery firsthand. My friend and I arranged for the psychic surgeon, Alex Orbito, to visit Hawaii, and conduct a spiritual healing mission. This is described at length in the first chapter. Following the healing mission, Alex invited my friend and me to visit the Philippines and produce a video documentary on his life and work. While there, I immersed myself in the fascinating world of Alex Orbito's spiritual healing center in Quezon City. It didn't take long to figure out that there was international controversy surrounding psychic surgery.

While parapsychologists were seeking a scientific explanation for how the human body can be opened and closed without leaving a scar, debunkers and skeptics insisted that psychic surgery was a fraud....a scam devised only to make money by offering false hope to the sick. The worst criticism of psychic surgery was precipitated by the discovery that operations often involved sleight-of-hand simulations of surgical operations. Within the parameters of Western medical ethics, any therapeutic intervention that involves the use of deception is considered to be unethical and, consequently, without merit. The discovery of sleight-of-hand operations led to a media blitz that portrayed psychic surgery as medical fraud, and psychic surgeons as criminals. Psychic surgery was thoroughly discredited. As a result, everyone assumed the final word had been heard, and psychic surgery was no longer discussed, except in derogatory terms.

Unlike most of the detractors of psychic surgery, I experienced psychic surgery as it is practiced in the Philippines. Having seen both sides, I believed that much of the confusion about psychic surgery existed because it was being represented out of context. In both Hawaii and the Philippines, I was impressed with the beneficial results of psychic surgery. Working at Alex Orbito's healing center in Quezon City, I found that skeptics were choosing to ignore the successes of psychic surgery and dwelling solely on the failings of the healers. In spite of the silence of numerous 'scientific experts,' I could see that many of the sick people who made the arduous trip to the Philippines were recovering from serious illnesses after receiving psychic surgery. In some cases, the dramatic cures I witnessed bore a strong resemblance to miracles.

The contradictions between what I had seen and the 'conventional wisdom' about psychic surgery puzzled me. Why were so many people getting positive results from something that the American scientific, legal, and medical communities claimed had no redeeming value? While psychic surgery was regarded as medical fraud in the United States, it was the subject of serious research in the Philippines and was taken quite seriously. The central question in early research efforts into psychic surgery was: What unknown laws of physics enabled the psychic surgeon to open and close the body? While foreign researchers speculated endlessly, the psychic surgeons identified the source of the healing phenomenon as the Holy Spirit. Researchers from around the world scoffed at the idea that the third person of the Christian Trinity was performing psychic operations through uneducated, impoverished Filipinos. These same researchers, who were quick to criticize the Filipino belief in the Holy Spirit as superstition and ignorance, never succeeded in identifying the underlying source of genuine psychic surgery.

They did, however, discover that much of what was claimed to be psychic surgery operations were, in fact, sleight-of-hand simulations of genuine psychic surgery. Despite the well documented evidence of genuine psychic surgery, the opponents of alternative healing chose to insist that *all* psychic surgery was a medical fraud. The situation degenerated to the point that both believers and nonbelievers began to analyze tissue and blood taken from the operations to determine if the operations had been "faked." Results from these tests remained contradictory and inconclusive. Meanwhile, oblivious to the heated debates going on around them, the psychic surgeons continued to successfully heal people from all over the world. At the center in Quezon City, there was absolutely no question that psychic surgery was a powerful healing method.

The cures brought about by psychic surgery, even when well documented, continued to be ignored or were deemed 'imaginary.' Yet, it was dramatically apparent that these cures were *not* imaginary. Many of the researchers I met were so intellectually arrogant that even empirical evidence of the restoration of health, such as X-rays and blood tests were disregarded. I could easily understand why the healers were fed up with researchers who privately admitted that they could detect no fraud, yet refused to publicly acknowledge what they admitted privately for fear of professional criticism. Alex Orbito addressed the irrational attitudes of the "scientific" researchers in saying that the purpose of the healers was "not to convince the people, but to cure the people."

Many early researchers into the enigma of psychic surgery found parallels between the healing work they observed, and a medical mystery known as the 'placebo effect.' They strongly suggested that these parallels be investigated. In my research, I have examined the practice of sleight-of-hand psychic surgery and identified therapeutic elements common to both it and the placebo effect. When studied in the light of modern scientific research into mind/body medicine I discovered that the sleight-of-hand simulations of surgical operations, the most reviled and discredited aspect of Filipino faith healing, was a valid healing method in its own right. I also learned that the American medical profession had done its own studies on what they called 'placebo surgery' and found that in their experiments, it produced better results.....than 'real' surgery. I was shocked to discover that even the so-called fraudulent sleight-of-hand operations could be understood as an innovative method of placebo delivery. A method that could be expected, based on medical research, to cure at least 35 percent of the patients who received it. Advances in our scientific understanding of belief-mediated physiological response suggests that those who judged the therapeutic use of sleight-of-hand to be an unethical scam were a bit premature in that judgment.

Though sleight-of-hand psychic surgery is a fact, much of the psychic surgery I had seen did not involve sleight-of-hand. I reviewed the studies that had been done on psychic surgery in the 1970's. These studies produced well documented proof that the paranormal phenomena produced by the healers was authentic. In the absence of any scientific explanation for the phenomena of spirit-directed psychic surgery, the only remaining explanation was the assertion of the Filipinos that the Holy Spirit was the source of their paranormal abilities.

The role of the Holy Spirit in the extraordinary healing activities of Jesus and the Apostles, is rarely regarded as having any direct bearing on contemporary Western Christianity. Jesus is central to Western Christian theology, and the Holy Spirit, when spoken of at all, is spoken of mostly in allegorical terms. Christian theologians have gone to great lengths to refute any connection between the work of the Holy Spirit and the paranormal. Western Christianity has long since abandoned any pretense of being a venue for the active intervention of spirits of any kind.

The Filipinos explained to me that in the person of the Holy Spirit, a Divine spiritual power, one that is positively good and beneficial, not only exists, but intervenes through those who were prepared to receive that power. During my discussions with the Filipinos about the role of the Holy Spirit in healing, they used the Bible as their sole reference to support their beliefs. Ultimately, they convinced me that, based on the biblical narrative, there was indeed plenty of evidence that supported their belief in the active intervention of the Holy Spirit.

As my research led me ever deeper into Christianity, I had to face strong personal aversions that I had developed growing up among Southern Baptists in Georgia during the civil rights movement. I attended a church composed mostly of lower middle-class Southerners who actively opposed civil rights for black people. Even as a child, I could see that racial hatred was the direct antithesis of Jesus' teachings. One of the turning points of my life occurred during a radio interview I heard on a black radio station in Savannah, Georgia, in the early 60's. The person being interviewed was Dr. Martin Luther King Jr.. During the interview, Dr. King indicted the racist elements of mainstream American culture and religion in the terminology of an erudite Christian minister.

In the face of racial violence, aided and abetted by mainstream southern evangelical and fundamentalist Christians, King pointedly challenged white Americans to live up to their own professed Christian values. In contrast to the sermons of white racist ministers, Dr. King's words emanated holiness. King seemed the very embodiment of Moses, with the Southern establishment playing the role of the stubborn Pharaoh. As I listened to King on the radio, I knew that he was telling the truth. Blatant hypocrisy existed in the spiritual life of white America. Having been raised in an environment where racism and bigotry were taught almost *as* Christian values, I realized that the ideological framework of Fundamentalist Christianity was directly in opposition to key teachings of Jesus. The failure of my Christian role models to "Do unto others as they would have them do unto them" and "Love their neighbors as themselves" led me to reject organized religion at an early age.

My rejection of Southern Baptists didn't change my feelings about God, or even Jesus. My experiences did, however, make it very clear that organized religion could easily become a front for mob rule. Seeing Christian ministers use Jesus' teachings to incite racist hatred convinced me that something was seriously wrong with them. Though it was obvious that Christians could be easily misled, I still found the Bible to be a fascinating and mysterious document. In my research in the Philippines, I was reintroduced to the Bible in a new and profound context.

According to the Filipino healers, encoded within the texts of the Bible were the means of communicating directly with the Holy Spirit. They assured me that they had established a dialogue with the Holy Spirit, and had been taught how to heal in the same capacity that Jesus and the Apostles had demonstrated in the biblical narrative of the New Testament. They also made it clear that God had intentionally led me to experience the dark side of literal fundamentalism to instill in me an intense curiosity about spirituality, and to motivate me to search until I found the truth. As I researched the anthropological and historical events that had taken place in Filipino culture, and which had enabled the Filipinos to conceive of and practice psychic surgery, I discovered a secret tradition from which the contemporary spiritual healing work of the Filipinos had emerged. The Filipinos brought to my attention the fact that, of all the founders of the world religions, only Jesus had modeled his work along the lines of a healing ministry. Jesus apparently saw healing as an excellent means of conveying the message that the power of the Divine was ever present, willing and able to interact with human beings in this world. Jesus taught his followers that, after he was gone, the paranormal healing work that was the cornerstone of his ministry would continue under the aegis of the Holy Spirit. In a culture whose pre-Christian religion revolved around establishing dialogues with spirits for purposes of healing and exorcism, the Filipinos found themselves in familiar territory in the biblical narratives about the paranormal healing activities of Jesus and the Apostles.

As a lifelong student of the healing arts, I realized that the Filipinos had discovered in the teachings of Jesus what I had discovered in Eastern philosophy: an intricate system of spiritual development. This system is the secret tradition from which all of the paranormal healing practices of the Filipinos emerged; it speaks to the original intent of Jesus and the purpose of the mission of hope that he tirelessly articulated. The doom-and-gloom scenarios of so many modern Bible 'scholars' may well have to be revised in light of the spiritual interpretation of the bible the Filipinos received from the Spirit of Truth. This understanding of the Bible, derived from the uniquely spiritual traditions of Filipino culture and the religious doctrine based on that interpretation, is known as Christian Spiritism. In the following chapters, I will detail the training in Christian Mediumship that I received from the Christian Spiritists. The esoteric healing ministry that I have documented in the Philippine Islands, among the poor, disenfranchised, provincial Christian Spiritists, sheds a great deal of light on some of the most perplexing and ultimately revealing practices of Jesus and the inferences of his teachings.

In the following pages the history of the emergence of the Holy Spirit in the modern world is brought to light. As might be expected, the Christian Spiritist interpretation of the Bible differs in many ways from conventional interpretation. It is possible that the Christian Spiritist interpretation of the Bible might offend and even outrage orthodox Christians. I am convinced, however, that anyone who believes in the veracity of the Bible will be hard pressed to find flaws in their theology. I also think that the information in this book is relevant to anyone whose lives have been touched by the Divine, no matter what their religious beliefs might be.

Over the last thirty years, events in the Philippines have placed the secret tradition in danger of being lost forever. Much of the material used in the writing of this book was derived from translations of the early texts of the Christian Spiritists, provided for me by the elders of the Christian Spiritist Church. I give my heartfelt thanks to those who have offered support and inspiration over the fourteen years I have spent gathering and organizing this information. These documents offer a comprehensive look at the specific events that led to psychic surgery. Events that transpired in the Philippines between 1904 and 1933 within the Christian Spiritist community.

On my many trips to the Philippines, I have been assisted and directed by spiritual forces that have protected me through many challenging times. This book is the final result of being in the right place at the right time, asking the right questions and receiving the right answers far more often than I would attribute to chance. The creative process that has produced this book has made me a true believer in spirit-directed (causal) synchronicity.

During the years I have spent studying and working with Christian Spiritists, I often felt as though I had been transported back through time and allowed to see and understand how the original followers of Jesus conducted their lives. In the Christian Spiritist community of the Philippines, their teachings and religious practices are those of a people who believe themselves to be living under the direct governance of the God's own spirit. Christian Spiritists are thoroughly unconventional; yet, in their practices there is an inner consistency, clarity, and power that illuminates events that took place two thousand years ago.

I have long since abandoned a belief in the supremacy of one religion or belief system over another. The validity of religious systems and beliefs can be measured by the extent that they convey hope, and the opportunity for human beings to grow beyond the confines of fear and materiality into the eternal mystery. In the following pages, I hope to convey the insights I received from the teachings and religious practices of the Christian Spiritists. My purpose in writing this book has changed as my understanding has grown. In writing this book, I have researched a wide range of seemingly unrelated subjects. A partial list of these subjects include spiritualism, mediumship, Fundamentalist Christian theology, placebo cure, imagery in healing, Filipino shamanism, the teachings of Allan Kardec, and the visionary revelations of a Catholic abbot who lived in Italy 700 years ago.

Each of these subjects have been like rungs on a ladder. As I have managed to put each piece of the puzzle into place, I have moved progressively higher up the ladder. Each step up the ladder has taken me further and further into a world that isn't supposed to exist: An inner dimension of Christianity discovered and brought into being in the *only* Christian country in Asia. Most of the following material has never been published before. This material not only contradicts the 'conventional wisdom' about psychic surgery, but Christianity as well. If you have fixed opinions about either, please suspend them for now, and read on.

Initially, I wanted to write this book to tell the other side of a story that has been monopolized by people who have not hesitated to slander and destroy good people who lack the ability to defend themselves. As my knowledge grew, however, I learned that the Filipinos believed that Divine spiritual forces were using the Spiritist community to deliver a message to the people of earth. According to them, psychic surgery was merely a ploy used by the Blessed Spirit to get our attention. The true mystery of psychic surgery lies in the *message* the Blessed Spirit is using healing miracles to deliver. The core of the message is that a transcendent intradimensional being has entered the material world to help us take the next step in our destiny as human beings. This wonderful, elevated spiritual being wants to heal us. Its calling cards are miracles.

This great Spirit of Truth has been working over the ages to spiritualize humanity. The very origins of Christianity lie in the coming of the Holy Spirit. The mass spiritual possession of the Apostles by the Holy Spirit marks the beginning of early Christianity. After pouring itself directly into the bodies of the Apostles at the Pentecost, the Holy Spirit activated spiritual gifts within them through which others were healed and converted. Since then, the Holy Spirit has continued the progressive revelation of the Will of God in a continuing series of events similar to the original Pentecost. These contemporary Pentecosts are similar to the original Pentecost in that they are characterized by the mass spiritual possession of human beings by the Spirit of God. They are different in that they have taken place during different eras of our history and have been interpreted accordingly.

Through these strategically placed ancient and contemporary Pentecost-like events, the stage is being set for the collective spiritual awakening of humanity. Jesus foretold not only the Coming of the Spirit of God, he foretold a new form of worship, one that the true worshipers of God would practice. He called it "Worship in Spirit and in Truth." This Coming of the Holy Spirit, prophesied by Jesus two thousand years ago has been deemphasized in Western Christianity. In the place of this unique form of worship, a Christian doctrine conceived of and interpreted solely by the clergy, condemn all forms of worship unlike their own.

A close reading of Jesus' prophesies, however, foretell a new epoch of human history. One that should have dawned after his ascension into heaven. After the Pentecost we are given a brief glimpse of the Church as an organization defined not by clergy, but by the Holy Spirit. In the new age foretold by Jesus, the Holy Spirit would occupy the summit of earthly power, and the prophets of the Holy Spirit would serve as arbiters of Divine purpose. Despite Jesus' assurance that the Holy Spirit would establish an intradimensional theocracy, a religion governed from another dimension, it didn't take place. Or did it? In the following chapters you will discover, as I have, the hidden history of this age of the Holy Spirit, where it began, how and why it was suppressed, and what we can expect, as we awaken to the presence of the Holy Spirit within us.

These are the secret teachings of an obscure religious sect that inadvertently rediscovered "Worship In Spirit and in Truth" in the context of their own native culture. Worshiping in this manner brought about a contemporary Pentecost in the Philippines. It was in this outpouring of the Divine Spirit that they received the power to heal. I have come to believe that the descendants of these original Christian Spiritists and the paranormal healing work they do is an atavistic resurgence of precisely what Jesus practiced and taught. As I am confident in my own beliefs, I will now leave it up to you to draw your own conclusions about my discoveries. I invite you to accompany me on this journey into the heart of Filipino Christian Spiritism and decide for yourselves the merit of my humble observations. All that I ask is that you, the reader, proceed with an open mind.

In Spirit and In Truth
Harvey Martin

Chapter One

Miracles on the Big Island

*I*n the late 1960s, members of the so-called "hippie" counterculture began arriving in Hawai'i in search of the ideal place in which to create a peaceful life-style in harmony with nature. Blessed with a mild tropical climate that borders on perfect, Hawai'i offered the optimum setting for exploring human potential, unencumbered by the harsh realities of icy winters and scorching summers. By the early 70's, the counterculture had transformed Hawai'i into one of the most successful centers for alternative life-styles in the United States.

The Islands of Hawai'i are a truly transcendent place. The perfect weather, vibrant foliage, and the power of the ocean all combine to cast a spell that no one in their right mind would want to break. In the multi-cultural environment of the Hawaiian Islands, exposure to the exotic is the norm. Although the Islands of Hawai'i are part of the United States, Americans who live in Hawai'i for any length of time become familiar with and embrace concepts and cultural norms very different from those they left behind in mainstream America. Idealism flourishes in the relaxed ambiance of the trade winds and brilliant sunshine of Hawai'i.

The exodus to Hawai'i began with the surfers from California, who were, of course, looking for the "perfect wave." But the exodus to Hawai'i by the counterculture began in earnest after the rock superstar, Jimi Hendrix, organized a series of famous concerts which came to be known as the Rainbow Bridge Concerts. The first took place inside Diamond Head crater on Oahu. The second concert was in the rural town of Ulupalakua, on the beautiful island of Maui. The concerts were filmed, and the movie "Rainbow Bridge," was produced. Upon its release, images of a surreal new culture, spawned in the paradise of Hawai'i, were seen in theaters across the country. Hendrix christened Hawai'i the "Land of a New Rising Sun" in a song of the same name.

The members of the burgeoning "hippie" counterculture who moved to Hawai'i discovered that traditional Hawaiian culture contained many elements which reflected their own longings. The spirit of Aloha emphasized the unselfish ideal of working together and sharing the fruitful abundance of nature. The concept of Ohana....the extended family in which everyone was seen as legitimate and beloved members of the human race....blended well with the tribal instincts of the holistic community.

The tradition of Aloha Aina, in which the land is seen as sacred and the object of heartfelt love, satisfied the environmental concerns of the holistic community. Reverence for nature and a desire to preserve the natural beauty of the islands provided common ground in a diverse population. Those of us who had rejected the tenets of contemporary American culture as being destructive to nature and human dignity, now resolved to create a new culture: a culture nourished with organically grown pesticide-free food, powered by energy produced by the sun, and kept in good health by a health care system that integrated the best of holistic healing from around the world. We proceeded with the absolute assurance that anything was possible. With deep faith in our vision of a truly brave new world, we embraced the islands of Hawai'i as a match made in heaven.

The amount of sunlight that falls on the state of Hawai'i made it possible to develop new types of housing powered exclusively by electricity produced by the sun and solar heated water. Natural energy sources also included constant trade winds......ideal for wind-generated power. With mail order sources like the Whole Earth Catalog, and the homespun wisdom of the Mother Earth News at our disposal, we were able to transform our living environments....and our lives. Though NASA invented solar photocells to power spacecraft, it was the holistic community that voluntarily began to scale down the applications of photovoltaic technology from satellites to homesteads.

It was truly an inspiration to realize that, for the first time in history, we had the technology to provide the creature comforts we loved without negatively impacting the environment.

Ironically, our discovery of photovoltaics and solar heated water coincided with the OPEC oil crisis. To our delight, the Carter administration mandated that the island of Hawai'i (Big Island) become energy independent by 1990, and offered to pay fifty percent of the cost of installing residential solar water heating and electrical systems in the form of a solar tax credit. By 1978, I was living independent of the power grid, on a completely solar-powered farm on the island of Hawai'i where I had purchased eight acres of land.

By two o'clock in the afternoon on any given day, my battery bank would be fully charged with electricity generated by Hawaiian sunlight. My photovoltaic system produced enough electricity each day to meet all of my energy requirements for a week. I was astounded by how simple it was to live "off the grid" in Hawai'i and, by logical extension, anywhere in tropical or sub-tropical regions of the world. The solar electric system I installed was fully automatic, had no moving parts, and the only maintenance was refilling the batteries with water every three weeks. We saw the freedom that solar technology offered as the final flowering of a decentralized society in which advanced technology allowed us to become fully independent. Even more important was the fact that solar was environmentally friendly. Unfortunately, the utilities saw our energy independence in terms of lost revenues. Following Ronald Reagan's election as president, the Department of Energy discontinued its development of solar technology, ended the tax credit, and concentrated instead on nuclear research.

Fortunately, we made the transition to solar independence before big money began to sabotage a sustainable future. Having achieved energy independence, we turned our attention to developing chemical and pesticide-free agricultural methods. We were shocked to discover that a place as beautiful as Hawai'i had the most toxic chemical-intensive agricultural practices in the world. The amount of fertilizers, pesticides, and herbicides used in farming sugar cane, pineapples, papayas and flowers bordered on genocidal for the farm workers and those who lived in or even in proximity to agricultural areas. In response, organic gardening, hydroponics, permaculture, biodynamic farming, and many other alternatives to chemical and pesticide intensive agriculture were established.

Holistic Healing in the Land of the New Rising Sun

Having discovered the means to produce clean energy and wholesome food, we then saw the need to create an alternative system of health care. Once again the diverse knowledge and experience of our holistic community was brought together and analyzed. From this analysis emerged a unique synthesis of the healing traditions of many cultures. In addition to the wide range of alternative therapies we brought with us from the Mainland, the Islands were rich in indigenous alternatives to main stream medical practice. From the Japanese and Chinese came shiatsu and acupuncture, tai chi chuan, and chi kung. From the Hawaiians came the therapeutic system of the Kahunas, which ranged from herbal cure to lomi-lomi massage and hooponopono (a forgiveness process.) In the relaxed Hawaiian environment, healers of many races became friends and freely shared their knowledge with one another. Close examination of the multicultural healing methods revealed that there were elements within the different systems that complemented each other and "worked" independent of the context they were originally developed in. As we experimented, combining these essential elements, new eclectic systems began to emerge.

Though we didn't develop the Touch for Health system, we used it extensively. Touch for Health is a prime example of a hybrid healing system derived from cross-referencing otherwise unrelated systems. BioKinesiology (BK) is the science of using muscle testing to determine the strength or weakness of an organ. Usually, BK is used in the context of Western medical science and has never existed in China. Dr. Joseph Goodheart saw a correlation between BK and the Chinese system of medicine in that acupuncture meridians are also directly related to specific organs. Goodheart reasoned that BK might be used as an alternative form of organ diagnosis. In China, this diagnosis is traditionally accomplished through the reading of the pulses on the wrist, and is very difficult to learn and master. Goodheart tested his theory and found that it worked. Using muscle testing instead of pulse examination, and acupressure with the fingers (Shiatsu) instead of needles for treatment, Goodheart succeeded in combining elements from Chinese, Japanese, and Western medicine, and producing one of the best *natural* health care systems to come out of the East-West synthesis.

Beyond a certain point, the study of healing becomes the study of subtle energetic processes and, ultimately, psychological and spiritual processes. Our knowledge grew daily and we believed, with good reason, that further revelations of the inner mechanisms of healing were not only possible but probable. We learned, for example, that Oriental cultures possessed medical systems based on the understanding of a subtle life force that operated in the physical body. We sought out oriental medical practitioners, studied with them and learned how to manipulate these subtle energies....through laws unknown to Western medicine...for the treatment of the physical body. We tested the oriental medicine systems extensively and found that they worked both in theory and in practice.

While acupuncture points can be easily detected with specialized electronic devices, the life force, which the Chinese call Chi, has eluded detection. Though Western science has failed to verify the existence of Chi, the scientifically proven existence of the acupuncture points and meridians suggested to us that Chi will eventually be proven to exist as well. For us, the fact that energetic medicine produced good results in practice was the only validation we needed. After all, the skillful manipulation of Chi, using the laws of Chinese medicine, has kept the most populous nation in the world healthy and reproducing for at least three thousand years. As our knowledge grew, we were humbled by the ever-expanding horizons that presented themselves to us, leading us deeper and deeper into the rarified realm of spiritual healing.

Having discovered so much in so short a time instilled in us a deep faith in the spiritual dimension of life. None of us doubted that there was much about healing that we had yet to discover, and that an open mind was a necessary requirement of our work. By 1977, a number of healers within our holistic community were deriving most of their income from healing work. The success of the healers was beginning to draw unwanted publicity. The medical establishment reacted to the growing numbers of healers, first with indifference, and finally with hostility. If we used these systems we had discovered, however successfully, we were breaking the law. We needed to find a way that we could conduct our healing research, and at the same time, offer our services legally. In order to protect the rapidly growing holistic healing community, we incorporated a religious, charitable, and educational organization. In 1977, The Church of Living Truth held its first meeting. We discussed the need to develop healing centers where a spiritual way of life and a sustainable future could be taught and practiced. With the help of the community, the first church center was built in the small Hawaiian village of Kapaahu on donated property. Kapaahu was the site of the oldest Kahuna ceremonial center in the Hawaiian Islands, the Waha'Ula Heiau.

The center was a holistic health care facility and research organization centered around the belief that the body was the vehicle of the spirit; therefore, any activities leading to the recovery or continuation of health in the body, perpetuated the ongoing work of the spirit. In addition to the healing program, we agreed that the Church should become involved in growing food organically and that the healing centers should be powered with solar photovoltaic systems and solar water heating systems. By 1979, the healing center at Kapaahu had become a self-contained, solar powered showplace, and conclusive proof that our vision was attainable. Within the holistic community, the growing interest in Chinese medicine had led a number of healers to seek out and study with the Asian masters of Chinese medicine and acupuncture. A hospital/school in Colombo, Sri Lanka, had become the largest hospital outside of China to offer hands-on training in Chinese medicine to students in the English language. This educational program, offered at the International College of Acupuncture, was sponsored by the World Health Organization. At the hospital, medical doctors as well as healers from around the world, worked side by side in a clinical environment under the supervision of Anton Jayasuriya, its director.

I went to Sri Lanka to study in September of 1980. While I was there, the International College of Acupuncture sponsored the Seventh World Congress of Acupuncture. Delegations of acupuncturists from around the world shared their scientific and experiential findings with their fellow participants. As well as being an extremely enriching experience, the Congress resulted in the creation of an international network of acupuncturists and alternative healers who offered each other endless opportunities to study and develop their skills as healers.

Upon returning from Sri Lanka, I went back to work at the healing center in Kapaahu. One day, a friend and fellow church member named Mark Olmstead, paid me a visit. As he drove up, he saw me nailing a roof onto the building with a great deal of difficulty. He immediately offered to help. Mark was very knowledgeable about matters such as organic farming and low-cost construction methods, and contributed a great deal of time and labor to the Church. Though Mark was an avid and experienced surfer, he had dislocated his shoulder in a series of surfing accidents which had left him partially disabled. In spite of occasional relief, his injury refused to heal and continued to dislocate. Doctors had suggested that surgery might correct the problem, but would offer no guarantees. Mark's injury also seemed beyond the capabilities of the local alternative healers. He had become increasingly depressed. Then, on the day when he dropped by, he told me that he had finally found a 'possible' answer to his problem.

The Advent of Psychic Surgery on the Big Island

One of his friends had recently been to the Philippines with his father to investigate the work of Filipino faith healers. They had returned with a videotape showing a Filipino man performing what appeared to be surgical operations barehanded. Dale, Mark's friend, explained to him that the "psychic surgeons," as they were known, were able to enter human bodies with their bare hands, extract tumors, as well as other obstructions from the body, and then, withdraw their hands from the bodies of their patients without even leaving a scar! Mark's description of the videotaped operations sounded impossible. In spite of my doubts, I kept an open mind and hoped, for Mark's sake, that it turned out to be a reality. Mark had been deeply affected by the videotaped footage of the psychic surgery.....it seemed to offer my friend hope in a hopeless situation, a *supernatural* solution to a very real problem.

With hardly a second thought, Mark departed for the Philippines to experience the work of the psychic surgeons firsthand. Two months later, he returned with photographs of his psychic surgery operation. He explained to me that the healer's assistant had held a mirror over his shoulder, and a Filipino friend of his had taken the photos via the mirror while squatting on the floor. The photographs showed the bare hands of the healer opening and then folding back the skin and muscles until the joint was exposed. Blood was clearly visible in the photographs, and I asked if the operation had been painful. He assured me that the operation was nearly painless, and lasted only two or three minutes. Another photograph depicted the psychic surgeon displaying what seemed to be a piece of dark tissue about the size of a dime.

He explained to Mark that scar tissue had formed when his shoulder had initially dislocated, and that it had prevented the shoulder joint from rejoining properly. Although his shoulder was not yet fully healed, Mark said it was greatly improved and he was satisfied with the results of the operation. The improvement in his shoulder, however, was almost insignificant compared to the transformation in his spiritual demeanor and perspective. Mark returned from the Philippines virtually radiating an aura of reverence and gratitude for the miracle that he had received. As much as psychic surgery was a method of healing that led to improvement in Mark's shoulder, it was also a spiritual event that had left him in...a state of grace.

Doubt no longer lingered in my mind as to the reality of psychic surgery. I began to regard the arrival of psychic surgery on the scene as the logical next step in the research that we had all been involved in for years. If the Chinese could manipulate and awaken subtle health restoring energies with needles, and muscle testing could be used to diagnose and treat the body by merely applying finger pressure to acupuncture points, other processes had to exist that produced even more extraordinary results. While in the Philippines, Mark had shot super 8 film of the healers performing psychic surgery. Upon his return to Hilo, he shot the rest of the roll of film and took it to the camera shop to be developed. To his shock and dismay, all of the footage he had shot in the Philippines was blank; the exception being the footage he had taken at the Hilo airport upon his return. The fact that the footage taken at the airport had developed seemed to prove that the camera was in good working order. The failure of the rest of the film to develop was a mystery. Mark even speculated that the film had not developed because he hadn't asked permission of the healers before he filmed them. It remained a mystery.

After being home awhile, Mark came to an uncomfortable realization. He had to readjust to and deal with people who had not experienced what he had. When he tried to share his experiences, even with many of his close friends, they simply did not believe him. This caused him a great deal of frustration. To unbelievers, his encounter with the psychic surgeons seemed to have led him to a "conversion experience." But, conversion to what? To what mysterious force could one attribute an experience of this magnitude? It was increasingly apparent to Mark that if he was going to tell anyone about his encounter with psychic surgery, he had better have some proof. Without proof.....and when related with the fervor of someone who has just been miraculously healed.....a description of psychic surgery could easily lead anyone to assume that you had completely lost your mind.

Among members of the holistic community on the Big Island, word spread fast. Soon, the topic of psychic surgery dominated many conversations. Yet, with the scant evidence, speculation was rampant. In this surreal environment, opinions ranged from unquestioning belief by those who were astonished by Mark's explanations of his paranormal experience, to total derision by those bastions of common sense who were certain that psychic surgery was some vile form of deception. In spite of all the speculation, no one, including Mark, knew what to make of the phenomenon of psychic surgery.

The Unbearable Proof

Mark decided he had no choice but to return to the Philippines and gather more substantial evidence. To lend objectivity to his findings, he was accompanied by another member of the holistic community. Margaret was a wonderful healer herself, and well respected. She suffered from congenital scoliosis, a condition in which there is curvature of the spine from birth. They left for the Philippines with a great deal of fanfare and high expectations.

During their visit in the Philippines, Mark met Alex Orbito. Alex was among the most prominent of the psychic surgeons and healers in the Philippines. Mark explained his dilemma to Alex and asked him if he would allow himself to be filmed as he performed psychic surgery. Alex readily agreed, much to Mark's relief. Meanwhile, Margaret had been busy getting treatments for her condition, and was affected very deeply by the local healing environment. In spite of her belief in the amazing capabilities of the various psychic surgeons and healers she had seen, her scoliosis was not corrected through psychic surgery. One of the healers, obviously frustrated by his inability to cure her, resorted to acupuncture. The moment he inserted the needle, Margaret felt a sharp, agonizing pain which was accompanied by dizziness and mental disorientation. Acupuncture, while an amazing tool in the hands of an expert, can also do a great deal of harm in the hands of the inexperienced.

After Margaret's unfortunate experience with the amateur acupuncturist in the Philippines, she rested for a few days, and resumed her search for another healer. Mark, on the other hand, having been able to film Alex Orbito performing psychic surgery, was ready to return home. Margaret decided to stay in the Philippines, and Mark returned to Hawai'i, this time with undeniable proof. At the Manila airport, prior to boarding his return flight to Hawai'i, he noticed that Margaret was speaking in a weird tone of voice. He didn't know what to make of it, but neither did he think anything was seriously wrong.

The super-8 footage Mark filmed came out much to his satisfaction, and a date was set for the highly anticipated, first public screening to the holistic community. The showing was held at Ke Ola Hou, the newly established center for holistic healing in Hilo. On the evening of the screening, a large number of curious people came, filling the building to capacity. The excitement and anticipation was almost tangible as everyone waited for the film to begin. No one knew what to expect, except Mark, and he had remained silent. Suddenly, there appeared on the screen a series of images that were truly from another world. The images depicted a Filipino man performing barehanded operations on a man who was lying on a table. No one had anticipated that this long-awaited film providing proof of the impossible, would repulse and horrify all who saw it.

Having no idea what to expect, the enthusiasm of the viewers immediately gave way to exclamations of revulsion. Within the first five minutes of the screening, several people passed out and had to be revived. One of the operations performed by Alex Orbito appeared to be the lancing of a boil about the size of a baseball on a man's leg. When Alex popped open the boil with his hand, putrid matter in the boil literally sprayed the entire healing room. Alex was so repulsed that even he, whom one would think would be used to these things, became nauseous and immediately left the room.

Unfortunately, the film had a similar effect on everyone who watched it. Those who had come to see the footage, came because they wanted to witness a miracle that had been experienced and verified by a member of their own peer group. The film showed example after example of a man performing operations with his bare hands, and removing all sorts of disgusting material from the bodies of his patients. Even so, the 'miraculous' aspect of the operations was immediately overwhelmed by the visceral reactions to the sight of blood, blood clots, and whatever else it was that Alex was extracting from the bodies of the Filipinos in the movie. If Mark's goal had been to provide proof of the reality of psychic surgery, he had clearly outdone himself. It became dramatically evident that there was a vast difference between Mark's personal experience of psychic surgery and the experience of a group of healthy, curious individuals watching a movie of a stranger being operated on.

In the case of someone who is suffering from illness, the possibility that malignant tumors may be painlessly extracted without even leaving a scar (and for an almost insignificant donation) is seen as a Divine miracle and a new lease on life. For someone who is merely curious, the remarkable aspect is quickly replaced by revulsion, and a denial of the possibility that such a thing can even exist. A natural reaction to blood and disease is abhorrence, and this reaction can be sufficiently strong enough to negate any context they are seen in.

In the chaotic aftermath of the showing of the psychic surgery film, Mark turned off the projector and an uneasy silence filled the room. This soon changed to confusion, as those who remained wandered about, trying to comprehend the incomprehensible. The already extraordinary situation then went off the scale when Margaret suddenly began to speak in a tone of voice that seemed to be that of an old Filipino woman. Hearing Margaret keep repeating "everything is wonderful" in a squeaky little voice quite unlike her own, was unsettling to say the least. Given the circumstances, it was unmistakable that everything was *not* wonderful. Margaret's husband was thoroughly shaken and, after some effort, he convinced her to leave with him. As the master of ceremonies for this strange event, Mark found himself at a total loss for words.

None of us had any idea what was happening to Margaret. There was speculation about spirit possession, a subject we knew next to nothing about. None of the healers present knew how to deal with Margaret's bizarre behavior. Margaret's husband was furious, and blamed Mark for his wife's condition. The reaction of the holistic community to his footage, combined with the hysteria caused by Margaret's 'apparent' possession, left everyone feeling confused and apprehensive. Finally, the famous Hawaiian Kahuna, Moornah Simeona successfully treated Margaret and she resumed as normal a life as she could under the circumstances.

Unlike many of the participants at the screening of Mark's footage, I didn't let the chaotic series of events through which psychic surgery had arrived obscure the fact that a man whom I knew like a brother had been cured of a very serious condition with the technique. In spite of his best efforts, however, the phenomenon of psychic surgery still remained as mysterious as ever.

In the aftermath of my first film encounter with psychic surgery, I moved to San Diego, California, to study video production. In February of 1983, Mark telephoned me. He had recently returned from another trip to the Philippines, and said that he had decided that the only way to properly introduce the miraculous abilities of the healers was to bring one to Hawai'i. He felt that Alex Orbito was the best healer and Alex accepted Mark's invitation to do a healing mission on the Big Island. He asked if I would return to Hawai'i and help sponsor Alex; I readily agreed to do so.

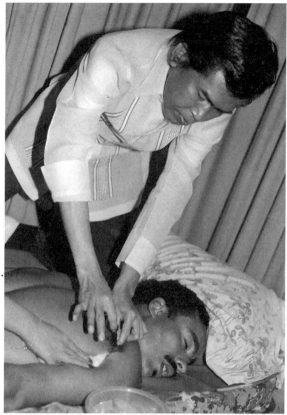

Alex Orbito operates on Mark's shoulder in the Philippines

The Psychic Surgeon Arrives

Among the many races that call Hawai'i home, Filipinos constitute one of the largest minority populations, yet there are very few institutions that represent Filipino culture in Hawai'i. Having no idea what to expect, I went to Honolulu with Mark to meet Reverend Alex Orbito at the airport. He arrived at three o'clock in the morning, and I was immediately impressed with him. He was a positive, friendly person who exuded charisma....even at three in the morning and after a ten hour flight. We spent the night at a friend's house in Honolulu and left for Hilo the next morning. Mark had several appointments, so I was given the responsibility of being Alex's tour guide and procurement agent. I asked him what he needed to perform the surgery. He said he needed only cotton and alcohol. After buying his minimal requirements at a drugstore, I took him on a tour of Volcano National Park and along the Chain of Craters road.

Alex dressed well, and I was surprised to see that he wore a very expensive gold Rolex watch. The great majority of Filipinos in Hawai'i are agricultural workers and certainly can't afford Rolexes. I noticed that his had a coat of arms emblazoned on the watch face that appeared to be of Arabic origin. When I asked him about it, he said that the king of Saudi Arabia had contacted him and asked if he would come to Saudi Arabia to try to heal the king's brother who had some very serious health problems. Alex was being called as a last resort. When Alex arrived in Saudi Arabia he was given a proposal. The king told him that if he could cure his brother, he would be given a large amount of money, as well as other gifts. Then, he warned Alex: If his brother died while under his care, Alex would be beheaded, as was the custom among the Saudi royals. Alex told the king that he'd consider his offer, and then retired to his guest quarters in the palace. There he prayed and meditated.

After several hours of meditation, Alex felt he was ready to help the king's brother and sent word to that effect. He was then brought to the room where the healing was to take place. After performing psychic surgery on different areas on the body of the king's brother, Alex indicated that he had done his best and was taken back to his quarters. Alex said that, as he waited, he was confident, yet concerned. Finally, after what seemed like an eternity, Alex heard a knock on his door. He opened it to find two uniformed guards ready to escort him to see the king. The guards remained silent, and Alex began to worry. However, upon seeing the smiling face of the king, Alex relaxed. The king told him that he had done well and gave him a large sum of money, and the Rolex watch. Alex used the money to purchase his healing center in Quezon City.

During our drive, I questioned Alex about psychic surgery. He told me that his healing was the work of the Holy Spirit. His reference to the Holy Spirit surprised and puzzled me. When I asked him to explain what he meant, he said that the Holy Spirit was the spirit of God.....the aspect of God that performed miracles in this world. He said that he was merely an *instrument of the Holy Spirit* and that he did not do the healing; rather, it was done *through* him. For the first time, I found myself in the presence of a healer whose healing was rooted in a form of Christianity. In the holistic community, Christianity was rarely mentioned in regard to healing. I was aware, of course, that a few evangelists healed during their services, but overall, healing was not a priority in mainstream Western Christianity. Otherwise, the prevalence of televangelists badmouthing the counterculture while espousing right-wing politics, did little to allay my suspicion that Western Christianity was a front for a government plot to establish a right-wing theocracy.

I was struck by the paradox of a Filipino Christian psychic surgeon, capable of opening bodies with his bare hands, coming to Hawai'i to do a healing mission among dedicated members of the American counterculture who had not only rejected mainstream Christianity, but had been dedicated students of the entire spectrum of mostly oriental spirituality for years. I was particularly drawn to Tibetan Buddhism and the ideal of the Bodhisattva. The Bodhisattvic oath to enlighten sentient beings and eliminate suffering was one shared by many of the members of the holistic community. On the Big Island in remote Wood Valley, we established a Tibetan Buddhist retreat center in the mid 1970s that has continued to grow through the years. The resident Lama at Wood Valley during Alex's visit was Nechung Rinpoche, formerly the high Lama of the Nechung Monastery in Tibet.

Dedicated to the ideals of Tibetan Buddhism, I had long since decided that I would do whatever I could to help people who lived a life of compassionate service towards others. I immediately wanted to help Alex because I could see that his intentions were the same as ours. In his humility and tireless efforts to help others, he seemed the very ideal of compassion. One thing was certain: Alex was not like any Christian I had ever met! Whatever Alex's religious background, he seemed the very embodiment of the intent to enlighten the living and eliminate suffering. In spite of our skepticism about Christianity, a bona fide instrument of the Holy Spirit was here in our midst, ready to perform the impossible.

As I drove on, I listened in fascination as Alex told of his incredible experiences in Africa, The Middle East, and Europe. I enjoyed his stories and it was evident that he was an exceptional person in every sense of the word. Upon our arrival in Hilo, I helped him to check into a hotel. Several hours later, Alex called and asked Mark and me to meet him in town for dinner. During dinner, I asked Alex for permission to videotape the healing sessions that were going to take place over the next three days. He agreed to my request. Then, both Mark and I questioned him extensively about psychic surgery and how it was performed. He told us that we all have two bodies, a spiritual body and a material body, and that different physical laws governed each of these. He added that when a person practices concentration, meditation, and cultivates the spiritual body, they will eventually reach the point where they become instruments, like himself, through which the Holy Spirit can 'intervene' in the material world. Alex then added that people who achieve this degree of spiritualization are often able to transcend the material laws of physics, and perform psychic surgery.

We had already decided to conduct the healing "mission," as Alex referred to it, at Mark's farm, which was located in a rural area of the Puna district, about thirty-five miles from Hilo. The farm was a perfect location for a number of reasons. Mark had cleared a large area which served as a parking lot. Mark's house and the grounds surrounding it were large enough to accommodate hundreds of people if necessary. The room we chose for the healing was a medium-sized bedroom that had nothing in it except a bed. We pushed the bed up against the wall and added a massage table, a chair, and a video recorder on a tripod with a chair for me to sit in as I operated the camera. The unexpected reactions and confusion that had occurred when Mark screened the graphic film of psychic surgery at Ke Ola Hou made it abundantly clear to us that we had to take great care in setting up this healing mission. We accepted the fact that there were going to be skeptics, including those who had seen the original footage and left with a bad impression.

For the sake of those who tended toward skepticism and disbelief, and with our credibility on the line, Mark and I had personally purchased everything that Alex was to use while healing, chose an empty room for the healing, videotaped the entire event, and took every precaution to set up the 'event' so that any sort of deception would be impossible.

Alex Orbito arrives in Hilo.

Witnessing the Impossible

Finally, the morning dawned on the first day of our healing mission. People began arriving at eight a.m.. At nine-thirty, Alex gathered everyone into Mark's house for a blessing. He explained, "we have two kinds of bodies: the material body and the spiritual body. The material body is from this earth, and the spiritual body is from God. The food that nourishes this material body is from the earth, but the food that feeds the spiritual body is from God. While the food that grows from the earth is harvested by the hand, the food that feeds the spiritual body is harvested through prayer, meditation, and sincere faith in God. That is the word of God. The spiritual body needs the food so that your physical body will become balanced. If your physical body is not balanced, when you come into contact with illness or diseases, it will have a negative influence on you. That is why you must balance your body with your meditation and prayer so that the sickness will disappear through your sincerity to God. That is why, brothers and sisters; I am here on a spiritual mission and want not only to cure your body, but to help you develop your spiritual self."

Alex's inspiring words ended with his request to join him in repeating The Lord's Prayer. Afterwards, Alex and I went into the healing room, leaving Mark to organize those who were there to be healed. As those who had come to be healed entered the room and laid down upon the table, I began to videotape one incredible healing 'operation' after another. During the first three operations I manned the video camera constantly focusing in on and panning the amazing events taking place before me. All of the 'patients' were locals of Hawaiian, Japanese, Chinese, Portuguese, and Filipino descent. I had known most of them for years. Overall, they were polite and cooperative. Most were nervous when they entered the healing room. After the third operation, Alex asked me if I would help him by holding the tray that held the tissue and blood extracted during the operations. I left the camera on and did as Alex requested. I stood two feet away from Alex during the following operations. I watched over and over as Alex somehow opened the bodies of his patients with his bare hands. Prior to operating, Alex would knead the area to be opened until a popping sound was made. The popping sound signaled the penetration of the skin and the appearance of blood. Shortly after the appearance of blood, Alex would remove bloody tissue of various shapes and sizes from the bodies of the patients. After finishing, he would simply press the opened area together and wipe off the blood.

Alex performed thirty-five operations on the first day, mostly for local people who had heard of Mark's recovery from his shoulder injury. As the healing proceeded, the atmosphere was transformed from one of anticipation to that of actualization of the sacred. The patients were spiritually inspired and emotionally overwhelmed by their transcendental experiences with Alex. The healing power that flowed effortlessly from God through Alex transcended the expectations of everyone involved, including me. No one present had ever experienced anything like the mystical atmosphere that had apparently been generated through the intervention of what Alex called the "Holy Spirit." At four in the afternoon, the first day of the healing mission ended. Within hours, the patients began to report positive results from the healings. In the aftermath of the first day of the healing mission, the word was out. Many of the local

Hawaiian people of Kalapana were Christians who believed in the power of the Holy Spirit, and were as different from mainstream Western Christians as Alex was. They were deeply moved by the work that Alex was doing. Several of them graciously invited Mark, Alex, and me to have dinner with them that night.

The next morning, we suspected that there would be a greater number of patients than there had been the first day, but we were not prepared for the deluge of people that began at seven-thirty. By nine o'clock, one hundred seventy-five people were patiently waiting outside. At nine-thirty, Alex repeated to the crowd what he had said the day before, but then added, "The spiritual vibration is to love one another. Loving one another is the bridge of healing to enter into your body. You know that we are brothers and sisters in one God. When I give spiritual healing to your body, as long as you are doing good, the cure will be effective. But if you are doing bad, the spiritual healing will disappear and the influence of the negative will return. That is why you must continue your spiritual development. That is for you, not for me. That is for you so that you can continue your obligation to God."

Once again, the people entered the little room one by one to be healed. During lunch on the second day, Alex was asked if he would do a demonstration for the group. All the healing up to that point had been performed behind closed doors. Alex said that he would consider it, but explained that he was reluctant to do a public demonstration because of the problem with people fainting. Mark and I agreed with him. After lunch, we had a special request from one of the members of the holistic community and his wife. They explained that they had tried unsuccessfully for some time to conceive a child. They had been told by their doctor that the wife had blockages in her reproductive organs. The couple asked Alex if he could help them and he said he would try. The woman then asked Alex if her husband could be with her during the healing session. Alex not only agreed to have the husband present, he told Mark that he would allow everyone to witness the operation.

About thirty-five people crowded into the small room, and watched as Alex began to knead the woman's stomach with both his hands. Suddenly, a clearly audible popping sound occurred, and Alex's hand appeared to plunge into her stomach. At this point, the husband suddenly gasped and fainted. As he fell to the floor, another man also passed out. Alex stopped what he was doing and went to revive the woman's husband and the other man. By merely touching each of them on the forehead, they regained consciousness immediately. The manner in which Alex revived them, and the speed of their recovery was nearly as impressive as the psychic surgery itself. Nevertheless, after reviving them, Alex looked at Mark, who immediately announced there would be no more demonstrations. After clearing the room, Alex operated on the woman again. Within the following year she conceived and gave birth to a much wanted child.

By the end of the second day, another hundred and twenty-five people had been treated by Alex, many of whom experienced and reported immediate improvement in their health. Some were disappointed, but still others began to report positive results later on that day and in the days following. The initial skepticism or confusion had been replaced by a growing sense of euphoria and gratitude. In the aftermath of the day's healing, everyone was united in a shared experience of spiritual transcendence. Mark was thrilled to finally communicate his experiences with supportive and understanding people. There was no question in our minds that Reverend Alex Orbito was a genuine *link between the spirit and the flesh*, and that our healing mission was succeeding beyond our wildest imaginings.

That evening, during our drive into Hilo to have dinner, Alex said, "As I see the crowd of sick people waiting for me to relieve them of their suffering, my heart is filled with compassion. I deeply and fervently pray to God to make me a channel of his healing power. As I pray, I am suddenly transformed into a Holy Man whose only remaining feeling is one of love, mercy, and compassion toward the sick. At this moment, I no longer think of myself as Alex Orbito, but as a mere channel of God's healing power."

After returning from dinner, we were told that the telephone had been ringing off the hook for hours.....people would now be arriving from the mainland, as well as the other Hawaiian islands for the third and final day of the healing mission. It was astonishing to see how quickly news had traveled by word of mouth. Other than telling friends about the healing mission, we hadn't promoted or advertised it in any way.

Back at Mark's farm, several of our close friends came over to visit. During the conversation, someone asked Alex how he was able to enter the body with his bare hands. He said, "When my spiritual mind is attuned to the Holy Spirit of God, my hand emits an energy that is more powerful than the physical makeup of the human cells, which merely give way to a more powerful force." Someone else in the room asked what the person being worked on should do in preparation for and during the healing? Alex replied, "If you pray while I am doing the operations you will not feel anything except maybe a little pain. You must pray and concentrate on God because your concentration is the way the power of God enters into your body. That is why I need your concentration and spiritual cooperation, so that the healing power is strong enough to enter into your body."

Alex continued, "My concentration is the way of my prayer. I concentrate first, pleading for the light of God to enter my being, to cleanse and remove all the negative vibrations from my body. Meditation and prayer give me the sense of holiness and fullness of spiritual vibrations. Before the actual healing, I feel a certain coldness in my forehead, which gradually spreads to my whole body. At that moment, I am completely overpowered by the Holy Spirit which gives me confidence and the complete assurance that all my movements come from the spirit who does the healing. Then, a surge of heat gravitates into my palms to signal my readiness for the operation." Everyone present was thrilled to hear Alex explain the techniques and the mind set that he induced before functioning as a healing instrument of the Holy Spirit.

Then, because the group was so receptive, Alex continued, "I would like to tell you something about the operation," he said. We all listened with riveting attention to his words. "When I put my hand inside the body, my hand is like a magnet. So, even if the sickness is a distance from my hand, it is drawn to me and I feel a current. When I feel the current, I know that the sickness is now in my hand and I remove it immediately. That is why the operations don't last very long. It is not I who opens the body, but the Spirit. After concentrating, I achieve a high level of attunement with the healing power of God.....and the healing power of the Holy Spirit enters my body. When I open the body of the patient, there is no pain, because it is not my hand, but the power which emanates from God, and is channeled through my hands, that performs the surgery."

Alex looked at his watch. It was time for him to retire for the night. In fact, we all needed to sleep.....our third and final day of the mission would be very busy. But some of us stayed up a while longer and discussed how totally amazing the "mission" was and how blessed we all felt to participate in such spiritual work. The next morning we were awakened by people arriving just as dawn was breaking. We had breakfast and watched as Mark's lawn filled up with cars. We received a phone call from a friend who had started directing traffic at the gate, asking if there was anyone who could help him handle the increasing flow of traffic. Mark went to the gate and saw a long line of cars stretching up the narrow road. A policeman drove up and offered to help direct traffic....he said his aunt had received a healing on the first day and it had helped her a great deal. He wanted to help, which Mark accepted and thanked him for.

Three hundred and fifty people had showed up and were waiting patiently, and reverently, for the healing to begin. While Alex seemed to take it all in stride, Mark and I were beginning to feel overwhelmed. Alex delivered a short version of the service that he had delivered over the last two days and then led everyone in prayer. An aura of spiritual providence permeated the crowd along with a mystical sense that miracles were imminent. At ten o'clock, the first person came into the room for healing. At six o'clock that evening, Alex finally succumbed to exhaustion. In those long, eight hours, two hundred and thirty-eight people received healing from Alex. Still waiting to be healed, were about forty more people who had arrived late, and had not been able to see Alex. I explained to them that Alex was just too exhausted to work on anyone else. This did not appease the group and they appealed loudly. Finally, Alex came out of the room where he had been resting. He told them that he would do distant healing for them if they would write their contact information on a piece of paper along with the health problems they suffered from. I had no idea what 'distant' healing was at that time but assumed it meant that Alex would pray for them and heal them from a distance. His announcement satisfied the crowd, and by seven-thirty the house was quiet once again.

Living In the Presence

During those three days, Alex Orbito had changed the lives of hundreds of people. Those most transformed by his work were Mark and me. It was hard to contemplate returning to our normal routines after having experienced what was surely a very real, divine intervention. During those three days, Mark, Alex, and I, had become very close. When we thanked Alex for so skillfully manifesting the wonderful healing mission, he told us that what we had experienced was as much a result of our participation as his. Alex asked if I would play back some of the videotapes of the healing. After viewing the footage, he asked us if we would come to the Philippines as his guests and produce a video documentary on his life and work. Mark and I were thrilled, after what we had seen, and wanted nothing more than to experience this remarkable phenomenon in the environment in which it had been conceived. We gratefully accepted his invitation.

We accompanied Alex back to Honolulu, and saw him off to the Philippines. When we returned to Hilo, we began preparing for our own journey. In the aftermath of the healing mission, it was clear that the Big Island had changed for the better. The local people had something both personal and meaningful in common with the holistic community. The experience enriched us all. The healing mission had been a real eye opener for the holistic community. It was the first time that any of us had ever experienced a living tradition of spirit-directed Christianity. Alex was an elder of the spiritual healing tradition of the Filipinos, a tradition that none of us knew anything about. In our studies, we had read about the Essenes, who were healers as well as contemporaries of Jesus. We had studied the Dead Sea Scrolls, Gnosticism, and other archaic traces of what Christianity had once been. But there was no mention in any available texts of a Christian ministry that revolved entirely around the teachings of Jesus as a healer, and the Holy Spirit as the right hand of Jesus the Healer. The Christian teachings I had learned as a child taught Christianity as a means of achieving a better life in the next world. The Filipino healing tradition that Alex embodied taught that, through the power of the Holy Spirit of God, we could receive empowerment *in this world*, and could use that empowerment to help and heal others as a means of teaching many of the deeper lessons of the spiritual aspects of life.

For many years, the holistic community had searched the world for spiritual teachings and teachers that would enable us to realize the potential of the spiritual presence that lived within us. In Alex Orbito, it seemed certain that we had finally found a human being whose spiritual beliefs produced true empowerment in the most profound sense of the word. Mark and I were both anxious to explore his world and familiarize ourselves with the source of his power. We counted the hours that brought us closer to our departure for the Philippines.

Chapter Two

Into the Realm of Espiritu Santo

The front gate at Alex Orbito's Healing Center

Into the Realm of Espiritu Santo

*I*n June of 1984, Mark and I arrived in Manila and checked into the Manila Midtown. Having traveled extensively in other parts of Asia, I had learned to hope for the best, and prepare for the worst, where lodging and food were concerned. I was surprised and pleased to find that our hotel offered a spa, several excellent restaurants, and reasonably priced accommodations. The following morning, Mark and I went to see Alex Orbito at his healing center in Cubao. Cubao is a suburban neighborhood, or barrio, of Quezon City, and Alex's center was located in a quiet area, away from the busy streets. I found the healing center to be a fascinating place for a number of reasons. Three times a week, Alex and his brother, Roger, held healing services at the center. The people who came to Alex's healing center represented a broad cross section of the human race. They included people from every economic level, as well as every nationality, race, and religious persuasion.

At the center, there were a number of other healers who worked with Alex and were members of his organization, The Philippine Healer's Circle, Inc.. Alex's fellow healers practiced diverse types of healing. Some performed what is known as magnetic healing, others did magnetic massage; still others prepared and dispensed herbal remedies and healing ointments. The magnetic healers were extremely skillful, and their healing work was often used in conjunction with psychic surgery. After the psychic surgeon was finished, it was the magnetic healer's job to energize the body and restore equilibrium following the operations. Though magnetic healing offered a valuable adjunct to the operations, the most popular form of healing practiced at the center, the one that brought people from around the world, were the astonishing operations performed by Alex and his brother, Roger.

The healing service that preceded the operations set the stage for a mystical experience, and was very successful in creating a state of openness and devotion to God that predisposed the patients to heal *in advance* of the operation itself. Healers, who also served as evangelists, delivered sermons in which passages of scripture that elaborated on the relationship between God and healing were read and explained to the Filipinos who attended the services. I wasn't able to understand the services, because they were spoken in the Tagalog dialect, the official language of the Philippines. The service often lasted from thirty to forty-five minutes, during which time the Filipinos, who were mostly impoverished and suffering from various illnesses, took the teachings to heart. When the sermon ended, The Lord's Prayer was sung first in Tagalog, and then in English. During the Tagalog version of The Lord's Prayer, Alex entered the room where the healing was to take place, sat down and prayed directly behind the healing table.

As the English version of The Lord's Prayer ended, Alex stood and blessed bottles of oil and water which would be used later in magnetic healing sessions. After the blessing, the patients entered the room to lie down on the table, one at a time. Usually, the Filipinos came in first, and Alex would perform psychic surgery on them. Filipinos received the treatment either without paying, or for a very nominal donation. After Alex finished with the Filipinos, he then turned his attention to the health problems of the foreigners. Foreigners generally gave a donation of about five dollars for the session. Hanging on the wall behind the table where Alex worked was an unusual looking banner, with the name "Union Espiritista Christiana de Filipinas" written in golden letters across the top. On the bottom of the banner was a scriptural reference. The scripture was James 5, verses 14&15, which says: "Is any one of you sick, let him call upon the elders of the church to pray over him and anoint him with oil in the name of the Lord, and the prayer offered in faith will make the sick person well. The Lord will raise him up and if he has sinned, he will be forgiven." The psychic surgery was performed in full view of observers and, while many of the operations were difficult to watch, they were often photographed and videotaped by foreigners eager to provide proof of their experience when they returned to their respective countries.

Alex prays, and concentrates to God.

Almost as soon as I arrived in Manila, I found that Alex had told a number of his associates about the healing center and Church in Hawai'i. They were impressed with the fact that the Church provided a sanctuary, as well as a venue, for those who possessed healing gifts. Alex and his fellow healers asked if I would help heal their patients at the center in Cubao. Of course, I said that I would. I worked at the Cubao healing center three days a week and fully immersed myself in their world. Since there is no equivalent to Chiropractic in Filipino folk healing, I adjusted the spines of hundreds of Filipinos for the first time. They could hardly believe how much better they felt. In the months that followed, I also did spinal work on foreign patients and worked on most of the healers as well. By helping the healers with their back problems, I gained their respect and support, which allowed Mark and me to work on the video project as fellow healers.

At Alex's healing center in Quezon City, I became deeply impressed by the fact that a significant number of people were being healed, and in many cases, miraculously healed. It was also apparent that whatever psychic surgery was, it seemed to be equally effective, regardless of the religious persuasion or customs of the person treated. Over and over, I observed Moslems being operated on by Alex after listening reverently as Christians sang The Lord's Prayer in the aftermath of a Christian worship service. The same was true with the Buddhists, Shintoists, and other Asians who came to the center for healing. In fact, it was quite common to hear enthusiastic testimonies to the psychic surgeons being offered in Japanese, Arabic, Chinese, English, and many other languages.

I could not imagine a better way to study the effectiveness of a healing technique than by subjecting it to the objective (and subjective) scrutiny of every conceivable belief system, including the various racial and religious biases of a broad cross section of the entire human race. It seemed reasonable to me that if any healing technique could produce consistent results given these conditions, the technique certainly had merit. Much to his credit, Alex did not seem bound by any particular religious dogma and, considering what I had seen, I could certainly understand why. The Filipino healers professed belief in Christ and claimed to derive their miraculous abilities from the Holy Spirit. Yet, when instructing those of different religious persuasions, Alex told them to *surrender to God in whatever form they perceived God to be.*

Japanese patients prepare for healing.

Living and working with the healers was enough to make a believer of me. While working at the center, I saw one planeload after another of sick people arriving from around the world. I came to know many of them personally. I listened to their stories of having undergone years of unsuccessful therapies, and then finally being told that they were incurable, inoperable...terminal. The debunkers of faith healing, and the watchdogs of the American medical profession, justified their repression of alternative healing on the belief that sick and vulnerable people were being exploited by unscrupulous healers. Ironically, many of the patients who came to Alex's center in Cubao insisted that they were the ones who had been horribly exploited by arrogant, greedy medical professionals. At the Center in Cubao, the cost of a treatment was five dollars for a foreigner, and fifty cents for a local. In most cases, it was the failure of the *medical* profession that prompted these people to seek alternatives. Many of the patients I met were the rejects, the embarrassments of conventional medicine, those who refused the doctor's final suggestion to die quietly. Not everyone is willing to lay down and die when science fails them. Some have a strong will to live; to keep trying in spite of the death sentences they've been given. Unfortunately, most of these brave people wait until it is too late to try to reclaim their health.

Working at Alex's Center in Cubao, I became deeply committed to my healing work. I felt fortunate to be able to offer my assistance to healers as dedicated as the members of the Philippine Healer's Circle. These people faced the endless human suffering that is caused by disease on a daily basis. At the center I observed the condition of the sick and infirm from the time they arrived, and it was apparent that, in spite of the terrible condition they were arriving in, many of these people were experiencing dramatic improvement from the combined efforts of Alex, Roger, and the magnetic healers. The critical patients received psychic surgery a number of times, sometimes staying for weeks. In some cases, patients experienced dramatic results after only one session, but generally, patients received treatment as often as they could. It was also common to see healthy but curious people receiving psychic surgery to enhance their already good health.

In trying to help those who suffered from illness, the healers clearly had taken on an often thankless task. Alex was under constant pressure to cure the incurable who were desperately clinging to life. The weight of this burden was squarely on his shoulders. In spite of my own commitment to help him, I was not sure that I was capable of handling the stress that he lived with day after day. Alex was obviously staggered by the endless life and death situations he faced in working with the terminally ill. The healing center in Cubao was equivalent to an emergency room where only incurable patients come as a last resort, demanding and expecting a miracle. Needless to say, Alex and the healers did their very best, but their task was endlessly frustrating. Further complicating the situation was the fact that those who were cured became staunch supporters of the healers and their methods, while those who were not criticized the healers and insisted that psychic surgery was a fraud. Of the many people I came to know who received treatment, both in Hawai'i and in the Philippines, most professed a great deal of relief from a variety of ailments too numerous to mention. Others were spontaneously healed in well documented cases. In rare cases, a small minority of the psychic surgeons have risen to prominence, even to become wealthy, as a result of their healing work. Not many outsiders, however, realize the high price these healers pay in the form of total sacrifice of their personal lives to the needs of others.

Spiritual Cooperation

As I've said earlier, Alex always advised his patients to pray and concentrate, and to cooperate in the process of their healing. Alex and the other Filipino healers believed that all healing comes from God; that they are merely instruments of God's will. They often told their patients that deep faith in God, and the surrender of the patient to the will of God is the most important factor in the restoration of health. Yet, however many times the healers advised their patients to surrender to God, or to meditate and pray, the patients would ignore their advice, and cling to the notion that the healer alone possessed the power to heal them. This is of course, in spite of, and at variance with, everything that the healer told them. This became a particular concern when the patient was not healed. The healer ultimately received the blame for the absence of a cure. It is much easier to blame the healer than it is to blame God, ourselves, or fate.

Among the Filipino healers, illness is divided into two main categories: material and spiritual. An injury received in an automobile accident is considered a material ailment. Spiritual ailments are defined as those caused by witchcraft, karma, and psychological factors. While the Filipino healers do not equate spiritual perfection with perfect health, they do recognize that illness can, and in most cases does, serve a higher purpose in the spiritual growth of the individual. When the ailment has a karmic basis, it simply means that the illness originates as the predictable result of the patient's personal behavior. Karmic illness can reflect a pattern of abusive behavior towards self or others. The concept that God uses illness as a tool in the task of bringing the soul to perfection is abhorrent to many. It is, however, a central theme in Christian healing. Throughout the biblical narrative, there are examples of God using physical illness to bring about spiritual transformation. For a few examples, read the first four chapters of the New Testament.

It is obvious that sickness can result from abandoning the words, thoughts, and deeds that we know to be true. What the healer is actually saying, when he or she asks you to pray and concentrate on God, is to *look within yourself.* Examine your words, thoughts, and deeds. Discern where it is that you may have deviated from your responsibility to the ultimate reality within yourself. It is within this deviation from the self that disease often originates. When someone is able to uncover the source of this internal deviation from truth, it may then be possible to resolve it. The resolution of these internal issues opens the door for miraculous healings to occur.

While observing those who came to Alex for healing, I asked them questions about themselves, and what they felt were the causes of their illnesses. I discovered that very few people can, or will, accept responsibility for their ailments. I met people who refused to accept that smoking cigarettes and drinking alcohol, even to excess, was undermining their health. They felt that a miraculous healer should be able to heal them despite their addictions. It is very painful to face the fact that *you may be your own worst enemy* and a victim of your own special brand of denial. This is especially so in the case of debilitating sickness. I found that when patients were able to confront these issues within themselves, rather than merely depending on someone else to heal them, they often heal. This process of internal introspection is not limited to Christianity, or to any religion; *The spiritual power that heals those who are willing to redeem themselves is universal and nondenominational.*

I mention this because some people who came to Alex's center apparently believed that traveling halfway around the world, checking into a hotel, and giving donations that ranged from five to hundreds of dollars, demonstrated that they had done their part. From the perspective of the healers, the requirements of the *spirit of truth* is very different than the economic and physical sacrifices we make in the pursuit of cures offered by Western medicine. When asked by patients if they can heal specific conditions, the healers often answer that *if it is the will of God, they will be healed.* The healers believe that, as instruments of the Divine, the relationship that they facilitate is the one between the *patient and God.* Openly admitting that they do not know the specifics of God's Divine plan, the healers suggest that one should pray or meditate to understand the spiritual implications of their situation; thus, the treatment of illness is addressed on the physical and spiritual level simultaneously. The Filipino healers often refer to a story told in the Bible. In it, Jesus is asked whether it was the sin of a blind man or his parents that had caused the man to be blind from birth. Jesus answers that it wasn't sin that had led the man to be born blind, it was God's plan that in curing the man's blindness through Jesus's miracle, many who were spiritually blind would learn to see. (John 9:1-7 paraphrased)

The Filipino healers also emphasize that the act of faith connects the individual to the healing power of the Divine. An example of this belief is found in the biblical account of the woman who had been hemorrhaging for twelve years. After suffering unsuccessful and expensive treatments from the medical profession of her time, she found herself penniless and still suffering infirmity. She heard about Jesus' healing powers and, in desperation, sought him out. She found him in the midst of a crowd of people. Approaching Jesus from behind, she believed that if she could only touch his cloak, she would be cured. She touched his cloak, and for the first time in twelve years, the hemorrhaging stopped. The telling part of this story is that Jesus was not aware that she was behind him; yet, when she touched his cloak, he felt what is described in the Bible as "power going out of him." After listening to the woman's story, Jesus replied, "My daughter, your faith has healed you, go in peace and be healed of your disease." (Mark 5:25-34) The lesson in this story is that strong belief and faith have therapeutic value that is intrinsic, that the act of faith establishes a link with the source of spiritual healing prior to and even in advance of the conscious involvement of the healer.

Videotaping the Miraculous

Shortly after arriving in Manila, Mark and I began videotaping the psychic surgery operations at the center in Cubao, three days a week from 10:00 a.m. until 2:00 p.m.. The crowded conditions in the healing room made it very difficult to record unobstructed footage. We solved our problem by constructing a crude scaffold on top of a ladder. At the end of the healing table, elevated above Alex and his many patients, we were able to videotape the unobstructed footage we needed to produce the documentary on Alex's life and work. Videotaping the psychic surgery was quite an experience. In addition to the many operations that were performed to heal physical conditions, we soon discovered that psychic surgery was also used to break curses that had been brought about by witchcraft.

The witchcraft cult that exists in the Philippines is ancient and powerful. In the operations conducted to end curses, the objects removed were very different from the blood and tissue extracted in operations performed on those with physical ailments. In one case, I videotaped the removal of several three-foot long strips of what appeared to be plastic from the body of a victim of witchcraft. In another, a box was filled with what appeared to be long strands of cassette tape taken from the stomach of an old Filipino woman. During these strange operations, about fifty people were watching closely and intently as the healer extracted yards and yards of bloody cassette tape from the patient's body! None of the observers, including myself, could detect any sign of deception or sleight-of-hand. The sheer volume of extracted tape made it difficult to imagine how anyone could palm or otherwise conceal it.

When these operations were over, I asked Alex to explain how enough bloody cassette tape to fill a cardboard box could get inside someone's body. He told me that a curse is a pattern of negative energy that is projected into a person by the ritually empowered will of the witch. Alex explained that when his hands penetrate the pattern of negative energy, the magnetic fluid that flows through him causes the negative energy patterns to condense into physical forms that are totally unpredictable. He added that although the forms are unpredictable, individual healers seemed to extract similar materials from one operation to the next. Alex believed the reason for this was that individual healers had unique perceptions of the form that negative patterns of energy would take. The subjective expectations of the healers interacted with and influenced the process in which *the negative patterns of energy were condensed into physical objects.* Alex said that he did not think that the witchcraft operations should be included in the video we were making. He felt that psychic surgery was more than enough for the viewing public to digest, and that expanding the parameters of the subject would only lead to further confusion.

One day, during one of the healing sessions I was taping, something very unusual happened. An American woman who had suffered a ruptured appendix that had never fully healed, wanted to observe the operations before deciding whether or not she would receive one. As she watched, Alex performed a series of unusually powerful operations. While he was operating, the environment in the small room we were in became excessively hot. The heat of the video lights, combined with the body heat of the tightly packed observers, caused sweat to pour off our bodies. Suddenly, in the midst of this stifling atmosphere, I experienced a sensation of coldness. The sensation was so powerful that chill bumps covered my skin. In addition to the sudden sensation of coldness, I felt as if I had been transported to a much higher elevation where the air was thin and ethereal. As I was trying to figure out what was going on, the American woman moved toward me, saying that she felt dizzy and thought she was going to faint. I suggested she leave the healing room and sit down. While trying to make her way through the bodies of the observers, she fainted.

As the Filipinos around her struggled to hold her up, I stopped videotaping and went to assist. Alex looked up from the operation he was performing, stopped, and made his way through the crowd to the woman. He bent over her, made some sort of a sign with his hand and then tapped the woman on her left shoulder. She immediately regained consciousness, and was led out of the room. Once she was comfortably seated outside, she told me that just prior to fainting, she had felt very cold. I said that I had experienced the same sensation. The evangelist/healer, Froilan Christi, who was sitting with us, explained that the coldness and rarified awareness occurs whenever Espiritu Santo (Holy Spirit) makes its presence known and felt. Froilan concluded that the fainting had been a positive event that demonstrated the woman's sensitivity to the spirit. This was the first of many such experiences in which the intensity of the healing increased as overheated rooms suddenly became cold. The phenomenon interested me so much that I began to analyze the group energy every time it happened. I began to suspect that the phenomenon was a result of the expectations of the group reaching a critical mass in which *expectation becomes actualized.* Whether this critical mass of belief facilitated the intervention of intradimensional or extra dimensional forces were unclear. When this phenomenon occurred, Alex seemed more distant and sometimes appeared anxious and distressed as he plunged his hands into body after body. Whatever the nature of the phenomenon, it was becoming clear that the Holy Spirit was manifesting its presence with great success.

After about six weeks of taping, Mark and I had what we felt was an excellent sampling of all the different types of psychic surgery operations. We had footage of men and women of nearly every race and nationality having operations on every conceivable part of the body. The footage was extremely graphic, but we felt that it depicted the full range of activity that went on in the practice of psychic surgery. Having finished taping the operations, we asked Alex if we could videotape some biographical material. Alex agreed, but told us that it would be a week or two before he would have the time to do it.

In the time I spent at the healing center I came to know the other members of the Healer's Circle who worked with Alex. I was surprised to find that some of his associates were jealous of his success, and attempted in subtle ways to undermine his authority. It upset me to hear this, and I told Alex that some of his colleagues were doing their best to convince me that he was greedy and oppressive, and was using them to his own advantage. Alex laughed, and told me not to worry. He said that, in spite of their criticism, they were loyal and he could always depend on them to help him; and furthermore, that most of their problems were imaginary. He then suggested that if their complaints bothered me, I should ask them to stop talking behind his back. I took his advice. They were shocked when I told them they should support Alex, because he was doing his best in a very difficult situation, and certainly did not deserve their criticism. I never heard another negative word about Alex from any of his associates.

While some members were jealous, others were dedicated healers. One Filipino woman, in particular, was very focused and highly effective. She asked Alex if he would lay hands on her head in an empowerment ceremony that was reserved for his advanced students. Alex agreed, and also allowed me to videotape the ceremony. After placing his hands on the woman's forehead, she appeared to go into convulsions. I was astonished at the power Alex was apparently channeling into the woman's body, which reacted as if she were being struck by one bolt of lightning after another. She later moved to Australia, where she has become a famous healer in her own right. Based on what I had seen at the center in Cubao, it seemed to me that the ability to perform psychic surgery was the result of a long and arduous process that began with Bible study and missionary work among the poor. If properly predisposed to the work of the Holy Spirit, the healer would eventually receive empowerment from someone who had already incorporated the power.

Juan Blanche, the Psychokinetic Psychic Surgeon

In his previous trips to Manila, Mark had met several other psychic surgeons whom he suggested I should meet. The first one we went to visit was a man named Juan Blanche. Of all the psychic surgeons, Juan was perhaps the most enigmatic. Mark told me that Juan was able to make incisions on the human body from a distance, without even touching the body, and then remove diseased tissue from these openings. Apparently there were two very different types of 'distant' healing. When Alex Orbito had offered 'distant' healing to his patients in Hawai'i, he prayed for them in absentia. I found it difficult to envision someone making an incision at a distance. I had only just begun to grasp the reality of opening the body with bare hands and had not even considered the possibility that there were psychic surgeons who used methods other than bare hands to open the body. I found the prospect rather overwhelming, and could not resist the opportunity to meet Juan and see for myself.

Juan Blanche had some unusual hours of operation. He would see patients only between two and six a.m.. He claimed his powers were strongest during those times. After a long drive into some of the more remote suburbs of Manila, we arrived at Blanche's healing center. It was 1:30 a.m.. The place was very much like Alex's with the Espiritist banner proclaiming the name of the center prominently displayed behind the altar. On the walls were laminated newspaper clippings that detailed the achievements of Juan Blanche in Germany, Sweden, Thailand, and numerous other countries. After our introductions, he invited us into his treatment room to receive a healing.

I had a painful lump on my lower back. Mark assured me that Juan was a specialist in the removal of tumors and growths both benign and cancerous. He had previously removed two such growths from Mark's scalp which he had given to him to keep. After I told Juan Blanche about the lump, he reached out, took my hand, and closed his eyes. After a moment of silence, he opened his eyes and told me that something was wrong with my leg, in the area of my shin, and asked if I had injured my leg. As he spoke, he seemed to look right through me. I thought it strange that he should mention my leg. While I had been resting earlier that night in preparation for the visit, I had felt a sharp pain in the area of my shin.

Until he mentioned it, I had completely forgotten that I had injured my leg while on vacation in Jamaica two years earlier. As far as I was concerned, my leg had healed and was no longer a problem. Juan told me that scar tissue from the old injury was obstructing the flow of blood to my lower leg and foot. He said that if it was not removed, I would probably develop problems within the next two years. I agreed, of course, to have him work on my leg right away. Juan also agreed to let me videotape the procedure. As I sat on the table, he wiped the area where he was going to operate with a cotton ball dipped in alcohol. He then proceeded to grasp Mark's hand and asked Mark to extend his finger. Then, while holding his hand, Juan made a pass over my shinbone with Mark's extended finger. As I watched my leg, small drops of blood began to bead up along an inch long, barely visible incision along my shinbone where Mark's finger had passed only moments before! As the blood became visible, Juan placed a coin on top of the incision, and then placed a piece of alcohol-soaked cotton on top of the coin and lit it with a match. As the cotton burst into flame, Juan placed an upside down shot glass on top of the flaming cotton ball and pressed the rim of the shot glass into the flesh on my shin. As the cotton slowly burned out, and consumed all the oxygen, a primitive but effective vacuum formed inside the shot glass.

As the vacuum increased, it suctioned the skin where the incision had been made into the shot glass. The pressure increased, the incision began to separate, and blood flow began to escalate. I was familiar with this technique, known as "cupping," which is widely used in Chinese medicine, Nevertheless, as Juan watched the blood fill the shot glass over the next ten minutes, I suspected that the Chinese had never used "cupping" in quite this way! During those ten minutes, Juan would periodically tap the glass and watch. Finally, he said that the scar tissue had reached the surface, pulled the shot glass off of my leg, and began to apply pressure to the area on either side of the incision. Suddenly, a wrinkled brown piece of tissue about the size of a dime emerged from the incision, and he removed it. He then rinsed the incision off with alcohol and smiled. Speechless, Mark and I stared at each other, and at the piece of tissue. Juan then had me turn over and removed the lump on my lower back. Both incisions healed rapidly with no complications. The first operation left a scar on my leg. The second operation left no scar, even though a much larger incision had been made

In two subsequent visits to Blanche's center, Mark and I were shown different but equally remarkable techniques that he used in his healing work. These, we also videotaped. One of Blanche's techniques involved pressing a tablespoon empty side up onto the abdominal area that would somehow 'fill up' with a fluid that he would empty. The spoon didn't penetrate the skin or even make a scratch, yet every minute or so, a milky fluid would fill the spoon! Blanche told us that the milky fluid was poisoning the patient's system and that removing the fluid would cure the stomach pain his patient was suffering from. His patient told us that he was feeling increasingly better even as we watched. In another very unusual technique he used to cure earaches, Blanche would take two stick matches, holding one in each hand between his fingers he placed them in the patient's ear. After prodding the ear with the match sticks, he removed what appeared to be a small piece of tissue. After meeting Juan, my perspective about the phenomenon of psychic surgery began to change. I realized that Alex, gifted and skilled as he was, was only one of many gifted, spirit-directed Filipino healers. It was also becoming clear that their attitudes and practices were derived from a common source. Without exception, all of the healers unanimously gave credit to the Holy Spirit for their success. Further, it was obvious that this select group of Filipino Christians had received some special insights into the workings of the Holy Spirit. I began to wonder just exactly what these insights might be.

I asked Alex if there had been any special preparations or rituals that he'd gone through in the early stages of his training as a healer. Though Alex had been *born* with powerful spiritual gifts, he said that he, along with many other Espiritistas, cultivated and expanded these gifts through specific spiritual practices. Like the Yogis of India, generations of Filipino healers prayed and meditated in sacred caves in order to learn concentration, and attain the inner peace that enabled them to fulfill their difficult missions as instruments of the Holy Spirit. I wanted very much to include some footage of these caves in the video, and asked Alex if he'd take Mark and me to see them. Alex agreed, and early one Saturday morning he picked us up at our hotel, and we departed for the northern Philippines. On our way to the caves, we stopped by the town of San Manuel, in the rural province of Tarlac, and visited the church of Alex's oldest brother, Reverend Marcos Orbito.

Interfaith Church

A Christian Spiritist Worship Service

Marcos Orbito is the founder and residing minister of the Interfaith Spiritual Church of the Philippines. The day we arrived was the fourth anniversary of the Interfaith Church and everyone was celebrating the event. Marcos Orbito's missionary efforts had raised the money to build

Into the Realm of Espiritu Santo

a very nice, modern church. He received us graciously and invited us to have dinner with him. Afterwards, Alex, Mark, myself, and a few church members who were still cooking, stayed outside while the rest of the Filipinos went into the church. I questioned Alex about the differences between their religious practices and those of Western Christians. Alex said that he didn't know enough about Western Christianity or the English language, to compare them. He suggested I go into the church to see the worship service and discern what those differences were for myself.

I went inside the church, sat down, and began to observe. I soon realized this was no ordinary Christian worship service. The church was filled with the sounds of hymns being sung in Tagalog and Ilocano, accompanied by guitar players. In the front of the church was a pulpit. On the right side of the pulpit, an elderly woman was sitting at a table facing the congregation. On the left side of the pulpit was a chalk board. At the pulpit, and next to the chalkboard, a man stood watching the elderly woman. My attention was immediately drawn to her. Tears streamed down her face as she gazed upward beatifically, oblivious to everyone else. She suddenly began to write very rapidly while continuing to gaze toward the ceiling. As she wrote, the man standing beside her watched intently. As she continued to write, the congregation sang hymns in Ilocano. The man would periodically turn to the blackboard and write phrases on it, which he was apparently translating from the text that the elderly female 'medium' was writing. I couldn't read the Tagalog phrases on the blackboard, but noticed that as soon as the old woman stopped writing, and the scriptural references were all there on the black board, the members of the congregation opened their Bibles and began to study intently. Suddenly, it dawned on me that the elderly female medium was 'channeling' scriptural references from the Bible.

Healer gives a spiritual injection to a young girl.

The congregation deeply contemplated the meaning of the scriptural messages as they applied to themselves, and then one of the members came to the front of the Church, stood behind the pulpit, and began to preach! The sermon he delivered was discerned from the scriptural references the congregation had just received from the Holy Spirit. After preaching for approximately ten minutes, he concluded his sermon and returned to his seat. No sooner had he sat down than another member of the congregation went to the pulpit and delivered another sermon. In the following hours, many more sermons were delivered. During the sermons, they explored every subtle nuance of the messages that had been sent to them for their enlightenment. Rather than preaching, some members sang songs they felt shed light on the messages from the Blessed Spirit. In all, about twenty-five people came up and shared their thoughts and feelings about the topics that the Holy Spirit had provided for them.

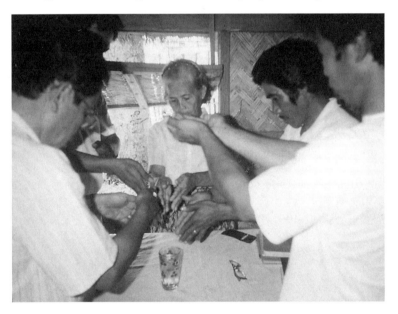

Charging water with Magnetic Fluid

As I sat and listened, I began to feel the growing presence of the Holy Spirit filling the room. After personally witnessing an elderly medium receive the contents of a religious service directly from the Holy Spirit, through what appeared to be automatic writing, I knew that this form of Christian worship bore no resemblance to Western Christianity. The man who had translated the writing was apparently gifted with the *interpretation* of spiritual revelations. In this church, founded by Alex's brother, spirit-directed sermons came through devout Christian mediums who possessed mediumistic abilities that they used solely in the context of church services. The authority within the church was not vested in any single person. Anyone who wished could preach from the pulpit about what they discerned from scriptures that had come directly from the Holy Spirit. I found this to be truly astonishing, extremely democratic, and spiritually evolved.

Western Christians have always maintained a strict hierarchy in the ranking of church officials, and any deviation from this rule of the church was considered heretical. The early Gnostics were the first in recorded history to conduct Christian religious services in which no distinction was made between the clergy and the lay members of the church. In the third century, the Catholic Father Tertullian bitterly complained that, "today one man is bishop and tomorrow another; the person who is a deacon today, tomorrow is a reader; the one who is a priest today is a layman tomorrow; for even on the laity they impose the functions of priesthood."

After about three hours I left the spiritual service which was still in progress and rejoined Alex. He asked me if I understood what the Filipinos were doing, and I told him I thought so. Alex said that Filipinos believe that during their church services, worshipers become filled with a subtle 'fluid' that emanated from the manifest presence of the Holy Spirit. When the Holy Spirit is fully present and the worshipers are filled with this spiritual essence, it is then dispensed in healing services which are open to the public. As the patients are healed, they become new members and the fellowship of the Holy Spirit grows. Alex then told me that the religious ceremony I had just witnessed was known as *Christian Spiritism*, and that Christian Spiritists taught that the Holy Spirit used the righteous as its instruments to fulfill the promise of Christ. I made a mental note to find out which specific promise of Christ Alex was referring to.

As I relaxed with Mark and Alex in an open shelter next to the Church, Alex stood up and announced in Ilocano that I was an accomplished spiritual healer from Hawai'i and I had offered to do spinal treatments for the people. For several hours I worked on a shaky little table, treating about thirty people. Afterward, Alex described a problem he had with his jaw dislocating, and asked if I would take a look at it. I gave him a meticulous treatment and adjusted his jaw successfully. After his treatment, we bid everyone farewell and proceeded on to Alex's country house in Burgos, Pangasinan.

The province of Pangasinan is revered as the heartland of Christian Spiritism. We arrived in Burgos around 4:30 a.m. and were thoroughly exhausted. We slept a few hours and awakened to a sunny day and the smells of breakfast. While Mark and I ate, Alex left to make preparations for our journey to the caves. When he returned, he asked Mark and me if we would do him a favor. He said that he owed the mayor of Burgos a favor, and that it could be repaid if we would videotape a greeting from the mayor and a pitch from him to invest in his town. Mark volunteered to videotape the mayor's greeting, listening to him profess his staunch support of both Presidents Ferdinand Marcos and Ronald Reagan.

The rock formation at the entrance of the "cave of the elephant."

The Sacred Cave of the Espiritistas

The following morning, we left for the caves in a jeepney that was well protected by four guards armed with automatic rifles. Before we set out, Alex's bodyguard, Ralph, explained that there were political problems in the area where the cave was located. He said emphatically that we had to be prepared, in case we were ambushed by communist insurgents! Mark and I hoped he was joking, though he assured us he was not. We watched anxiously for the next forty minutes as we drove deep into the rural countryside on a long, winding, dirt road. We were relieved when we finally arrived at the home of a farmer, located in a very remote area. Alex suggested that we rest and eat before we entered the sacred cave. After lunch, the keeper of the cave, who lived in a nearby house, opened the padlocked entrance and checked the cave out. An unusual rock formation above the entrance of the cave looked exactly like the head and trunk of an elephant. We were told that the cave was commonly referred to by the locals as the "cave of the elephant," (even though elephants had never existed in the Philippines.) Alex knelt and prayed at the entrance and then asked the magnetic healer/evangelist, Froilan Christi, who accompanied us, to go inside and look around. Froilan gave the okay, and we followed Alex into the cave.

Alex Orbito meditates shortly after we enter the cave.

The interior was exquisite. The walls glistened and sparkled in the reflected light that came through the entrance of the cave. As I turned my video light on, the pearly white limestone stalagmites and stalactites suddenly burst into a rainbow of shimmering color. I felt honored and humbled as my camera recorded the very first footage of the interior of one of the most sacred caves of the Espiritist healers. When we were well inside the cave, Alex climbed up onto a shining ledge and spoke about the spiritual and historical significance of the cave. Then he gave instructions as to how we should meditate when we were taken deeper into the cave to its meditation chambers.

After his discourse, we walked around the sparkling stalagmites and stalactites and into a very large and totally still chamber. Mark and I were then led to different areas of the chamber and left alone to pray and meditate in total darkness and silence. Having meditated for years, I marveled at what a perfect place this chamber was for profound meditation....dark, quiet, and comfortably warm. I began to meditate and to take slow, deep breaths. Suddenly, I was startled as a bat flew by and missed my face by inches. I immediately ceased my loud breathing and began breathing as silently as I could. Slowly, I sank into a deep meditation, one that filled me with peace and serenity. After nearly an hour and a half, Alex returned and said it was time to go farther into the cave, to a place he called the "healing waters."

Alex Orbito prays, asking for protection and guidance before we proceed deeper into the cave.

As we descended deeper and deeper into the cave, the floor of the cave became very hazardous to negotiate. I found myself precariously juggling expensive video equipment in semidarkness through eight-inch deep mud that was getting deeper with every step. In addition to the mud, water droplets fell from the ceiling onto the recording equipment. After what seemed an eternity of slogging through mud, the floor of the cave began to regain its solidity. Off in the distance, I heard the sounds of water flowing over rocks, the sound of an underground river. As we approached the fast-flowing water, Alex showed me one final and formidable obstacle. In order to reach the chamber of the 'healing waters,' I had to crawl through a three foot opening in the rock. The six inch deep stream flowed through the opening and water dripped down from narrow ceiling. I braced myself, and took a deep breath. I knew if I failed, thousands of dollars worth of video equipment could be ruined, and an essential part of the documentary lost. The only way I could make it would be to lie on my back and wiggle through, with the camera and recording deck resting on my chest. Somehow, I managed to squeeze through the opening and back stroke my way into the chamber of the healing waters with the equipment undamaged. Truly, a miracle.

I receive a blessing from Alex Orbito in a subterranean pool called "the healing waters."

Once inside the chamber of the healing waters, I was immediately captivated by its mystical beauty. Here, deep inside the earth of the northern Philippines, water flowed downward over seven terraced waterfalls to fill a large pool. It was as warm as a bath. Breathlessly, I set up the floodlights, flipped the switch and watched with satisfaction (and relief) as the lights came on and illuminated this magical grotto for the first time. As I videotaped, Alex prayed, and then began to bless us, one at a time, by immersing us into the water. After our immersion/blessing, a guide led us through crystalline openings in the cave walls up the seven levels of waterfalls into the uppermost level to the place where an underground river, the source of the healing waters, first entered the cave. When Alex announced that it was time to leave the sacred cave, Mark and I felt we had been spiritually renewed and were extremely grateful for the experience.

Froilan said it was not uncommon for aspiring Christian Spiritists to spend days, even a week or more, meditating inside the totally dark and silent cave. Froilan also pointed out that becoming a medium of the Holy Spirit did not necessarily mean one would become a psychic surgeon. He stressed that *psychic surgery was only one of many spiritual gifts bestowed by the Holy Spirit.* The ability to receive revelations through automatic writing was also a gift of the spirit, as was the ability to translate the revelations into scriptural references. In addition to psychic surgery, magnetic healing was a very powerful method of healing. Froilan emphasized that all aspects of spirit-directed healing were equally important. Seen in the overall context of Christian Spiritist healing, psychic surgery is unique only in that it is the spirit-directed healing practice that Westerners have found to be most fascinating.

Cultivating rice in Nueva Ecija.

We Visit Alex's Hometown

Shortly after our return to Manila, Alex called and said that he was ready to take me to his hometown in the rural province of Nueva Ecija, to videotape the biographical footage for the documentary. Alex, his bodyguard, and I drove north from Manila for four hours, then turned off onto a dirt road and drove for another hour through mud ruts and washed out areas until we finally reached Alex's birthplace. Alex Orbito was born on November 25, 1940, the youngest of twelve children in the remote, tiny village of Nagcoralan, at the end of a thirty-mile long dirt road. Very little had changed here in centuries. Alex's parents were among the founding members of the Union Espiritista Christiana de Filipinas and were devout healers. Upon our arrival, we were met by a large welcoming committee. Alex instructed several of his nephews to show me around Nagcoralan, and assist me in videotaping while he talked to his brother Joseph. Our first stop was the community church. The community itself, which consisted mostly of Alex's relatives, had constructed a building to house the local Christian Spiritist church. It was constructed in the rural style of house construction known as "nipa" style. In nipa style buildings, only native materials are used in construction. The walls of the church were framed with posts of bamboo and lashed together with strips of bamboo. The roof and the wall covering were thatched from the leaves and ribs of the nipa palm.

As a child, Alex had undoubtedly been profoundly influenced by his parents' preoccupation with the Christian Spiritist movement. It became clear that life in Alex's village revolved around two things: farming and religion. Rice is the primary crop in Nagcoralan, and is harvested in the same manner as it has been for centuries, using water buffaloes, (carabaos) to till and cultivate the rice paddies. After videotaping for several hours, and having dinner together with nearly all of Alex's family, we departed for Manila. It was mind-blowing to contemplate how the youngest of twelve children, born into an impoverished rural area of central Luzon would end up the subject of Shirley MacLaine's book *Going Within*.

Water buffaloes rest after a hard day's work.

In it she says, "I was talking with Alex while he operated on another friend of mine whose abdomen was open. Suddenly Alex took my right hand in his right hand. He closed his eyes and concentrated intensely. "Concentrate on God," he said to me. "I will show you what I experience while operating." After a few minutes Orbito took my right hand and held it above my friend's abdomen. "Now put your hand into his body," he commanded gently. I thought I'd pass out. With Alex's hand guiding mine, I put my hand into the abdominal wall. My hand was inside his abdomen up to my wrist and I felt absolutely nothing physical! In fact, the feeling had a dreamlike quality to it. It was as though I had plunged my hand into a warm mist. It simply made no logical sense." "This is how it is for me," Orbito said, "I never feel anything physical. The body is only 'thought.' It is only what we imagine it to be." As soon as I felt doubt, disbelief, and questions ripple intensely through my mind, Alex removed my hand. "Such thoughts will affect the patient," he warned. I removed my hand and looked at it. There was moisture covering it but no blood. It was as if my hand had a mind and spirit of its own, unconnected to my brain." Ms. MacLaine described her psychic surgery experience with Alex Orbito as, "a moment that will live with me always." Alex Orbito is surely a man of destiny.

Shortly after completing the videotaping in Nagcoralan, I returned to the United States with the final footage and met Mark in Los Angeles where we edited the documentary. Thanks to Alex, we had produced the only footage ever recorded of the sacred cave and a number of sequences of psychic surgery, as well as a narrative written with the full cooperation of Alex Orbito. Mark and I thought the video would sell well. Unfortunately, we barely recovered the money we spent making the documentary, and had to resign ourselves to the fact that the world was not yet ready for psychic surgery.

The Second Hawaiian Healing Mission

In September, 1984, Mark and I invited Alex to return to Hawai'i for another healing mission. I had contacted fellow church members on the Island of Maui and had asked if they would help me coordinate a healing mission on Maui. They welcomed the opportunity. Before moving to the Big Island, I had lived for several years on Maui and had grown to love the people and the island deeply. The dedicated members of the island's holistic community have been thoroughly organized since the late sixties and are an inspiration to me in many ways. Between 1973 and 1978, American devotees of Indian gurus, Tibetan Lamas, and teachers from the entire spectrum of spiritual traditions had moved to Maui, established themselves, and began to offer their teachings to the public.

By 1975, virtually every eastern religious tradition, both modern and ancient, had devoted representatives on the Island of Maui. The core group of the holistic community who had lived there prior to the influx of gurus, immersed themselves in very high-level, comparative religious studies. From the essential elements of Buddhism, Hinduism, Sufism, Theosophy, and many other spiritual philosophies and disciplines, Maui's holistic community was able to evaluate the spiritual teachings of diverse races and cultures simultaneously, and in so doing, developed uniquely eclectic insights.

I arrived on Maui several days before Alex to help organize the event. We secured the use of a private, and centrally-located house for the healing sessions. Virtually everyone who came, was impressed with Alex and the healing work he did. Alex had never been in the heart of the American counterculture before, and commented that he was thoroughly impressed with the deep eclectic spirituality of the Maui family. He expressed amazement at the range of spiritual practices he saw going on around him. On Maui, no one had to be reminded to surrender to God in whatever way they perceived God to be.

During the healing mission, an old friend of mine came from

Honolulu to participate. He brought along one of his business associates; both were anxious to witness a demonstration of Alex's healing. My friend was and still is a successful jewelry wholesaler and the friend who had come with him managed a black pearl farm in Tahiti. I asked Alex if it would be possible to give a demonstration. In spite of his initial misgivings, he agreed to do one. We went into the healing room and watched as Alex began. Soon, he was focused on the abdominal area of a woman who lay on the table. He energetically kneaded the woman's abdomen until a loud popping sound was heard and blood appeared. Suddenly, the room filled with a vile stench. Enduring the stench, we watched as Alex removed a large piece of tissue and what appeared to be clotted blood from her abdominal region. My two friends from Honolulu, who had arrived as skeptics, left as believers. They confided that they had discussed how the operations could be faked by palming tissue, or by hiding blood in cotton balls, but they couldn't conceive of any way for such a vile stench to be produced through fakery.

The second day of the Maui healing mission, we drove to the other side of the island to a subdivision in Kihei. The healing there went very well, except for one incident with a troublemaker whom we escorted out. After the healing session ended, Alex blessed us all while we stood in a circle holding hands, singing "Amazing Grace," Maui style. We left Maui the following morning, promising to return in two days so that Alex could deliver a lecture on healing to a fully booked group of yogis, doctors, chiropractors, hippies, and various other natural healers.

Upon our arrival on the Big Island, Alex said he needed to rest, but would be willing to work on a small number of people. This healing session was held at a friend's house on the slopes of Mauna Loa, in the quiet, rural community of Volcano Village. Forty people attended and Alex healed powerfully, and with very good results. During the sessions, a personal friend who suffered from a severe case of hypoglycemia, was cured instantly. Another patient who suffered from impaired breathing reported that his breathing had improved dramatically. His doctor later confirmed his subjective evaluation of his improved breathing. That evening, we had dinner together and left for Maui the following morning.

We were looking forward to two more fully-booked days of healing, culminating with Alex's lecture. After checking into a hotel in Kihei, Alex asked if he could speak to me privately. I went to his room, and he told me that the vibrations did not feel right. He wanted me to cancel the rest of the healing mission. We were all terribly disappointed by Alex's sudden decision. The Maui family who had worked very hard to organize the event, were now forced to explain the abrupt cancellation to the network of dedicated people who had made it possible. They tried to persuade Alex to change his mind, but ultimately accepted his decision and decided to make the best of the situation.

Despite their disappointment, the Maui family had been deeply impressed with Alex, and generously offered to help facilitate our healing mission in any way they could. They felt, as Mark and I did, that working with Alex was an inspiration. By helping Alex, we helped hundreds of people receive healing on many levels. We were all healers who had been involved in this work for many years, but Alex Orbito showed us how to expand our horizons far beyond anything we had ever imagined. It was also obvious that Alex himself found deep personal satisfaction and inspiration in his healing work. To be the instrument of powerful spiritual forces that transform the lives of people who suffer from illness is deeply rewarding. The inspiration that motivated Alex was clearly contagious. The Maui healers offered to accompany us to Honolulu and help us with our healing mission there. We gratefully accepted.

Upon reaching Honolulu, we temporarily went our separate ways. Alex to visit his relatives in Makiki, and I and my friends from Maui, to visit a friend in Kailua. Two days later, Alex called and invited us to come to Makiki and attend the church service at the Union Espiritista. I was surprised to learn that the Union Espiritista even existed in Hawai'i, and accepted his offer with enthusiasm. On Sunday morning, I met with Alex in Honolulu and proceeded to the Church. The service was very similar to the one I had attended in the Philippines, except for the fact that, rather than having an automatic writer as the medium, an evangelist opened the Bible, while under the 'inspiration' of the Holy Spirit, to random selections of scripture which served as the basis for the discussions that followed. In many instances, the discussions were long-winded and in the Ilocano dialect, which did little to fire my interest. Following the discussions, Alex and I performed healing work on the Filipino-American Christian Spiritists.

After these healing sessions were over, we all went to a hotel in the middle of the tourist belt of Waikiki, where we had reserved two adjoining rooms for our final healing mission. We chose this particular hotel for several reasons. Among these were economy, a large parking lot, and anonymity. One room was to be the office/orientation/waiting room, and the other room was to be used for healing. I called my jewelry wholesaler friend (who, since his return from Maui, had told a number of people about his experience with Alex.) He assured me that a great deal of interest had been generated, and to expect a large crowd. The following morning, Alex started working at ten a.m., and the deluge began.

While we worked in the orientation room, patients began arriving downstairs in wheelchairs inquiring at the front desk of the hotel lobby about the "spiritual healer." The normally sedate hotel bustled with activity as growing numbers of patients converged on it. The situation was rapidly getting out of hand. Finally, a hotel staff member asked if we could station someone in the lobby to direct patients. I went downstairs to the lobby and was amazed by the sight that greeted me. The lobby of the hotel looked like a hospital emergency room and the hotel management wasn't looking very happy. We calmly assured them that we would resolve the situation.

Back in the orientation room, I played and replayed the video that Mark and I had produced for the benefit of those who had come to receive treatment. Since the video had an instructive narrative, we sat quietly as one roomful of people after another saw the video, asked questions, and went to receive treatment. Many of the patients were Vietnamese, Thai, and Chinese immigrant workers who did not speak English. I tried to help them understand by using modified sign language, but I could see that I was getting nowhere. Finally, I decided to take the leaders of these various groups into the healing room to view the treatments, so that they could then explain it to their groups.

After seeing a demonstration of psychic surgery, the group leaders were excited, amazed, and apparently impressed their respective groups with whatever they told them. It was wonderful to see the power of spiritual healing once again bridging the gap between languages and cultures. Many powerful healings took place that day with some clearly bordering on the miraculous. The second day was even more powerful and toward the end of it those of us who had organized the healing event were filled with a deep sense of joy and spiritual accomplishment. Alex closed the mission with a circle prayer that summed up the profound emotions we were all experiencing. In the aftermath of our mission, we wanted nothing more than to perpetuate the healing work of the Holy Spirit.

Chapter Three

From Shaman to Christian

My first trip to the Philippines had raised as many questions as it had answered. I now knew that a Christian Spiritist church existed in Asia, whose members, among other extraordinary things, could open bodies with their bare hands, remove diseased tissue, and close them again without leaving a scar. These Filipino Christians held services in which the content of their sermons were received through automatic-writing mediums and translated into scripture by members with other spiritual gifts. Yet, in spite of all I had learned, the central mystery from which all these phenomena arose, remained unsolved. For every effect there is a cause, and I wondered what incredible series of events had transpired in Filipino culture that led to the emergence of Christian Spiritism among the Filipinos. Why was the Holy Spirit at the center of Filipino Christian Spiritism, instead of Jehovah or Jesus? I suspected that a great and profound truth underlay the manifestations of the Filipino Espiritistas and decided to explore the anthropological and historical basis of the mysteries I had witnessed.

On my second trip to the Philippines, I resolved to plumb the depths of the mysteries of Christian Spiritism and get some answers. It became obvious to me, as I lived and worked with the Filipino healers, that their Christian beliefs and practices were unlike any I had seen or heard about anywhere else. It was also clear that their unorthodox beliefs were deeply rooted in a cultural synthesis that had endowed them with abilities well beyond the capacity of ordinary human beings. I realized that if I were ever going to understand their remarkable abilities as healers, I was first going to have to gain insight into specifically what elements were present before, during, and after the synthesis occurred.

While controversy raged about whether the tissues and blood specimens extracted by the psychic surgeons were real or not, I began to look for answers in other areas. When asked what it was that gave psychic surgeons the power to heal, they always replied that it was the Holy Spirit. Assuming that the Filipino healers were talking about the Holy Spirit as it is understood by Western Christians, the scientists and parapsychologists and debunkers were quick to dismiss their explanation as simplistic, and chose instead to debate the nature of the operations. The ongoing controversy over the operations was not producing any worthwhile insights. I concluded that I needed to take a closer look at exactly *what* the Filipinos were referring to when they spoke of the Holy Spirit.

In the West, the Holy Spirit is rarely spoken of in any but Pentecostal churches, and then mostly in reference to the power that makes speaking and interpreting in tongues possible. Since Pentecostal churches are but a small minority in the mainstream of Western Christianity, the role of the Holy Spirit is obscure, and in many cases, viewed with skepticism and suspicion. The question I wanted to answer was: What had made the concept and expression of the entity known as the Holy Spirit so totally different in the Philippines than it was in the West. With the help of many kind and patient Filipinos, I was able to assemble a chronology of the evolution of the Filipino experience of the Holy Spirit, from its introduction in the early sixteenth century by the Spanish Catholics, to the present as the inspiration and underlying power of Christian Spiritist healing practices.

Planting rice in the terraced paddies of the Cordillera mountains.

Filipino Shamanism

Life in the remote provinces of the Philippines has a timeless quality in which the beliefs and practices of many stages of human development coexist. In 1978, a Stone Age tribe was discovered within hours of modern cities in the southern Philippines! From the terraced rice fields of Banaue to the sparkling beaches of the Sulu archipelago, living examples of the religious and cultural practices of archaic times still exist more or less intact. The coexistence of ancient beliefs and life-styles with the modern, makes it relatively easy to chart the changes that have occurred through the ages. It is well documented that long before Christianity was introduced in the Philippines, there existed a native religion based on the invocation and active engagement of various types of spiritual forces, some good and some evil. The lives of villagers were constantly beset with fears of being cursed by the servants of the destructive forces of evil, which they referred to as "kulam" or "gahoy." These terms are the terms for witchcraft, or the harm inflicted by a witch, in the Tagalog dialect.

A witchcraft cult has existed in the Philippines from time immemorial. In the Tagalog dialect, practitioners of kulam or gahoy are called Mangkukulam. The Mangkukulam were sorcerers and mediums of various types of dangerous and destructive spirits. One of the most dangerous was known as Ingkanto. Ingkanto demanded human sacrifice at least once a year for those on whose behalf they intervened, starting with a member of the sorcerer's family. After having forged an alliance with an Ingkanto, the sorcerer received the power to inflict insanity and sickness through curses, which, for a price, could be removed. The Mangkukulam also offered their services to members of the community who wanted vengeance for unresolved grievances.

Locked in constant struggle with the Mangkukulam were tribal shamans known as Mananambal. The Mananambal were the emissaries of the healing spirits and constructive spiritual forces. They spent most of their time actively dispelling the effects of evil sorcery. Since the evil sorcery most often manifested in the form of physical illness and insanity, the training of the Mananambal found its primary emphasis in the development and application of powerful methods of healing and exorcism.

Since ancient times, the Filipinos have possessed a highly sophisticated understanding of the inner workings of the spiritual realm, as well as the different types of supernatural power through which healing was accomplished. These powers are referred to as "Bisa." In F. Landa Jocano's book, *Folk Medicine in a Philippine Municipality*, he tells us, "In the Philippines no one pursues the art of healing without supernatural blessing or without supernatural power known as Bisa." A number of different types of Bisa are associated with healing. Some healers describe Bisa as a "ball or small stone that is inside the body of the healer or sorcerer." It is believed that this substance generates the power, strength, and ability to heal and overcome other individuals. This Bisa is said to be attached to the liver. Other healers describe Bisa as a "force emanating from the blood" that is thought of as a gaseous element akin to a vapor. It is believed that this Bisa condenses when the blood is stimulated to heightened activity by human emotions. Once it condenses, Bisa becomes a potent force for either healing or causing illness. Bisa can also be condensed by merely being in the presence of certain individuals who possess psychic power.

Long before the arrival of the Spanish, the Mananambal were familiar with Bisa. One, in particular, was considered a Divine gift, revered above all others. This Bisa was described as an unseen power that flows directly from God to the healers. It is further described as a type of electric current that can sometimes exert a paralyzing effect. The possession of this Bisa is considered to be a sacred trust. The healer who commands it is considered superior to healers with any other forms of Bisa. Healers who possess this Bisa do not charge for their services for it is considered a sacred endowment. Healers who use it are aided by elevated spirits who tell them exactly what to do when attending to their patients' needs. It is believed that the spirits are either ordinary benevolent beings, or special beings sent by God, to assist a healer who has been chosen for a special purpose. This Bisa is the one most desired by the agents of benevolent spiritual forces, and is the Bisa present in all spirit-directed healing phenomenon. I will refer to this Bisa as the *spirit-directed Bisa*.

The Arrival of Magellan

The religious beliefs of Filipino society at the time of Magellan's landing in Cebu in the 16th century paralleled the religious beliefs of Hebrews who lived in the Middle East during the time of Jesus. These Filipinos believed in hierarchies of good and evil spirits who were engaged in constant struggle. The ongoing rivalry between shaman/healers and the witchcraft cult certainly reinforced this belief. Pre-Christian Filipinos, like the Jews of the Middle East, believed in one supreme God that they called Bathala, and had the unusual distinction of being the only monotheistic society in Asia. Yet, even though ancient Filipinos believed in one supreme God, they also believed that Bathala was far removed from the affairs of human beings. As such, they felt they needed *intermediaries* to petition Bathala on their behalf. This led to the development of what Filipino anthropologists call "split-level theology," which exists to this day. In this split/level theology, animism and monotheism are reconciled. Filipinos believed, like the Hebrews, that extra dimensional entities who carried out the will of God could intervene in their affairs on God's behalf.

Within a short time after the Spanish explorer Magellan arrived on the island of Cebu, the Queen of Cebu converted to Catholicism. It is one of the ironies of religious history that the initial attraction of the Filipinos to the Catholic religion lay in the demonstration of its use as an instrument of healing and exorcism by the Catholic friars who came with Magellan to convert them! In the beginning of the 17th century, a Jesuit father, Pedro Chirino, recorded an example of an exorcism by a Catholic friar of a woman who had been bewitched and seized with trembling and paroxysms (convulsions, spasms.) Chirino wrote, "Our Brother was sent to ascertain what this disturbance meant, and when he learned what had happened, he called the husband and gave him a little piece of the "Agnus" in a reliquary, exorting him at the same time to have faith, and promising that his wife would soon be healed....The husband went home with the agnus, and no sooner had he applied it to his wife than she was freed of the trembling and terror and remained calm. This occurrence soon became public, and another Indian (the term "Indios" was used by the Spanish to refer to the people of the Philippines) who had been bewitched by the same Indian woman, on seeing this marvel, was convinced that God granted health to those who invoked him. Accordingly, he asked for the same relic, and he also was healed."

Apparently, the Spanish Catholic friars who traveled with Magellan to Cebu were so successful in their exorcisms and healing, that the Filipino tribal healers and exorcists acknowledged and accepted the power of the Catholic religion on the basis of their success. The Mananambal believed that the ability to heal and exorcise were manifestations of mediumship and, as such, considered the friars to be mediums. In their ongoing struggle with the Mangkukulam, the Mananambal relied on many different types of spirits. Most of these spirits, however, were unreliable, lacking sufficient power. In order to successfully counter the curses and spells of the Mangkukulam, the Mananambal had to invoke spirits who could wield greater power than the Mangkukulam. The Mananambal closely observed and evaluated the healing abilities of the friars. Seeing the friars effortlessly dispel evil spirits where they had failed convinced the Mananambal that the Catholics had somehow learned to incorporate the spirit-directed Bisa both predictably and exclusively.

The Mananambal knew that the paranormal gifts of spirit-directed Bisa were mediated through the assistance of elevated spirits, and they were curious about the identity of the elevated spirit that utilized the friars as mediums. The Mananambal eventually learned that the Spirit who worked through the friars was called Espiritu Santo. They also learned that this Spirit was nothing less than the Spirit of the One Supreme God, whom they called Bathala, and the Spaniards called Jehovah. The Mananambal observed that Espiritu Santo was a Divine Spirit who intervened directly on behalf of those who believed in and served the one true God. Though the Mananambal were familiar with spirit-directed Bisa, they were not able to consistently access the elevated spirits. As a consequence, they were forced to work only with the spirits that were within their means to access. The Mananambal desperately needed what the Catholics had, and concentrated their efforts on learning whatever was required to become mediums of Espiritu Santo.

The social conditions in Cebu at the time of Magellan were ripe for the introduction of Catholicism. The victimization of the Filipinos by their own indigenous sorcerers and witches provided the perfect opportunity for the Catholic friars to introduce Catholicism as an advanced system of healing and exorcism. In their conversion of the Filipinos, even baptism was offered in the context of a healing ritual. Having had Christianity introduced as what appeared to the Filipinos to be a highly developed form of spirit-directed healing and exorcism provided the Mananambal with fertile ground for incorporating their own ancient system of shamanism into Christianity.

Converted by God's Spirit

The Mananambal strongly identified with the person of Jesus, and his trials, as these were conveyed to them by the Catholic friars. That the One Supreme God of the Spanish had sent his only Son, to be born into the flesh in the role of a Divine healer and exorcist, was seen as an act of great significance to the native Filipino healers, one that they could closely identify with. As witnesses to the power of the Spirit that worked through the Catholic friars, a consensus was reached among the Mananambal. It was acknowledged that the teachings and religious practices of the Christians were the means through which the Mananambal would gain access to spirit-directed Bisa. They now believed that as long as they were aided and supported in their work by this supremely elevated and most exalted spirit, the Holy Spirit of Christ, no evil force could prevail against them.

In their understanding of Jesus, as the highest possible manifestation of their own works and aspirations, the Christian teachings that were received from the Catholics were understood as shamanic instructions designed to elevate the shaman to the sacred status of an instrument, or medium, of the Holy Spirit. Inspired by their goal of becoming mediums of the Holy Spirit, the Mananambal practiced the teachings and instructions of Jesus to the letter, and became *very* devout Christians. Ultimately, the Mananambal sublimated an ancient system of shamanic healing into the mission of Jesus Christ. This paradoxical occurrence was the first of several events within Filipino culture that led to the emergence of the powerful form of spirit-directed healing known as psychic surgery.

The Spaniards dealt harshly with those who disagreed with them.

During the Spanish colonial period, most of the indigenous healers and shamans of the cultures conquered by the Spaniards were killed, and their teachings destroyed, as a result of the irreconcilable differences between their beliefs and those of the Spanish. In the conversion of the Philippines, however, the parallels that existed between the religious practices of the Filipinos, and the Christian teachings of the Catholics, cleared the way for an easy, and pretty much bloodless conversion to take place. One that inadvertently empowered an ancient system of shamanism to find new expression, and survive the persecution and eradication that had occurred in other similar circumstances.

The Spanish, who considered their Filipino subjects to be ignorant savages, had no idea how the Filipinos interpreted the religious teachings they had received. They assumed the Filipinos did not have the capacity to understand, much less assimilate, their religious precepts. The term that describes the process through which a converted culture assimilates a foreign theology is 'indigenization,' The process of indigenization is characterized by an ongoing assimilation of an introduced theology into the prevailing system of beliefs of the culture into which the new theology is introduced. Eventually, a new synthesis is reached that addresses the religious needs of new converts in the context of their native beliefs.

The victorious Catholics eventually became aware of the unorthodox beliefs of the worshipers of the Holy Spirit, whom they concluded were heretics of the worst sort. Through the use of the most violent forms of torture and repression, the Spanish Catholics succeeded in forcing the great majority of Filipinos to submit to the orthodox interpretation of Catholic dogma. Under the Spanish, Filipinos were forced to abandon the leadership of the Mananambal and become orthodox Catholics. The Mananambal who survived the persecution recognized the danger involved in openly discussing their insights. The incorporation of the spiritual practices of the Mananambal into the work of the Holy Spirit became, of necessity, a closely guarded secret, a mystery religion conceived and brought to fruition in the obscurity of the rural Philippines.

Jesus confronts demon possessed man at Gadara.

The Pope Acknowledges Christian Pluralism

In 1974, at the Third General Synod of Bishops in Rome, Pope Paul VI spoke of the inevitable emergence of new forms of Christianity based on the ongoing indigenization of Catholicism in the African and Asian cultures. Pope Paul said, "Indeed we admit that a certain theological pluralism finds its roots in the mystery of Christ, the inscrutable richness whereof transcend the capacities of expression of all ages and cultures. Thus, the doctrine of faith which necessarily derives from that mystery calls for constant fresh research..."

Jesus exorcizes demons into a herd of pigs.

Christian Spiritism is one of the oldest examples of a hybrid Christianity derived from the heart of an Asian culture. In most cases, the races that were conquered by Spain adopted the outer form of

Christianity, but continued to worship their own ancestral gods. A case in point is Haiti, where there is widespread worship of the West African Voudoun Loa spirits. Likewise in Central and South America where the religion of Santeria flourishes. In the Philippines, however, the acceptance of the supremacy of the Holy Spirit led to a true conversion, albeit a conversion based on their own unique, and very different, understanding of Christianity. In the Christian Spiritist concept of Christianity, they saw no contradiction in using their highly developed, mediumistic practices and psychic abilities in the service of Jesus Christ.

In Filipino culture, trance and trance possession have always been viewed as the means through which the spiritual realm can be entered into and communed with. While in trance, Filipino shamans enter altered states of consciousness. This expanded perception allows the shaman (whether male or female) to enter this spiritual realm, study the landscape, meet the inhabitants of this 'parallel dimension,' and form relationships with them. As the inhabitants of this spirit filled dimension can be persuaded to share their information, the shamans gain access to information that is inaccessible to 'ordinary' human beings. The shaman is then able to intervene in the affairs of the mundane world with a degree of insight that enables them to find solutions to problems that otherwise would be impossible to resolve. In most cases, when the shaman is in the spirit world, his or her body is unconscious. This ability of the trance-shaman to enter the spirit world and "speak" with spirits has been a cornerstone of Filipino spiritist practice throughout its entire history.

As early as 1604, the Jesuit writer, Father Pedro Chirino, described the use of trance in a rural setting of the Visayan region of the Philippines. "The house is the usual place for the sacrifice, and the victim is a dog or cock. The mode of sacrifice is to slay the victim with certain ceremonies, and with dance movements which are performed by the priest to the accompaniment of a bell, or kettledrum. It is at this time that the devil takes possession of them, or they pretend that he does. They now make their strange grimaces, and fall into a state of ecstasy; after that period, they announce what they have seen and heard..." The belief that the information received during the trance state came from the "devil" is common to 16th and 17th century Spanish theology. A morbid fear of the devil is an element so pronounced in Western Christianity that virtually all spirit intervention was, and in most cases still is, seen as demonic. My Christian Spiritist mentors were quick to point out that if all forms of spirit intervention are demonic, then how are we to categorize the Pentecost, and the miracles that *Jesus* performed through the power of the Holy Spirit?

Jesus was accused of doing the devil's work in the 11th chapter of Luke. Some of the witnesses to the exorcism of a man who could not speak, said that, "He casteth out devils through Beelzebub, the chief of the devils." Jesus replied, "Every kingdom which is divided against itself shall be destroyed; and a house which is divided against itself shall fall. And if Satan is divided against himself, how can his kingdom survive? And yet you say that I am casting out demons through Beelzebub, by what means do your sons cast them out? But if I cast out demons by the finger of God, then the kingdom of heaven is come near you." (Luke 12:14-20)

The Role of the Holy Spirit in Christian Spiritism

The group of elders of the Christian Spiritist Church who relayed the information to me regarding the transition from shamanism to Christian Spiritism, did so verbally, in the form of an historical overview. In my efforts to cross reference their story, I read everything I could find on the subject of Filipino anthropology. I discovered that the Jesuit order of the Catholic Church had meticulously maintained records, from the time of their arrival in the Philippines in the early 16th century, to the present. A contemporary Jesuit writer whom I felt was the most qualified and erudite of the Filipino Jesuits was Father Francisco Demetrio, a Jesuit professor at Xavier University in Cagayan de Oro City, on the island of Mindanao. At the time I met with him in 1986 he was Professor of the Department of Philippine Studies-Folklore and Folklife Research Center. After reading several of his anthropological studies, which I found to be both enlightening and well researched, I wrote to him in Mindanao. I told him what I had learned from the Christian Spiritists and asked him if he considered the account I had been told by them to be accurate.

In his reply he stated, "Indeed there has been a continuity between the ancient shamanic healing before the advent of Christianity and the present day Mananambal among our people. I don't doubt that the Holy Spirit is operating through them now, even as He was in the past through their own culture and spiritual development." Father Demetrio also reaffirmed that, as a means of employing the assistance of spiritual forces among the Filipinos, the trance state has remained the entryway for communing with the realities of the spiritual realm. In the Philippines, ordinary Catholics use prayer as a means of entering into religious trance, which is evident in the crucifixion rituals that occur every year during Easter.

In order to facilitate their total domination of the Filipinos, the Spanish did not allow them to learn to read and, consequently, the Mananambal were not able to learn of the biblical teachings of Jesus, or the attributes of the Holy Spirit, until long after the arrival of the Spanish. As a result, the early Mananambal used references and constructed their Orasyones (magical prayers) from the catechism and used exclusively Catholic terminology in their rituals. As Spaniards and Filipinos intermarried, the repressive forces began to loosen their iron grip, and the Filipinos gradually gained access to the intellectual life of European civilization. Having acquired this newfound freedom, they began to study the bible in earnest. The widespread references to prophesy and the intervention of spirits in the stories of the Old Testament prophets, and the instructions of Jesus concerning the Holy Spirit, gave the Filipino Mananambal a great deal of insight. They began to suspect that the Spanish had unwittingly introduced them to a teaching that could be understood and utilized in the context of their long-standing traditions of spirit worship, in ways that were impossible for European Catholics, who had been too spiritually and emotionally traumatized by Inquisitions and witch hunts, to even contemplate, much less grasp.

As the Filipinos studied the bible, they learned that Jesus had identified God as Spirit, and that Jesus had defined the proper form of worship as worship "In Spirit and In Truth." (John 4:23-24) Jesus spoke of his return to heaven and the coming of the Holy Spirit that would follow His ascension into heaven. (John 16:7-16) Jesus further elaborated on the nature of the Holy Spirit when He said, "And I will ask of my Father and He will give you another comforter, to be with you forever, even the Spirit of Truth that the world cannot receive, because it has not seen Him and does not know Him; but you know Him because He abides with you and is *in* you." (John 14:16-17) Jesus, in conclusion, tells the apostles, "But the Comforter, the Holy Spirit, whom my Father will send in my name will teach you everything, and remind you of everything which I tell you." (John 14:26)

In searching for the cultural and anthropological roots of psychic surgery, I found a culture in which the Holy Spirit had survived the materialism of Descartes, and the rationalism of Newton. While Western Christians define the historical mission of Jesus in terms of the propitiation of the sins of humanity through His crucifixion and resurrection, Christian Spiritists define the primary historical mission of Jesus as overseeing the *Coming of the Holy Spirit* from God into the members of the body of Christ on earth. Jesus details the event in his prophesies and succeeded in preparing a select group of followers to become instruments of the wonderful power that he, himself, relied on and used to demonstrate the supremacy of God's power over the forces of evil.

The last words that Jesus spoke before He ascended into heaven were, "When the Holy Spirit comes upon you, you shall be witnesses to me both in Jerusalem and Judea, also in the province of Samaria and to the uttermost part of the earth." (Acts 1:8) Jesus's *first* commission to the apostles was to "heal the sick, cleanse the lepers, and cast out demons." In the time of Jesus, disease, leprosy, and demonic possession were believed to be the work of evil spirits. In order to successfully treat these conditions, the intervention of the Holy Spirit was required. Jesus apparently wanted his disciples to have a practical working knowledge of the applications of the powerful gifts of the Holy Spirit. It was through total immersion in the healing ministry, that Jesus taught his followers the ways and means through which the gifts of the Holy Spirit could be exercised. Jesus' commission to his apostles was the first step in preparing them for the second part of his mission, which was the sending forth of the Holy Spirit. In reading the scriptures, it becomes apparent that Jesus felt that initiating this outpouring of the Spirit into his chosen was a mission of utmost importance.

According to the Christian Spiritists, the Coming of the Holy Spirit at the Pentecost marked the fulfillment of Jesus's mission. It was during the Pentecost that the transmission of Divine power that Jesus had prophesied occurred. It came in fiery tongues of flame that descended upon the heads of the apostles (Acts 2:2-3) who, at that moment, were possessed by the Holy Spirit and immediately thereafter found themselves able to perform spiritual works that paralleled those which Jesus had performed. The Apostles were able to discern the exact nature of the gifts that they had received and classified these gifts of the Holy Spirit into three categories. The first were the gifts of **Revelation,** which include (1) Words of Wisdom, (2) Words of Knowledge, and (3) The discernment of the True Spirit. The second category were the gifts of **Power**, which include (4) The Gift of Faith, (5) The Gift of Healing, and (6) The Gift of the Working of Miracles. The third and final category, the gifts of **Inspiration,** include (7) The Gift of Prophesy, (8) The Gift of Diversity of Tongues, and (9) The Gift of Interpretation of Tongues. (1 Corinthians 12:1-12)

When the Christian Spiritists were finally able to read and study the bible, they discovered a sound doctrinal basis for the continuation and further development of Christian Spiritism. They strived to develop their spiritual gifts in the service of Christ, and chose the Christian healing ministry as the classroom in which they would perfect their skills as instruments of the Holy Spirit. And so, the ministry of the Christian Spiritists was modeled on Jesus's healing ministry. Training of new members was structured in the same way that Jesus trained the apostles. Aspiring mediums of the Holy Spirit were sent on healing missions that ministered to the legions of impoverished Filipinos, who suffered from sickness and infirmities of various types. In the interactive context of the healing ministry, each developing medium discovered for him or herself how the Holy Spirit operates.

Decoding Jesus's Teachings

By 1850, the Christian Spiritist community began organizing itself into a practicing congregation and started holding worship services in strict secrecy. They were severely persecuted by the Catholic Church, as well as medical authorities, but persevered in their spiritual work. Belonging to a culture steeped in spirit-directed religion, the instructions of Jesus concerning the Holy Spirit was one of the main topics of discussion in their services. Of special interest were the revelations of Jesus in John 14:26, wherein he says, "*When the Spirit of Truth has come, He will guide you into all the truth, and He will not speak from Himself; but what He hears He will speak;* and he will make known to you things which are to come in the future, he will glorify me, because he will take of my own and show it to you."

The biblical reference about the Holy Spirit speaking not from Himself, but instead speaking only what he heard, inspired great interest among the Filipino mediums who began to suspect that the instructions of Jesus in the Bible *were coded in a way that concealed a great mystery, nothing less than the means through which the Holy Spirit would "speak" to the members of the body of Christ,* the true Church. In the Philippines, people possessing strong religious conviction in conjunction with highly developed mediumistic abilities are quite common. They are well aware of the abilities of spirits to "speak" through mediums. As such, they immediately interpreted Jesus' references to the Holy Spirit 'speaking' in the context of their indigenous Spiritist practices. The Filipinos make a distinction between trance-possession mediums, who leave their unconscious bodies and 'travel' in the spiritual world, and mediums whom spirits enter into and 'speak' through while they are still conscious. These conscious or semiconscious mediums, are able to 'see' spirit phenomena with their eyes open or closed, and 'hear' the spirit 'speak.' In either case, they report what they learn from the spirit.

The Filipinos also make a clear distinction between demonic possession and possession by benevolent, beneficial, evolved spirits. If a spirit offers advice or healing services that fulfills immediate needs in their society, the spirit is regarded as 'elevated,' and celebrated as an ally and protector against the intervention of lesser spirits. Like the Filipinos, many of the apostles apparently possessed strong mediumistic gifts in conjunction with deep religious convictions. In the New Testament, the Apostle Paul discusses his perception of his experience as an instrument of the Holy Spirit. Paul begins by telling his followers, "When I came to you, I did not speak eloquently, nor was I able to preach to you with the authority of one learned in the mysteries of God. Except for my spiritual encounter with Jesus, I was totally unprepared for the work I now do. With great reverence for God and trembling I preached. The words I spoke and the preaching I did were not the result of prior training and education, rather, they were the words and preaching of the Spirit spoken powerfully *through* me. The Spirit has demonstrated its power and wisdom *through* me so that your faith might not rest in the wisdom of men, but in the power of God." (I Cor. 2:1-5 Paraphrased) Like the best of the Filipino mediums, Paul's intellect was undeveloped. Yet, in spite of this, he found himself delivering profoundly moving sermons. Paul readily admitted that the Spirit allowed him to function in ways that went beyond his normal capacities, and explained that the Holy Spirit was using him to inspire faith in the power and wisdom of God as the ultimate source of revelation and instruction.

Paul explains how he received his ability to "speak" on behalf of God's Spirit by saying, "How do we convey wisdom that we have derived from the Spirit, a wisdom and understanding not of this world? An undying wisdom unlike that possessed by worldly rulers who pass away.

We receive the wisdom of God in a mysterious, hidden way, that God ordained before the world for our glory. Had the rulers of the world known the truth, they would not have crucified Jesus. The eye has not seen and the ear has not heard and the heart of man has not conceived the things which God has prepared for those who love him. But God has revealed them to us by his Spirit; for the Spirit searches everything, even the depths of God." (I Cor. 2:6-10 Paraphrased)

When Paul discusses the nature of spirit-directed communication, he tells his followers, "For what man knows the mind of man, save the spirit of man which is in him? Even so, *no one knows the mind of God except the Spirit of God.* Now we have received the spirit that is from God, that we may understand the gifts that are given to us by God. For the things we discuss are not dependent on the knowledge of words and man's wisdom, but on the teaching of the Spirit, thus explaining spiritual things to the spiritually minded. The material man rejects spiritual things; they are foolishness to him; neither can he know them, because they are spiritually discerned. But the spiritual man discerns every thing, and yet no man can discern Him. For who knows the mind of the Lord that he may teach it? But we have the mind of Christ." (I Cor.2:11-16 Paraphrased)

Speaking with the Holy Spirit

For the Filipinos, the underlying theme of spirit-revealed knowledge was a familiar one. Not only were they well aware of the phenomenon of spirit communication, they were also experienced in producing the ceremonial setting that enabled the Spirit to communicate through mediums. They reasoned that what Jesus was referring to was the possibility of invoking the Holy Spirit into the body of a sanctified Christian medium. If this could be achieved, they could receive instructions directly from the Holy Spirit and be "taught everything" as Jesus had promised. The Christian Spiritists devised a ceremony unique in its goal of establishing an intradimensional dialogue with the Holy Spirit. Special hymns were written and sung to simultaneously predispose the mediums, and invoke the Holy Spirit. Their efforts were rewarded by the Holy Spirit, who sent the Spiritual Messengers of Christ to speak directly to them through their devout Christian mediums exactly as Jesus had promised.

The Christian Spiritist elders told me that the period between 1845 and 1850 was when this intradimensional dialogue was first established in the Philippines. Having accomplished the knowledge and conversation of the Holy Spirit, they questioned the Holy Spirit about the meaning of Christ's teachings, which the bible taught could only be interpreted and elucidated by God's own Spirit. In addition to their indigenous discoveries, they were becoming aware of developments taking place in the United States and France that would serve to confirm and articulate their own understanding of spiritual intelligence and purpose.

Chapter Four

The Union Espiritista Christiana de Filipinas

The Union Espiritista Christiana de Filipinas

The Philippine Islands were a colony of Spain for nearly 400 years. During the colonial period, Catholicism ruled the cultural, intellectual, and spiritual lives of the Filipinos. Toward the end of the colonial period, Christian Spiritists were caught between very powerful forces. The Catholic church openly attacked Spiritism and, in 1856, Pope Pius IX prohibited mediumship as "heretical, scandalous, and contrary to the honesty of customs." The Spanish Catholics, however, were the most hostile opponents of Spiritism. In 1861, the Bishop of Barcelona ordered that three hundred spiritist books be confiscated and publicly burned. In the Philippines, Spanish Catholic rulers insisted that Christian Spiritism was heretical and went to great lengths to destroy it. Among Filipinos, however, it was seen as a profound revelation, derived from spiritual insight unique to their culture, a sacred trust.

The Bishop of Barcelona ordered that Spiritist books be confiscated and burned.

By the end of the 19th century, Filipinos began to organize and rebel against the Spanish. One of the underlying causes of the Revolution of 1896 was freedom of religion. It is no coincidence that many of the leaders of the revolt were Christian Spiritists. As such, they considered Christian Spiritism to be an important component of the emerging identity of a new breed of Filipinos, free from colonial oppression and able to worship as they pleased. The birth of Filipino nationalism and the struggle for independence went hand in hand with the legitimization of Christian Spiritism. The Revolution of 1896 concluded with a pact in which the

Spaniards promised independence and autonomy for Filipinos. The pact was soon broken and the struggle resumed. In 1898, Philippine independence was finally won. On June 12, 1898, the American Navy, led by Commodore George Dewey, arrived in the Philippines and completed the defeat of the Spanish Armada in Manila Bay. After fighting a long terrible war for their independence, Filipinos now found themselves annexed by the United States as one of the spoils of the Spanish-American War.

With the American annexation of the Philippines, Filipino revolutionaries splintered into three groups. The first group continued the military struggle against the Americans; the second formed the Philippine Independent Church and seceded from the control of the Vatican. The third group, led by Juan Alvear, Agustin dela Rosa and Casimiro Pena, incorporated the Union Espiritista Christiana de Filipinas, The Christian Spiritist Union of the Philippines Inc., (hereafter referred to as the "Union.")

Juan Alvear was a highly educated and articulate man. He completed his law studies at the University of Santo Tomas in Manila. When the Revolution of 1896 broke out, he became a writer for "La Independencia," the newspaper of the Katipunan, the revolutionary political party. In addition to being a lawyer and publisher, Alvear was deeply interested in theosophy and theology, and was also gifted with the ability to heal. The Union was founded on February 19, 1905, and registered as a corporation on January 21, 1909. Under the Colonial rule of the United States, Christian Spiritists could conduct their services and propagate their beliefs without fear of persecution, for the first time in nearly 400 years. Members of the Union believed the Holy Spirit to be the *Divine minister* and guide sent by Jesus to illuminate the mysteries of the Bible, and to help them establish the kingdom of heaven on earth. The study of scriptures under the tutelage of the Holy Spirit was high on the agenda of the Union members, as was the ministry of healing.

Under the pen name, J. Obdell Alexis, Alvear wrote the first textbook of the Union. He called it *Antikey A Doctrina Espiritista* (A Short Spiritist Doctrine.) A dear friend and mentor of mine, the Reverend Benjamin Pajarillo, located an original copy of the book and managed to find a translator who, with a great deal of difficulty, translated it into English. The reason the translation was especially difficult was because it was written using a combination of three languages: Spanish, Tagalog, and a dialect of Northern Luzon known as Pangasinese. On the cover page of the Doctrina Espiritista were the words, "Adopted from the writings of the first apostle of Spiritism, Allan Kardec, and the result of thorough research by the author on true Spiritism."

The first textbook of the Union Espiritista

Allan Kardec

While the Bible was the first and most widely read book among Christian Spiritists, Alvear and many of the other members of the Union were well versed in the writings of those authors whose work illuminated and articulated the subject of Spiritism. Foremost among these was the French professor, Denizard Hippolyte-Leon-Rivail. Born in Lyon, France in 1804, Rivail was in his early fifties when he first became interested in the wildly popular phenomenon of spirit-rapping. Rivail was well educated, and knowledgeable in many subjects. As a professor he taught mathematics, astronomy, physiology, French, physics, chemistry, and comparative anatomy.

The Spiritualism movement began with what Allen Kardec termed typtology. Typtology is a mode of spirit communication in which spirits lift and tilt a table during a seance to produce rapping sounds. In organized seances, a number of people would sit around a table, hold hands, concentrate, and ask questions of the spirits. The spirits would then answer their questions through a series of raps, or knocks, similar to someone knocking on a door. In order to question the spirits, sometimes a simple yes or no would be indicated by a prescribed number of knocks. In another method, called alphabetical typtology, letters of the alphabet were recited and when the letter that the spirit wanted to draw attention to was called, a rap could be heard; thus spelling out words, sentences, and so on. Using this method, it was possible to hold lengthy, detailed conversations with the mysterious entities responsible for spirit-rapping.

The first recorded spirit-rapping began in America in 1848 with the playful efforts of Margaretta and Kate Fox to communicate with the spirits of the dead. Much to their astonishment, they succeeded in establishing a ghostly dialogue with the spirit of Charles Haynes. Using rapping noises as its means of communication, Hayne's spirit conveyed the message that he had been killed and buried in the basement of their home. When bones were found in their basement, what had begun as innocent fun became a sensation. From these humble beginnings, what came to be known as the Spiritualism movement took root and grew to international proportions. As a result of their spiritualistic activities, the Fox sisters were condemned and lived in constant danger. They were attacked by religious fanatics in their community, and besieged by angry mobs several times. They were also exploited, and eventually betrayed by their own sister, Leah, who was said to have been the beneficiary of most of the donations collected from those who came to the Fox sisters for spiritual counseling.

Margaretta and Kate Fox

As the spiritualism movement got underway in America and Europe, the strange but well-documented manifestations of spirit communication such as spirit-rapping and seance channeling were regarded as weird and unexplainable events. The great majority of Americans and Europeans viewed it as nothing more than a bizarre form of entertainment. For those who took the spirit communications seriously, however, it quickly became apparent that something more was happening. Many of the messages received from the spirits were discovered to be quite accurate. In addition to the messages, other phenomena were being witnessed and verified by many of the most credible individuals in American and European society. By 1854, spirit-directed paranormal phenomenon had reached the level of an intradimensional invasion. Leading spiritualists in the United States decided that it was time to undertake an official investigation. The erudite and well-respected spiritualists petitioned Congress to appoint a scientific commission to investigate the perplexing paranormal phenomenon that had been witnessed by so many people.

The petition entitled 'A Memorial' described the phenomenon produced by the spirits in great detail. The object of the investigation was described in the petition as: 1) an occult force, exhibited in sliding, raising, arresting, holding, suspending, and otherwise disturbing, numerous ponderable bodies, apparently in direct opposition to the acknowledged laws of matter, and altogether transcending the accredited powers of the human mind; 2) lights of various forms and colors, and of different degrees of intensity, which appear in dark rooms, where no substances exist, which are liable to develop a chemical action or phosphorescent illumination, and in the absence of all the means and instruments whereby electricity is generated or combustion produced; 3) sounds which are extremely frequent in their occurrence, widely diversified in their character, and more or less significant in their import; and 4) how the functions of the human body and mind are often and strangely influenced in what appear to be certain abnormal states of the system, and by causes which are neither adequately defined nor understood.

This document was delivered by the former governor of Wisconsin, Nathaniel Tallmadge, to Senator James Shields to be presented before Congress. Much to the consternation of the petitioners, Shields scorned the spiritualists by saying, "the prevalence of this delusion at this age of the world, among any considerable portion of our citizens, must originate, in my opinion, in a defective system of education, or in a partial derangement of the mental faculties, produced by a diseased condition of the physical organization. I cannot, therefore, believe that it prevails to the extent indicated in this petition." Responding to Shield's criticism, Eliab Capron, a chronicler of the spiritualism movement, wrote, "It is not probable that any of the Memorialists expected more favorable treatment than they received. The carpenters and fishermen of this world are the ones to investigate new truths, and make senates and crowns believe and respect them. It is in vain to look for the reception or respect of new truths by men in high places." The widely documented and verified invasion of the spirits described above never received a plausible explanation and is still regarded as a mystery.

While controversy raged in the United States, however, a very significant spiritual event was developing in France. Rivail had an experience that deepened his commitment to understanding the phenomenon which was to change his life forever. He describes this event in his own words. "I was confronted with a fact that was contrary to the laws of nature as we knew them, and repugnant to my reason, but one night in May, 1855, at the home of Madame Plainemason, I myself witnessed the phenomenon of tables circling around, jumping, and even running, as it were, in such conditions that any doubts were dispelled. That was a fact: there must be a cause, I thought. Something very serious is behind all this stuff that serves merely to entertain the spectators."

In his efforts to comprehend the paranormal, spirit-directed phenomenon he had personally witnessed, Rivail began to gather transcribed texts of spirit messages from his wide circle of acquaintances. As time went on, a great number of manuscripts detailing these question and answer sessions with the spirit world became available. Rivail studied the channeled messages of his colleagues and was quite impressed with the inner consistency and universal, philosophical overview that existed in many of the texts. Because of his achievements as an educator who had written popular books on grammar and spelling, his colleagues decided that he was the person best qualified to write a book on the material that had been channeled. His fellow researchers handed over more than fifty notebooks of channeled information to Rivail, and asked him to write a book on the material.

Some of the notebooks contained trivial writing, but a significant number of them espoused elevated moral teachings of a spiritual, philosophical, and even religious nature. The manuscripts revealed the messages of entities who referred to themselves as the Spirit of Truth, the Comforter, and the Messengers of God. Early on, these spirits claimed that they had arrived to fulfill the prophesy of the Bible concerning the advent of the Holy Spirit. Much to his amazement, as Rivail continued to systematize this great body of information, a mystical religious doctrine began to emerge, one that was consistent, coherent, and inspiring.

In 1856, Rivail decided to change his approach. Rather than merely editing the work of others, he decided to write an exhaustive list of questions which he presented to the spirits himself. In the preface to *The Spirit's Book*, Anna Blackwell describes Rivail's introduction to a friend whose two daughters were mediums. While most of the messages the daughters received were as lighthearted and frivolous as they themselves were, when Rivail sat with them, their demeanor changed from lighthearted to serious. Inquiring as to the reason for this dramatic change of demeanor, the spirits that spoke through the mediums told him that "spirit entities of a much higher order than those who habitually communicated through the two young mediums came expressly for him, and would continue to do so, in order to enable him to fulfill an *important religious mission*." In 1857, he published his first book, *The Spirit's Book*. It was laid out in a format comprised of 1,018 questions and answers. He covered many topics under four general headings which were, 1) Primary Causes, 2) The Spiritual World of the Spirits , 3) Moral, Natural, and Divine Law, and 4) Repentance, Heaven, Purgatory, and Hell. During one of these sessions Rivail was told that, in a former incarnation, he had been a Druid with the name of Allan Kardec. He liked the name and decided that in all future writings of a spiritual nature, he would publish under the name from his former life. Rivail went on to write three more books, entitled *The Book of Mediums*, *The Gospel as Interpreted by Spiritism*, and *Spiritualist Initiation*.

Allan Kardec

The published works of Allan Kardec elevated spiritualism to an intellectual doctrine which he called the Spiritist Doctrine. A doctrine derived entirely from the direct revelation of spirit-directed mediums, it had a profound influence on the Filipino Christian Spiritists, and was integrated into the doctrine of the Union. The spiritist communities in the Philippines, as well as in Brazil, saw in Kardec's teachings an eloquent articulation of many of their own deeply held, indigenous beliefs about the reality of the spiritual realm of existence.

For centuries, the people of the Philippines and Brazil had suffered the indignity of having their native beliefs and spiritual practices either dismissed outright as superstition stemming from ignorance, or actively persecuted as heresy. In Kardec, they found a vindication of the superhuman efforts they had gone to in order to keep their cultures alive, and both embraced the teachings of the spirit via Kardec. While the bible contained specific references to the Holy Spirit, these references were circumspect and incomplete. In contrast, the Spiritist Doctrine provided an unprecedented explanation of the nature of the spirit world and its inhabitants. For Christian Spiritists, the Spiritist Doctrine articulated not only their own indigenous beliefs, it also articulated their beliefs about the Holy Spirit.

The Spiritist communities of Brazil and the Philippines share the unusual distinction of practicing very similar methods of paranormal healing within the gospel message of Jesus' healing ministry. These traditions of spirit-directed healing, when articulated by the spiritual revelations in the books of Allan Kardec, and applied within the context of the miraculous healing ministry of Jesus, produced two communities on opposite sides of the world from which psychic surgery has emerged as one of the primary modes of treatment.

The Decline of Spiritualism

In the fifty years that elapsed between the publication of Kardec's books and the incorporation of the Union, the spiritualism movement declined in the United States and Europe. Numerous scandals undermined the credibility of some of its foremost proponents. By 1888, both of the Fox sisters confessed that they were cheats. In fact, both sisters had developed serious drinking problems over the years. At the behest of her sister Leah, Kate Fox's children were taken from her by the Society for the Prevention of Cruelty to Children, and placed in foster care. This act led to a great deal of bitterness and anger against Leah by both Margaretta and Kate. Feeling exploited and betrayed by their sister Leah, who had collected and spent the great majority of the money paid to them...Margaretta and Kate appeared publicly at the New York Academy of Music. Margaretta confessed that she had made all the rapping noises that fostered the movement by means of a double-jointed big toe. Kate remained silent and would neither confirm nor deny the confession of her sister. It was later learned that a reporter had offered $1,500 to them if they would confess and give him an exclusive on the story. Desperate for money and liquor, the sisters apparently agreed, and then proceeded to drink their earnings away. Margaretta recanted her confession in writing shortly before she died in 1895. Kate never recanted, and died shortly afterwards. Both sisters were buried in pauper's graves.

True Spiritism Emerges

As spiritualism fell into decline in America and Europe, what Allan Kardec called true or Christian Spiritism flourished in the Philippines and Brazil. True or Christian Spiritism was the culmination of the enlightened teachings that Kardec received from the spirits. Kardec's revelations directly contradicted the teachings of orthodox Spiritualism. Prior to Kardec, spiritualists taught that we lived only once. The spirits told Kardec that we in fact reincarnated. This dispute created a schism that led Kardec to call his doctrine Spiritism in order to distinguish his teachings from those of the spiritualists. Like Kardec before him, Juan Alvear methodically questioned the spirits. Based on his conversations with the spirits, Alvear tells us, "The prophesy stated by God in the prophet Joel 2:28-31, that His spirit will be poured upon all flesh is being fulfilled. What Jesus foretold about the arrival of the Spirit of Truth, the Holy Spirit, in John 14:16-26 and John 16:7-13, is also being fulfilled. In the church, the coming of the Spirit of Truth will elucidate the meaning of Christ's teachings and they will be interpreted in real spirit and truth, which is known only in spirit."

Alvear goes on to say, "Fifty years have elapsed since the aforementioned (spiritualistic) manifestations happened. Spiritualism has gained ill repute in the Western countries where they occurred. Christian Spiritism has flourished as the other forms of spiritualism have fallen into decay. Here in the Philippines, the forces of Christ in the spirit world made themselves manifest through our mediums as *medicine* called *magnetic fluid*, which flows from the spirit world through the mediums to introduce Spiritism through healing. The pulpit and the learned claim that the appearance of spirits was the work of the devil who settled in the Philippines. Nevertheless, there is an increasing number infused with Spiritism, which is spreading to the provinces and its result is none other than morality and sanctity and the knowledge of God's spirit. So it has become clear that Spiritism is a good tree because its fruit is good. Now, it is apparent that God has manifested in the Third Person of the Holy Spirit, announcing to the world that those who believe will be saved."

In contrast to the derision and incredulity that plagued the advent of spiritualism in the West, the phenomenon was described by Alvear as the first attempts of the Holy Spirit to communicate a new spirituality, a form of Christianity in which the Holy Spirit manifested itself through highly evolved Christian mediums. The same spirits who tried so hard to prove their existence to skeptical and incredulous Westerners, were well received by the members of Christian Spiritist organizations in the Philippines. Christian Spiritists teach, that after the death of the Apostles, the sacred spirits of the spiritual realm, as well as the earthbound spirits and the souls of those who have passed from this life into the next, began to communicate with the living. In the Doctrina, Alvear tells us, "In the days of the Apostles, the spirit communicated with mankind through supernatural means such as burning bushes, writing on walls, and revealed itself through its servants who became prophets and seers. In the same manner, we now witness the wonders of heaven which have happened before but much more so now because these wonders have spread across a much wider area on Earth than during the times of the Apostles."

While a great number of Americans and Europeans were scratching their heads in disbelief as tables waltzed across rooms and thunderous rapping sounds echoed, the Filipino Spiritists immediately recognized and cooperated with the manifesting spirits who identified themselves as the "spiritual messengers of Christ." Alvear defined the unique insight of the Christian Spiritists when he wrote, "The presence of spirits as mentioned, voice pulsations, music, noises, lights, etc., and occurrences in other nations have been widespread. But today's events are different because spoken words and writing are being received through sanctified Christians who, through their sanctification, have become vehicles of the Holy Spirit of Truth as prophesied by Christ. Is this not what happened to the prophets who received the word of God, which they wrote? Now, spread all over the world are the new prophets who receive the word of God through His spirits. Thus, is fulfilled the word of God which said: "On the last day, my spirit shall pervade all mankind, your sons and your daughters shall be the prophets, the young men shall see miracles, and the old women and men shall dream new dreams."

With the wisdom and insight borne of their unique sensitivity, the Filipino Christian Spiritists clarified the mission of the spirits. In the following dialogue with the Blessed Spirit, Alvear asks:

Alvear: From the time that man appeared on earth until now, was there ever a time when spirits did not talk or communicate with human beings?
Spirit: None whatsoever, there were always spirits talking to men until now, however, because of fear of speaking with lower spirits and abuses that came to be, such were prohibited.
Alvear: What is the fundamental moral doctrine of Spiritism?
Spirit: It is none other than Christ's teachings. (Do unto others as you would have them do unto you.) That is why it is called Christian Spiritism.
Alvear: Does Christian Spiritism come from the teachings of Christ?
Spirit: Yes, and it also comes from the true spirit as foretold by Jesus

Christ.

Alvear: What do we derive from this doctrine?

Spirit: The important and various teachings of the Holy Spirit which we learn from questions and answers.

Alvear: But what is the purpose of these manifestations of the spirit?

Spirit: It is God's will that the concept of man be changed with regard to the dead, and to the spirits so that they can be understood, and in order to understand that the spiritual world is a source of strength on Earth, amidst the turmoil and darkness, and this spiritual world guides men on Earth to their destiny, which is the will of Christ.

At Alex Orbito's healing center in Quezon City, one of the main topics discussed by the many foreigners who came to research the phenomenon of psychic surgery, was whether the ability to perform this paranormal surgery was an inborn ability, or whether it could be learned. Though I had no desire to become a psychic surgeon, I began to wonder why the question seemed to be avoided. My curiosity eventually prevailed and I decided to see if I could find the answer. I reasoned that, if there was anything the psychic surgeons had in common, I might find the answers I sought by researching whatever commonality they shared among themselves. On the surface, there appeared to be very little that the psychic surgeons had in common. Some were public figures who enjoyed the limelight, while others worked only in the middle of the night. Some were rich; others were very poor. Some of the psychic surgeons were playboys; others were pious recluses.

As I expanded my research and met more psychic surgeons, magnetic healers, and Christian Spiritists, I finally began to notice something they all had in common. At every healer's center that I visited, there was a banner from the Union Espiritista prominently displayed on the wall in close proximity to the table where the healers worked. On the banner was the name of the center, as well as scriptural references. Whether the healers who worked at the respective centers were affiliated with Alex Orbito or not, the banner was always present. Eventually, I found three things the healers had in common. They all professed the Holy Spirit as the source of their healing power. They all were either active members of the Union, or had been at some time in their lives. Finally, they all had the banner of the Union prominently displayed in their healing centers.

Early in my research I managed to find a copy of the amended Constitution of the Union Espiritista, dated 1950. Since I was primarily interested in finding older texts that documented the early history of the Union, I was not overly excited by the Constitution. On first glance, the corporate structure of the Union seemed to be a straightforward combination of parliamentary procedure and bylaws. In the table of contents, the chapter headings dealt mostly with the duties and responsibilities of the officers, elections, and issues dealing with charter requirements. The amended Constitution seemed in every way to be a normal corporate document. Then, one day, I took a closer look at it and found a chapter entitled "Spiritual Direction of the Association." I opened the booklet and read the following, *"The Spiritual Direction shall be the Supreme Authority of the Association. This shall integrate a court of Spirits of Light, officially known as Spirit Protectors, who shall be under the superior and unique direction of our Lord Jesus. These Spirits are the ones who shall direct the works in general of the Association, principally scientific, philosophical, moral and spiritual, through medianimical communications."* I was astounded to discover that this duly registered corporation which seemed normal in every way was officially directed through mediums, by spirits from another dimension of space and time.

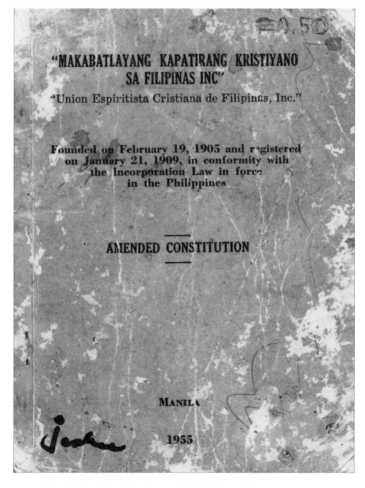

The Constitution of the Union Espiritista

The existence of a large organization whose administration was based solely on the revelations of spirits through mediums was hard for me to comprehend. Yet, after what I had seen and experienced with the psychic surgeons, I didn't let the limitations of my knowledge stand in the way of my research. One Sunday, I decided to visit the headquarters of the Union in Quezon City. Accompanied by two Filipino friends, we made the difficult journey through Quezon City's side streets and neighborhoods. Eventually, we arrived at the General Center of the Union Espiritista where services were in progress. We sat down to observe. The man presiding over the service asked me to introduce myself. I told the worshipers that I was a healer and a writer and was very much interested in learning about Espiritism. I offered my healing services to them, and gave them several copies of my book *The Healing Ministry of Jesus Christ*.

As the service drew to a close, one of the spiritists came over and introduced himself to me as Brother Cypriano Ramos. He told me that he was the archivist of the Union, and published their newsletter. He impressed me as someone who could tell me what I needed to know about Filipino Espiritism. Brother Ramos thanked me again for my book, and said that the Union had recently published a book entitled *God is Spirit*, and gave me a copy. I briefly summarized my research and told him that I was trying to locate information about the formative stages of Espiritism in the Philippines. I asked him if the Union had published any other books. He said that other books had been published, but were long out of print, and difficult to find.

We then discussed psychic surgery. I said that I had noticed that most of the psychic surgeons were members of the Union. He confirmed that they were. I asked him if the Union offered any courses of instruction in the development of healing powers. As I had suspected, he told me that they did. Trying to contain my excitement, I asked him if the psychic surgeons had received the training offered by the Union. He replied that they had all been trained since childhood to function in varying capacities as instruments of the Holy Spirit. There, in the pew where we sat, I learned that the psychic surgeons had all received what Brother Ramos called *Christian mediumship training*! He candidly explained that the training had been revealed to the Christian Spiritists directly from the Holy Spirit over many years. I assumed that they had received the training in a way similar to that in which Marcos Orbito's Interfaith Church members received their sermons.

In addition to whatever gifts the psychic surgeons had been born with, they had also received *religious training* from the Union Espiritista. I asked Brother Ramos what percentage of people who complete the mediumship training became psychic surgeons. He replied that very few of their mediums were psychic surgeons and explained that mediumship training predisposes a person to receive the Holy Spirit, but once the medium is able to receive the Holy Spirit, their spirit-directed activities may vary greatly. In discussing psychic surgery with Brother Ramos, I got the distinct impression that it was not nearly as important to the Espiritistas as it was to Westerners.

He told me of certain prayers they had received from the Holy Spirit. These prayers, when spoken either verbally or in silence, facilitated the intervention of the power of God into the task at hand. These sacred prayers are referred to as Orasyones and have a long history among Filipino folk healers. Finally, I asked if it would be possible for me to receive mediumship training. He smiled, and asked why I would want to study mediumship training. I replied that I had studied the spiritual teachings and practices of many cultures; but I felt that Christian Spiritism offered me something closer to my roots, something I had been led to by destiny. After asking me several more questions, Brother Ramos, apparently convinced of my sincerity, offered to train me himself.

He then gave me his address in Manila, and after giving me a copy of their newsletter, he left. Shortly after this first meeting, I went to see him one morning at his home. Brother Ramos and his wife were gracious hosts, going out of their way to extend their hospitality to me. After a while, we began to discuss mediumship training. As he spoke, I took copious notes. He first suggested that I become a vegetarian and meditate at certain special times. I was confused by his suggestions because, of the forty psychic surgeons whom I knew personally, none were vegetarian. I also asked him if the mediumship training that he proposed to teach me was the same training that the psychic surgeons had undergone. He admitted to me that it wasn't; that they had received their training in the rural provinces from an older group of mediumship trainers, most of whom were now dead.

Brother Ramos explained that the Union had changed a great deal over the past twenty years, and had integrated many practices which had not been observed by the early Union. He also said that there was no longer any uniform training for Christian mediumship; that the elders of the Union taught mediumship training in varying ways. I explained to him that I had received training in Yoga and other Oriental disciplines, but I had never known of any yogis who could open the body with their bare hands. I then told him, as tactfully as I could, that I would prefer to experience the most traditional form of Christian mediumship training; hopefully, the same one that the psychic surgeons had received. He thought for a minute, and told me that only a few of the original mediumship trainers were still alive. He warned that they lived among the poor in the remote provinces of Northern Luzon in areas controlled by the communist insurgents of the New Peoples Army (NPA.) He cautioned that it would be very dangerous for me to travel to those areas. As our meeting came to a close, I mentioned in passing that should he come across any books or written materials that might help me in my research into the cultural events that led to psychic surgery, I'd appreciate it if he would contact me. He escorted me to the door, and as we said our farewells, Brother Ramos eyes suddenly lit up. He asked me to wait, and went back into his house. Several minutes later, he returned with a large, dusty book. I could see from its condition that the book was very old. He said that he had almost forgotten about this book. It had been recovered from an old Spiritist center in the province of Pangasinan which was being razed to make way for new construction. As I held the book in my hands, a chill went down my spine. I asked him what he thought it contained, and he admitted that he did not know. I carefully opened the book and was surprised to see that the entire book was handwritten in a beautiful, cursive style of old Spanish. Old Spanish was the language and educational standard of the Philippines during the Colonial period.

For several moments we both stood in silence, staring at the book and at each other. The pages were cracked and flaking from age. Our curiosity grew as we carefully turned the pages of the book. Yet even with the utmost care, merely turning the pages caused them to crumble. I expressed my concern to him that if some sort of copy wasn't made, the book, and whatever information it contained would soon be lost forever. He agreed. We discussed our options and came to a mutual agreement. He agreed to let me take the book with me. I agreed to make a copy of the book, find a translator, have a complete translation done, and give him a copy of the translation. Though I knew I was undertaking a great responsibility, I had a gut feeling that this old, disintegrating book might contain the information I was seeking.

I was very concerned about the book being damaged by handling, and promised to be as careful as possible with it. However, if it were damaged, I did not want him to be angry with me. He said that the book had been lost for 45 years and even if it were damaged in an attempt to translate it, he felt that it was worth the risk. He knew that translating a book of this size and age would be expensive, and doubted that such a project would ever be undertaken by the Union. Much of the archival material had already been lost, misplaced, or destroyed by time. He handed the book to me. I thanked him profusely, and left Brother Ramos's house with my work clearly cut out for me.

Chapter Five

The Spiritual Messengers of Christ

The Corporate Minutes of the Union Espiritista (1919-1933)

The Spiritual Messengers of Christ

After my meeting with Brother Ramos, my priorities became crystal clear. First, I had to have the book translated. Second, I had to find the right person to teach me Christian mediumship training. In January, 1986, I received a telephone call from Alex Orbito, who asked me to meet him at his office in the Manila Midtown Hotel. Alex was in an exuberant mood and told me that the Philippine Healers' Circle was having its annual meeting to elect officers and that he very much wanted me to attend. He took me to the conference room where we were seated. It was an impressive gathering of nearly forty psychic surgeons. In the three years since I'd first arrived in the Philippines, I had come to know all the members of the Philippine Healers' Circle Inc.. In spite of their great healing abilities, I found that none of the psychic surgeons were experienced in spinal adjustment, and that was the area of healing in which I am most skilled. While working at Alex's center I had adjusted the spines of not only the psychic surgeons, but their families as well, and they all seemed extremely satisfied with the results.

The meeting was called to order with Alex presiding. He immediately made a motion that I be elected as a member of the Board of Directors and be named regional Vice-President of the Healers' Circle. The motion was seconded, and I was unanimously elected as a Director and Vice-President of the Philippine Healers' Circle for the USA. The election to that office was an honor that had never been extended to a non-Filipino. I was flattered and grateful to be held in such high esteem by a group of people as dedicated and gifted as these were. In my capacity as Regional Vice President of the Healers' Circle, my duties consisted mostly of organizing healing missions to the United States. I enjoyed organizing healing missions, and felt that they did a great deal of good. However, after meeting with Brother Ramos, I had learned that psychic surgery, and all that it accomplished, was only a small part of a much larger picture. In learning of the mediumship training, I knew that I was getting closer to the source. After meeting Brother Ramos, my research priorities changed. My natural curiosity about any form of training that enabled human beings to become psychic surgeons, left me thinking about little else. In the three years I had spent within the healing community in Manila, no one, either foreign or Filipino had ever mentioned mediumship training. I had read a few brief references to the religious practices of the Espiritistas, but no one had specifically stated that all of the psychic surgeons had received Christian mediumship training from the Union.

At the election ceremony, I met a psychic surgeon who was to play a major role in helping me achieve my goals. His name was Reverend Lino Guinsad, of Baguio City. Lino was the youngest of all the psychic surgeons and was a genuine, loving person. After the meeting, Lino and I went back to my apartment and I showed him the still untranslated book. He took one look at the book and was visibly impressed. He was also surprised when I discussed my knowledge of Christian mediumship training with him. He said that, among the members of the Healers' Circle, certain subjects were not discussed with foreigners, and mediumship training was high on the list of the forbidden topics. I did not need to ask him why.

I explained to Lino that the archivist of the Union Espiritista had not only told me about mediumship training, he had offered to train me. I also told Lino about my meeting with Brother Ramos and what I had learned from him. Lino was very amused that I had turned down Brother Ramos's offer of mediumship training. He said that, had I been Filipino, I would have become a vegetarian rather than risk offending someone as erudite and well respected as Brother Ramos. I assured Lino that I meant no offense by my refusal. I then told him that Brother Ramos had also said there were still mediumship trainers among the provincial Espiritistas, who taught mediumship training as it had been taught in the early Union. When I told Lino that I was anxious to meet such a trainer, he smiled. He said he knew just the person I needed to meet. He assured me that this particular mediumship trainer was the best in the Philippines, and that, even though the elderly healer did spend a great deal of time in communist-controlled areas, he lived in Baguio City with his wife and two children.

The Translation

Finding someone who could translate old Spanish manuscripts into English proved to be very difficult. With the long history of Spanish colonial rule in the Philippines, I expected that finding a translator would be easy. I found instead that most Filipinos had bitter memories of the Spanish, and had long since abandoned the Spanish language in favor of English. I finally located a translator through an apprentice of one of the members of the Healers' Circle. In March of 1986, I rented a big, beautiful house in Baguio City and convinced the translator to relocate from Quezon City to my new house, and to begin work translating the book on a full-time basis. The translator, who had the unlikely name of Siegfried Sepulveda, belonged to one of the very few Filipino families who still spoke Spanish among themselves. Siegfried was an aspiring actor and playwright who had fallen on hard times. He was happy to have what he viewed as a paid vacation in Baguio City, a place dearly loved by all Filipinos. Shortly after the translation work began, I was called back to Manila for a week. Upon my return to Baguio, I arrived in the evening, and was shocked to find Siegfried drunk and acting very sullen and depressed. The following morning, I asked Siegfried what was wrong. He returned my question with his own questions about the book. He asked where I had gotten it, and if I knew what it contained. I replied that I did not, and he proceeded to tell me that he had never before seen anything like the manuscript.

He explained that the book was the corporate book of minutes of the General Center of the Union Espiritista between the years of 1919 and 1933. I asked him what was so unusual about that. What was unusual, he replied, was the format of the business meetings. In typical corporate settings, business meetings are presided over by corporate officers and the items on the agenda are put to a vote. In the meetings of the Union, however, all of the decisions were made by *spirits* who spoke through mediums who were present at the business meetings. I recalled the chapter I had read in the Constitution of the Union about the spiritual direction of the association and took a deep breath. I asked Siegfried to show me what he meant. He opened the book and pointed to the column on the left side of each page. Laid out in a question and answer format, the entire book was an ongoing dialogue between a group of spirits that worked under the aegis of the Holy Spirit, and the President of the Union. My mind was staggered by the implications of having obtained the only existing copy of the corporate minutes of the early years of the Union. I recalled how effortlessly the elderly female medium and the scribe had channeled the contents of the spiritual service at the Interfaith Church. But the mind-boggling inferences of the spiritual intervention at the Interfaith Church were child's play compared to the level of spirit intervention revealed in the astonishing book we were about to translate.

Seigfried found the idea of translating a document that recorded the progress of an organization governed by spirits to be a little overwhelming, even intimidating. I discussed my research with him and reassured him that not all spirits were bad; that some of them were Divine spirits, who served God and humanity. I pointed out that I believed that the spirits whose messages were recorded in the Minutes, could very well be the same spirits referred to in the Doctrina as the Spiritual Messengers of Christ. This group of spirits had first contacted the Espiritistas in the formal evangelical conferences that Alvear refers to in the Doctrina. I pointed out to Siegfried that if such were the case, then the Minutes were a detailed chronological record of the origins of Filipino Espiritism, a subject that he might find to be quite interesting. Siegfried admitted that he had never even considered the possibility that such a thing existed, but it was clear that his curiosity was quickly replacing his fear. He asked me where I had learned about the Spiritual Messengers of Christ and I showed him my translation of Juan Alvear's book, the *Doctrina Espiritista*. Siegfried spent the afternoon reading the *Doctrina Espiritista* and, after finishing, he calmly resumed work on the translation, which he now found to be quite fascinating.

Like the works of Allan Kardec, the *Doctrina Espiritista* is written in a question and answer format. In the *Doctrina*, Alvear specifically discusses the arrival of a group of spirits he calls the Spiritual Messengers of Christ. Following the arrival of the Divine Spirits, Alvear describes the "founding of schools of moral evangelism which arose from the knowledge of the Holy Spirit" and proceeds to write that, "From this time came the true Spiritism in formal mediums followed by the emergence of conferences and evangelical sessions." Alvear describes the Spiritual Messengers as, "messenger spirits or spirits who are ministers of Jesus Christ; they are in charge of planning, *they direct and govern the unrefined spirits*, they are chosen to fulfill God's will." As for the ultimate purpose of the Messengers of Christ, the Spirit tells Alvear of "Big things that heaven has in store in the end, which is the revelation or appearance of the Holy Spirit."

While Seigfried was busy translating, I studied, organized, and arranged the translated Minutes into a coherent body of information which I am publishing in this chapter. It is the Minutes which illustrate the inner workings of the organization whose activities and discoveries laid the foundation from which the enigma of psychic surgery emerged. Before reading the Minutes, I often wondered what events in Filipino culture had led these people to conceive and create a healing practice as unique as psychic surgery. I was amazed to discover that the central cultural event underlying the manifestation of their paranormal healing, was the equivalent of a contemporary Filipino Pentecost in which a group of spirits...the spiritual messengers of Christ...decided to cultivate and expand their relationship with the Filipino mediums of the Holy Spirit. The messengers of Christ provided the Filipinos with a mission and the means to accomplish it. The mission of the Christian Spiritists was the establishment of an organization through which the citizens of earth could learn of and prepare themselves for the coming of the Holy Spirit. In order to accomplish their mission, the mediums received a training that expanded and fine-tuned their capacity to function as *instruments* of the Holy Spirit. As instruments of the Holy Spirit, they dispensed the healing power of God's Spirit through their healing ministry to win converts.

In recounting the series of events that led to the Christian Spiritist Pentecost, it seems that the stage of history had been meticulously set in the Philippines. Is it mere coincidence that Friars brought to Cebu by Magellan, and even Magellan himself, *successfully exorcised powerful demons* and taught baptism as a healing ritual? I wonder how often other conquistadors used spiritual healing and exorcism as a means of paving the way for the colonial policies of Spain? The cultural evolution of the Filipinos produced individuals who were instinctively and intellectually predisposed to fully and voluntarily cooperate with a covert mission of the Holy Spirit. The Minutes of the Union are nothing less than proof that elevated spiritual forces are manipulating the genetic and historical strategies of the human race.

Friends have asked me what I consider to be the most convincing evidence that paranormal healing in the Philippines is genuine. I tell them that it is the chronological record that describes the unfolding of the relationship of the Christian Spiritists and the Spiritual Messengers of Christ. The very existence of the Minutes is definitive evidence of the dawning of a spiritualized world in which the Holy Spirit has emerged to

The Spiritual Messengers of Christ

play a fundamental role. In the Doctrina, Juan Alvear suggests that as the progressive revelation of the Holy Spirit continues, its work would become increasingly *externalized*, and spirit-directed models of religion would become more common. In the introduction of the Doctrina, Alvear tells us that, "Through the revelation of the Holy Spirit, the resistance of the Church and other opposing groups to the advent of Spiritism will slowly disintegrate because all will come together in the teachings of the true Spirit which will reign at the second coming of Christ to fulfill a mission in accordance with the will of God on earth, a mission *no longer directed by the minds of men* (italics mine) but received from the spirit directly in the fulfillment of the Holy Spirit." In the meantime, the Doctrina teaches that individuals who are properly predisposed to receive and cooperate with the Spirit of Truth will transform the world in ways that are presently inconceivable. Among the Filipino Christian Spiritists this is a work in progress.

The Minutes of the Union are unique in that they illustrate the specific details of the difficulties the early Christian Spiritists faced as they tried their best to follow the instructions they received from the Holy Spirit. These selfless disciples of the Holy Spirit were determined to establish the means through which the highest and most profound source of spiritual power could intervene in this world for the good of all. Travel back with me in time to the Philippines of 1919 to take an intimate look at the supernatural dilemmas and surreal struggles that confronted these courageous and dedicated people.

In order to understand the activities of the mediums in the Minutes of the Union, I must first explain the terms "influenced," "protector," and "apparatus." When Christian Spiritists refer to the word "influenced," they are referring to the *direct induction of trance* in the mediums. The Director of Mediums is responsible for inducing the trance state in the mediums and discerning whether or not the communicating spirit is one of elevated status. The Director of Mediums works exclusively with experienced mediums who possess highly developed moral and spiritual qualities. These mediums willingly allow elevated spirits to communicate revelation and instruction through them. The spiritual and moral authority of the Director of Mediums is derived from an in depth discernment of trance phenomenon, and years of experience preparing mediums to receive the Holy Spirit, and participate in the mission of the Spirit of Truth. As I have previously implied, this ability to "influence" is fundamental to the teaching of Christian mediumship training.

The word "protector" was borrowed from Allan Kardec, and refers to a wise trustworthy spirit of high degree. The "protector" is also regarded as being sufficiently elevated and powerful to ensure protection against unevolved spirits within the context of their spiritist activities. In the Christian Spiritist understanding of the term it refers to the Holy Spirit which is seen as presiding over a group of sanctified spirits who serve God in the spiritual awakening of humanity. The spirits are referred to in a number of ways in the Minutes, i.e., the Blessed Spirit, the Spiritual Messengers of Christ, the Master Spirit, and simply as the Spirit. The "apparatus" is a wooden tripod upon which sits a circular table top. On the table top are the letters of the alphabet and the numbers one through ten. The apparatus is used by certain mediums to receive messages from the spirit world.

The spirits who presided over the meetings of the Union, as recorded in the following text, identified themselves as the Spiritual Messengers of Christ. Before the meetings began, the medium was placed into a deep trance by the Director of Mediums, and through the entranced bodies of the mediums, the Spirit would speak. In the following pages, you will learn, as I did, what these Spirits told the Filipinos. I have selected examples of meetings that detail the conversations and instructions that 1) describe the spiritual training that the members of the Union received, 2) depict the spiritual transformations that were taking place in the individual members of the Union under the guidance of the Spirit, 3) illustrate the problems that faced the Union and how they were resolved, and 4) explain how spiritual authority was established within the Union. Out of respect for the descendants of the Christian Spiritists, I have put blank spaces in place of the names of the members referred to in the minutes.

The Minutes of the Union Espiritista

Before we explore the more profound Minutes of the Union, I will first give an example of a typical meeting wherein nothing particularly extraordinary takes place. This meeting was held on September 14, 1919, in a small town outside of Manila:

President: We pay homage to your presence, beloved Protector.
Spirit: Why have you "influenced" only now?
President: This is due to the state of the weather conditions that have prevailed lately.
Spirit: Well, all right. Do you wish to consult me about something?
President: Yes, to give an account of the Board's resolution and also to inform you about the bad condition of the Center due to the past flooding.
Spirit: Very well.
President: (Gives an account of the agreement that in case of emergencies like floods, the General Center can perform its works at the La Paz or Progreso Centers instead.)
Spirit: That's all right.
President: (Gives an account of the investment of the Union's funds, which investment is highly advantageous for the Union.)
Spirit: (acknowledges that it is beneficial.)
President: Take into consideration the inauguration of the Center "El

Sol" (The Sun of Truth) in San Pablo, as well as others wishing to apply for membership in the Union.
Spirit: Yes, approved.
President: (Gives an account of a letter received from the secretary of LaPaz Center referring to the decision of the Spirit on the distribution of the portrait of one of the deceased members of the center.)
Spirit: And the inscription?
President: According to the letter, the Protector of that center said that what is written, is written, and should stay that way.
Spirit: How was it written? Have you already written about the photograph?
President: Yes, in a model meant for the sole use of that center.
Spirit: In that case, why consult me yet?
President: Because I wanted to make the distribution with the same inscription.
Spirit: Well, tell him that I'm now changing the inscription on the photograph.
President: Over the original?
Spirit: Yes.
President: Well, I shall do so.
Spirit: Yes, and what else?
President: (Gives an account of the orders received last Wednesday for the Protector's consideration as it is the first time that orders (directives) have emanated from entities in centers other than the General Center and therefore petitions for instructions concerning the proper course of action.)
Spirit:- Counsels of that nature are all right. They can receive them, you understand? But not instructions, because they are moral counsels for the advancement of their mediumship. What else?
President: Only to let you know that we do not find teachings from the communications we, as of now, have received.
Spirit: Well done. It is up to you to bring this to their attention. Besides, a lot depends upon the morality of the mediums and the state of enthusiasm when they are being "influenced," as well as the state of mind (courage) of the medium. Tell them that.
President: I feel the same about that as you and intend to tell them so.
Spirit: Well, what else?
President: (Renders an account of the new center's work and is skeptical of the language used in the communications which they have noticed.)
Spirit- The objective in using this type of language is to convince the profane members. For you, it sounds bad, but to the profane members it does not. Think about this and tell me next time.
President: (Gives further accounts of the brothers who have applied for membership.)
Spirit: Approved!

President: (Gives an account of the letter.)
Spirit: We shall resolve that later.
President: (Renders an account on the studies concerning psychic experiments.)
Spirit: Bring the minutes at the next meeting.
President: Very Good.
Spirit: Be more punctual.
President: And when should we come back?
Spirit: The last Sunday of the month.
(Session ends at 12:40 P.M.)

    In reading these Minutes, it is apparent that the Spirit supervised and oversaw even the most mundane matters of the organization. In the period that these Minutes were written, the Union was expanding rapidly. If a message, or counsel, was received in the sessions held in the smaller centers, it was sent to the General Center for verification by the Blessed Spirit. In the example recorded here, one of the centers had received orders from a spirit while in session and while the orders were not detailed in the Minutes, the spirit indicates by its response that the orders were moral counsels. The president objects that the counsels of the spirit were irrelevant and the Protector encourages him to bring this to the attention of the members of the center where they were received. The Protector also tells the president that the quality of the counsels that are received are directly related to the level of morality and enthusiasm of the mediums when they are being "influenced."
    The president obviously felt that the mediums who received these counsels were lacking. The president then reads the orders to the Protector and the Protector replies that the orders were sent to convince the profane members, to whom it made sense. The Protector advises the president that, in some cases, orders will come through solely for the benefit of the profane; that, even though the orders may sound bad to the experienced, they will still serve a purpose.
    The Protector examined and supervised far more than the mundane aspects of the Union. The members of the Union were actively working to develop their mediumistic abilities. As they advanced, they would come to the attention of the trainers, who would bring them before the Protector/Spirit for confirmation of the medium's progress. An example of this is found in the Minutes of October 5, 1919:

President: (Renders an account of the psychic works which took place last night and also about the faculty of the new medium brought by a brother of the Tiaong center to submit to the General Center.)
Spirit: Has she been initiated?
President: Not yet, sir.
Spirit: What else?

The Spiritual Messengers of Christ

President: I submit for your consideration....the identification of the faculties of this sister.
Spirit: Let her come in.
President: The sister is now present.
Spirit: Good.
President: (Renders an account of the verified manifestations by the sister from Tiaong last night.)
Spirit: She should dedicate herself to study the Gospels at least a half an hour every day.
Sister: Yes sir, I will do so.
Spirit: Do not ever abuse your faculties (gifts.)
Sister: Yes, sir.
Spirit: Your spiritual gifts should be used only for moral objectives.
Sister: Yes, sir.
Spirit: That is all!
Sister: I pray and beseech thee for a key or sign that will assure me that I am assisted by your Protector or any other high (elevated) spirit.
Spirit: That she cannot determine by herself. Only the brethren present can do so.
(Note-the moral level of a spirit can most accurately be observed while the spirit is communicating through the medium.)
President: It is because she has a protector, and according to her, she assures us that it is Mary. That is why she is insistent, because she wants to be certain.
Spirit: Well, by the light (or manner) in which the spirit presents itself, yes, it is clear (bright, illustrious.)
Sister: That is true, sir, according to the protector of our center, she who assists and protects me is the mother of humanity.
Spirit: Yes, it is she.
Sister: Thank you, sir, and I hope that you will continue to protect me.
Spirit: Well, that is all.
Sister: (Gives thanks and departs.)

While the identification of one's individual protector is an important step, it is only the first fruit of mediumship training. The next step is clairvoyance training. Clairvoyance training is related to the Pentecostal gift of the discernment of the True Spirit. An example of this is recorded in the Minutes of November 9, 1919, wherein the Spirit/Protector tests the ability of a medium to discern the true spirit:

Spirit: Do you wish to consult?
President: Beloved Protector, as per orders received from the Protector during last Thursday night's sessions, the medium seer____has been ordered to attend this General Center session today.
Spirit: What have you instructed her to do?

President: Nothing sir, just for her to attend. If you wish, she is outside waiting.
Spirit: Let her come in.
President: (Presents the sister.)
Spirit: Do you see spirits?
Sister: Yes, sir.
Spirit: How do I seem to you?
Sister: I see you as a master wearing a very bright white tunic.
Spirit: What about the other spirits?
Sister: I see Mary wearing a gray colored dress. Michael in a warrior suit, and Raphael with a long crozier (shepherd's staff) and with a fish.
Spirit: And the light?
Sister: As for the light, sir, I see a brilliant ray coming from the apparatus.
Spirit: Good! When you see inferior spirits, what do you do?
Sister: I pray for God to give them the necessary light, and I also invoke our captain, St. Michael, so as to drive them away and send them to their proper (corresponding) places.
Spirit: Good! And how do you drive them away?
Sister: Sir, first of all, I ask forgiveness for my faults and then I ask a light from the Father for all of these poor brothers, and that is how I comprehend it to be, sir.
Spirit: Good! When you perform sessions at home for consultations, try to do it with more concentration on your part, and do it in a private room and not in a place where just anybody can pass by.
Sister: Yes, sir, that is how I shall do so. May I please leave now, sir?
Spirit: Yes, (Spirit now addresses the president) And to you, in your family consultations at home....it is not proper to have in your room other people who are not concerned or interested.
President: Very well, then. At the next session, we shall hold it in an isolated sitting room where the consultees shall enter one by one.
Spirit: This is not just for mere form but because, there being less people, it becomes more conducive for meditation and concentration.
President: Very well, sir.
Spirit: That is all.

Not all aspiring mediums of the Holy Spirit were properly predisposed to receive a protector of high rank, and some attracted and were victimized by spirits of low rank. When this occurred, the directors of the session conferred with the elevated spirit protector to receive instructions on how to resolve the desperate situations they found themselves in. In these situations, the welfare of the medium was the responsibility of the Protector and the director of the session. An example of this is recorded in the Minutes of October 26, 1919:

President: We pay homage to your presence.

The Spiritual Messengers of Christ

Spirit: Well, any consultations?

President: Yes, beloved Protector. In compliance with your orders as directed during the last session, we wish to inform you that the concentration sessions, as mandated, took place during the last two Mondays. The same was transmitted to the provincial centers and it has been scheduled every third Monday of the month. Also, there was poor attendance from the El Progreso center.

Spirit: Why did they not attend?

President: Their excuses still have not been sent in.

Spirit: (Gives acknowledgment.)

President: The proofs (trials) of the sisters ___ and ___ for them to form a group brought good results, and thus they request the protector to assist them, submitting for your approval, to use them in works for apparatus, consultations for diagnosis/treatment of diseases, sessions and studies, and family consultations, which they shall alternate with the other groups.

Spirit: Yes, approved.

President: I will now give you an account of the nature of the communications (messages) received during the sessions. I will also describe the visions which the spirits manifest and transmit through the seers, so that in case they do not merit your approval, I would then beseech you to order or give spiritual directives (guidelines) that would serve to warn (prepare) the spirits as to the form (shape) or norm (standard) which they should follow, thereby preventing our works from being discredited or placed in ridicule.

Spirit: Why?

President: The messages received through the apparatus order the seers to see the vision and later tells them to tell the public what they have seen. This, I believe, should be restricted.

Spirit: During the next session we shall tell you how you should proceed accordingly.

President: Very well. (He then gives an account of the accident which occurred last night to the medium from Tiaong during her mediumistic exercises.)

Spirit: Good, what about the exercises?

President: Mediumistic exercises?

Spirit- Yes.

President: We are performing them Saturday, as per instructions.

Spirit: Good.

President: And will you please tell us what to do with the medium from Tiaong who has been attacked by sickness that causes her to lose consciousness for long periods of time? This has already been going on for six hours.

Spirit: Do you believe that she is in danger?

President: It seems to be a nervous attack (hysteria) and the fourth group

is asking for influence so as to receive orders for treatment.
Spirit: Do not consult concerning that.
President: What should we do then?
Spirit: Give her magnetic treatment.
President: Very well then, but afterwards what?
Spirit: Due to the state she is in, suspend her from her duties.
President: The exercises and some of the works?
Spirit: Yes, all she needs is rest...not less that one month. How did you perform the exercises?
President: In conformity with instructions. However, she was like a somnambulist. She would stand up and talk, and then a syncope would supervene and she would lose consciousness.
Spirit: Have we not already warned you about this?
(Note: We, in this case, is used in first person, plural.)
President: Yes, sir. However, the protector orders her to talk and we just can not do anything about it.
Spirit: In her case, the only thing that you can do is to distract her from her thoughts through other activities, like having her take charge of household chores, or take her for a stroll. If she sits down and then meditates or tries to concentrate, then she becomes predisposed to receiving....Do you understand?
President: Yes I do. And should we do it here or in her hometown?
Spirit: She can go home.
President: Very Well.
Session ended 11:20 a.m.

In the Minutes of November 9, 1919, the Protector called for changes in the format of the sessions. Prior to this meeting, the sessions had been devoted to training mediums through inducing trance in groups of aspiring mediums. It became obvious, however, that the mediums had all sorts of misconceptions that led to negative results in the sessions. As a result of the problems arising from an apparent lack of knowledge in the mediums, the Protector decided that the members of the Union should educate themselves by studying and teaching subjects relevant to Christian Spiritism in their sessions, in addition to their mediumship training. The Protector gave the following instructions:

Spirit: Each session should have an announced program (agenda) two weeks beforehand. During each session, the medium seers should refrain from receiving visions. From now on, you should prepare the programs for each session or conference.
President: You mean to say that we should eliminate our present procedures?
Spirit: It should be restructured.
President: What we now have are printed materials for each month.

Spirit: From now on, each speaker will have a separate topic that they will study and be prepared to deliver to the group.
President: Very well then, sir.
Spirit: When are the mediums influenced?
President: In all the sessions.
Spirit: In what part?
President: During the opening of the meeting.
Spirit: At the next session (seance) we shall give the programs two weeks in advance.
President: Very well, sir, and what about this coming Thursday?
Spirit: This coming Thursday, the session will be structured as follows:
1) Opening- A chapter from the Gospel will be read by Brother_____.
2) The doctrine of the association and its significance in meaning by Sister_____.
3) How the small Espiritist groups can help in furthering the propagation of Spiritism by the president of the La Paz chapter, Brother_____.
Spirit: In your propagation work, you should place more emphasis on the moral side of Spiritism. Always tell them that the spiritual side of Spiritism is fraught with danger because of the risk of getting in contact with inferior spirits. Those who wish to dedicate themselves to Spiritism should, at the least, be highly moral, for it is in this, therefore, that one takes part in its essence.
4) Concerning the private lives of mediums, on the proper development of their faculties (powers) by Brother_____.
5) Spirit communication with apparatus and shutdown.
Spirit: The speakers should prepare well and study their topics and they should find out the best method of making sure that their listeners do not go to sleep, which is usually due to a lack of technique on how to develop the topic in such a way as to make it more attractive to the audience.
President: In this case, this program should be for next Thursday?
Spirit: Yes, that is all. Go.
President: When should we meet again to receive the next program?
Spirit: Influence on Sunday.
Session ended 11:45 a.m.

It was through the act of "influencing" (inducing trance in) the mediums, that communication with the spirit was established. Once the aspiring mediums had been "influenced," they were opened to the spirit. The level and type of spirit that manifested corresponded to the degree of moral, intellectual, and spiritual development within the medium. In individuals who craved power, the spirit who came would often be a domineering, power-hungry tyrant. Jesus illustrated this principle of spiritual affinity in the Beatitudes where he says, "Blessed are the pure in heart, for they shall see God." (Matt.5:8) The mediumship trainers saw that the opposite was equally true. It is for this reason that the Protector commented that the spiritual side of Spiritism was fraught with danger and that in order to practice Christian Spiritism, the medium had to be a highly moral person.

As the number of members increased, and many chapters were formed in the provinces far from the oversight of the General Center, it became more difficult to monitor the activities of the rural centers. In the absence of scrutiny, negative spirits would impose themselves. An example of this is recorded in the Minutes of December 14, 1919:

<u>President</u>: There is a brother member from"Luz de la Verdad" (Light of Truth) center of Tayug, Pangasinan, who is waiting outside wishing to consult you, if you would so allow.
<u>Spirit</u>: Bring him in.
<u>President</u>: (Presents the brother.)
<u>Spirit</u>: What do you wish to consult me about?
<u>Brother</u>: I come to you as a last resort because of my wife who is a medium-speaker and incorporator (trance-medium)_____ from the Light of Truth center. Having met with no affection I believe that she should discontinue her spiritual practices with the Union. I believe that she is deviating from the Law of Charity due to the following reasons: Her mediumistic activities have convinced her that her protector is master Jesus. She also believes that Jesus has placed her under the charge of the spirit of brother____(one of the deceased founders of the Union) as her guide. Yet, it is apparent to me, that by his manner of being, and in his manifestation, that her protector is not Jesus. As for the spirit of the brother who guides her, he discredits a lot of the teachings of Spiritism due to his works which are not in accordance with Spiritism or with reason. He also gives us unreasonable demands, the majority of which are impossible to fulfill. Another reason I have come here is to seek advice on what I must do to bring my wife back to her senses as she seems to be under the spell of what I consider to be negative spirits. She has completely neglected her domestic duties and our home life has become chaotic. Please help me to convince her to listen to my advice concerning her duties, as it is written and commanded in the Gospels.
<u>Spirit</u>: Thank you for bringing this to our attention. At the next session, we shall dictate instructions expressly for her that she will receive by mail.
<u>Brother</u>: I also wish to bring to the attention and knowledge of the spiritual management that the spiritual director of Light of Truth Center gives orders and directives that are not in conformity with those exercised or complied with by the Union. We are prohibited from complying with the specific orders of the General Center. He has prohibited the cures (healing sessions) for instance, and he has changed the time of the sessions from morning to evening which last until midnight or later, in studies that we

The Spiritual Messengers of Christ

derive no benefit from. The spiritual director also interprets verses of the Gospel inaccurately, therefore I am exposing it all. I beseech the spiritual management to take the proper measures because, if this deception continues, it is possible that we will disband and form another center, because as I see it, the majority of our members are already fanatics. I pray for and implore the Father's mercy, and hope that the spiritual management will normalize things so that we will still form a part of the truth. Not that I am telling you in advance what to do, but may I suggest that all the mediums of that center be brought here for examination by the General Center and, if so ordered, we will attend and get the confirmation from this management. Nonetheless, all of these matters are under the power, justice, and knowledge of the Father and up to the spiritual management of this center to decide.
Spirit: Well, what you have said is the truth. You should combat fanaticism because it is precisely the one thing that Christian Spiritists cannot tolerate, and all messages that you receive from the spirit should pass through the sieve (screen) of your knowledge and discernment, both scientific and moral, before you follow or obey them.
President: In that case, should all their mediums come and report here?
Spirit: Yes.
Brother: I wish to find out from this board who is the Protector of the Light of Truth center. Is it the master as claimed by_____?
Spirit: Yes, it is, but I must warn you that there are many spirits who falsely claim to be master_____.
Brother: I beseech you, respectable master to send another protector who is not master_____ and, if that is not possible give him instructions not to squeeze us so.
Spirit: All right, how many times do you presently communicate?
Brother: Sir, the protector wishes the work to be continuous (every night.)
Spirit: Well, from now on, you should not meet more than three times a week for communication purposes.
Brother: Very good, sir, and thank you.

In the next meeting held on December 22, 1919, the wife of the brother from the Light of Truth center is brought to the General Center in Manila.

Spirit: Why did you influence?
President: Sir, it is because the members from the Light of Truth center wish to consult you if you would so allow. They are in the antechamber waiting.
Spirit: Bring the wife of the brother in.
President: She is present.
Spirit: Why did you not come when we asked you?
Sister: Because the protector did not permit me to, and because of my

household duties.

Spirit: And you give the protector of your Center more credit than you give the spiritual management of the General Center? Do you believe more in those spirits who communicate with you?

Sister: Sir, I know nothing. I believed that all that I have received were from elevated (high) spirits and protectors.

Spirit: How do you judge if a spirit is good or bad?

Sister: Sir, I am ignorant. I wish you would explain that part to me.

Spirit: How do you distinguish one from the other?

Sister: According to the spirit who protects or assists me, he claims to be _____.

Spirit: Ask the spirit for some teachings, and then study them and if they are in conformity with the doctrine of Christian Spiritism, then you may have faith in the spirit who communicated with you. The spirits of light do not come for purposes of entertainment. They come to give you moral counsel and to guide you in your way of living. The spirits of light do not expect you to spend all of your time communicating with them. They also want you to spend time at home with your family. The spirits of light communicate with you, directing you with good thoughts. The only thing you have to do is to invoke them and be predisposed to them. Henceforth, do not abuse your mediumship. Make use of it once a day, at the most, and not more than five minutes. Study well the messages you receive before totally accepting them. Read spiritist works instead of devoting so much time to other things. Read the communications in your manual instead of solely communicating with the spirits as you used to do. What else?

Sister: Sir, I therefore ask the spiritual management if I am really intended to be a medium at the Light of Truth center which are the gifts granted by the Father, for my benefit and that of humanity. Will you please grant me a director or spiritual guide so that I may not be used as an instrument of slanders and altercations among the brothers of humanity, and that these mediumistic works will be true and perfect? You, sir, know what has happened in our Light of Truth center. You know that, due to my ignorance and my lack of discernment, I was instrumental for falsehoods too numerous to mention. Forgive me, sir, for all of this is due to my imperfections. For this reason, if it is not necessary for my advancement and progress, I wish to resign my position as a medium. Sir, not my will but the Father's, make known your will and it shall be so.

Spirit: Well, for now, I advise you to cease using your mediumistic powers for two weeks.

Sister: All right, sir. I would like to request from you the flag and standard of our center.

(Note: When new centers were started, the protector would instruct the General Center to issue banners or flags which hang on the walls of the centers. These banners were considered to be symbols of the covenant

that existed between the Holy Spirit and the individual congregations of Christian Spiritists, and were specifically designed based on information provided by the Spiritual Protector of the General Center.)
Spirit: At the next session.
Sister: Sir, I would like to know if the spirit who assists me can stop, and give me peace for a while? Because he is always dominating me, and the more I wish to reject him, the more he orders me to do.
Spirit: (Gives instructions to the president to send a medium and gives the medium instructions as to a specific method of magnetic treatment to give to the woman suffering from the negative spirit.)
President: How many times must the treatment be done?
Spirit: Twice, in the morning and before she retires at night.
President: Later, should it be done during the hours for healings?
Spirit: Yes.
Sister: Sir, I do not wish to be a medium anymore, so as not to be easily under the influence of any spirit, and I am afraid that the spirit who assists me will come back to molest me as he used to back in Tayug.
Spirit: We will help you.
President: Does that mean, sir, that she should reject any and all suggestions by any spirits?
Spirit: Yes, she should occupy herself with other activities.
President: Very well then, sir.
Spirit: She should not predispose herself to concentrating her thoughts on only one thing.
Sister: But sir, I am afraid of the spirit who assists me. I am so suggestible to his influence and I do not have the courage to resist him.
Spirit: Yes, we will help you. You may go now. We shall give the standard at the next session. Go!
(In this situation and similar ones, the Spirit gives this advice to the President concerning the mediumistic works and the spiritual protection of mediums:)
Spirit: Take advantage of the opportunity to counsel all the mediums, healers, and others possessing faculties (spiritual gifts) that they should not abuse their mediumship in order that Spiritism and the association to which they belong will not be censored, nor placed in ridicule by the profane world, due to the evil results obtained thereby; it is better not to receive any communications than to receive them from a perturbed spirit. That way one does not carry the risk of being obsessed nor tricked into evil paths. Do not forget about this, because the time is coming when you will spend more time and effort combating fanaticism among spiritists than you will spend propagating Spiritism. Spiritual protection depends upon the predisposition of the mediums, the sifting of the messages is the task of the presiding officer of the sessions. Thus, there should always be constant discernment of Spiritism, so as to be able to distinguish the good messages from the bad ones. Abuse of mediumship results in the

interruption of good messages due to the interference of the evil spirits. The only protection which the Blessed Spirit can give you is to guide you in your works, but if the mediums are not properly predisposed before the sessions, or if they abuse their mediumistic powers, then they, and only they themselves, are responsible for the evil results thus obtained. The spirits are free, and they communicate with people who are conditioned to receive communication from them.

The problem of improperly predisposed mediums being used by inferior spirits, who would assert themselves as leaders of the Centers and issue directives, continued to be a problem. The Blessed Spirit sought to resolve this problem by insisting that all centers be required to submit to the authority of the General Center. In the Minutes of April 10, 1921, the Protector revealed the new administrative structure of the Union:

Spirit: The administration of all centers, those of Manila as well as those from the provinces, shall from this time on, be under the general directorate of the General Center in every matter with respect to the administration of the local directorates. Do you understand?
President: Yes, sir.
Spirit: Nominations of mediums in the different centers should first be sanctioned by the local directorate and then these should be submitted to the General Center for review or revision. (All mediums must be pre-approved.)
President: In that case, shall I ask for the names of the mediums of all the centers, Manila and provincial?
Spirit: Yes, along with the comments of the local directorates in regard to their mediums.
President: Very well.
Spirit: The programs of works shall be under the jurisdiction of the General Directorate. Spiritual directions should likewise be referred to and consulted with the General Directorate, especially changes in the dates of the anniversary celebrations. The General Center shall dictate the dates wherein consultative studies and sessions would be done.
President: Very well.
Spirit: The installation of the new centers shall be under the jurisdiction of the directorate. Only the General Center shall be allowed to name the centers and determine the colors of the banner and flag of the new centers. In cases of conflict of jurisdiction among the different centers, the General Directorate shall decide. Do you understand?
President: Yes, sir. (Relates to the Spirit the recent events which happened in the La Paz center where the brothers refused to obey any orders from the General Directorate and, instead, would only follow orders from the spirits that they were contacting in their local centers.)
Spirit: That would be all right if they were certain that they were communicating with good spirits and always used the same mediums

The Spiritual Messengers of Christ

that were known to be predisposed toward the good spirits.
President: I have pointed that out to the rebellious members already but they continue to influence questionable mediums with bad results.
Spirit: Yes, and if you have false mediums, how will you be then? It would be better, therefore, for the General Directorate to have the authority to decide which mediums are actually qualified.
President: I agree, sir, but the majority of the brethren do not want to hear and obey anyone except the spirits contacted in their local centers.
Spirit: Tell them that should not be the case and if they are to remain part of the Union that this will not be allowed.
President: Very well, sir.
Spirit: Spiritism is still in its infancy and that kind of thinking has already been the cause of the demoralization of many of the earlier members, like _____ and the others.
President: Very well, sir.
Spirit: The secret of good administration of your organization, as compared to those of others, is in the centralization of administration, spiritual, as well as that of the directorates in general. Do you understand?
President: Yes, sir.
Spirit: We shall continue later.

The President faced a difficult task in imposing order on the rebellious centers. The discernment of the true spirit was the issue. The President needed a means of identifying whether or not the spirits who communicated through the mediums were the messengers of Christ. This identification had to take place at the beginning of the sessions. Such a means of identification was provided by the Protector. The first reference to the "Keys," as they were called, was mentioned in the minutes of the meeting held on December 18, 1920:

President: We pay homage to thy presence, beloved Protector. (Reads minutes.)
Spirit: Good, in that case, the mediums of the second group shall "influence" with the moral apparatus with the broad counter just as it is; and a medium from the first group will receive the "Key" and will tell the president if it was given correctly. Or the President General will receive the Key in case one of the mediums of the first group can not receive. Do you understand?
President: Yes, sir, but in that case I do not know the Key yet.
Spirit: It will be given to you in time or it will be written down and sealed in an envelope that must not be opened unless told to do so. Do you understand?
President: Very well, sir.
Spirit: This should be safeguarded by the president. (Pres. Makes some

observations concerning the mediums from the second group who cannot function due to sickness.) We shall name as substitutes two mediums from the second group in case those of the second group cannot receive the Key. All the powers shall be decided in the general directorate.
President: Very well.
Spirit: And the second group shall not be used to receive instructions, but solely to receive moral counsels.
President: Very well.
Spirit: Nothing pertinent to the administration of the association. What else?
President: Tells the protector about a Key which only brother____ knew, and in having the Key was invested with an authority against which nobody could prevail.
Spirit: Do you know how it was given to brother____?
President: No, sir. He died with the secret.
Spirit: You should search the Minutes.
President: It would be impossible, due to the fact that, as I understand it, they did not write down the proceedings then for archival purposes as we do now. I beseech thee, beloved Protector, enlighten me by explaining why the Key is exclusively for certain persons, and what virtue does it have?
Spirit: Yes, I will, but you are too impatient. The explanation of the virtue of the Key of Jesus will be given in January. The Key that will be given is the Key of the Lord Jesus. You will receive many Keys but only one will be given for now.
President: (asks the protector to explain the nature and purpose of the 'key.')
Spirit: It depends on you. The Key will be sealed inside an envelope before the anniversary of the Union.
President: Asks if the Key shall be hereditary for all future presidents?
Spirit: Yes.
President: In that case, thou may consider that it shall serve as the testament which every president shall leave to his successor.
Spirit: It should not be given except to the president, who is a true Christian Spiritist, who has passed the necessary trials, and who has demonstrated that his faith in Christian Spiritism is genuine.
President: (Objects that the Key and the exclusive manner in which it is bestowed will be seen as a special privilege and will cause problems.)
Spirit: The Key will be given only to the first group because that is the group that will receive instructions relative to spiritual administration.
President: Very well.
Session ends.

In reading the plight of the President, it is clear that serious measures had to be taken to prevent the Union from falling apart. The promise of

The Spiritual Messengers of Christ

the Spirit to deliver the Key that could be used to establish order in the sessions became the main topic of the sessions. In the Minutes of the meeting held on January 23, 1921, the session begins with questions about the Key:

Spirit: Very well then, concerning the Key, it shall be given on the second Sunday of February. Once again, you must put it in the envelope and seal it. On the envelope should be written: "Key of the General Center" in the handwriting of a medium from the first group whose name will be given later. She, herself, will write in the Minute Book the Key as a means of confirmation. Do you understand?
President: Yes, sir.
Spirit: The President General will keep and safeguard the Key. The Key has two purposes. First, it is a sign of identification of the presence of the spirit of light and second, as proof of the veracity of the mediumship of the mediums. Do you understand?
President: Yes sir, but what if the President and the mediums of the group were not present? Who would receive the Key?
Spirit: What? (Spirit expresses concern about the President's insecurity)
Spirit: That has already been foreseen.
President: What if none of the designated mediums can make it, and I myself were indisposed to receive the Key? Does that mean that we will not have a General Center?
Spirit: No! In that case, the matter of the Key will be postponed for now, or until the President is ready to receive it, or until a new President is elected.
President: Very well then, sir. (However, he makes observations concerning the difficulties encountered with regard to convening the members of the first group and also the probability of one of them being absent on the occasion.)
Spirit: In that case, the first group shall be dissolved, and the second group shall be the first group.
President: (Objects and asks whether it is possible to name the recipient now so that a substitute may also be named in case of the absence of the former.)
Spirit: They should then come from the second group, because the members of this group have faculties on a par with those of the first group.
President: Does that mean that, in case of such an eventuality, the members of the second group can receive the instructions?
Spirit: Yes.

The hesitation on the part of the Protector to deliver the Key obviously strained relations between the President and the Protector. The Key was a document revealed by the Blessed Spirit that contained the "names" or "passwords" by which the Spiritual Messengers of Christ could identify themselves once they were present in the mediums. Without this Key, it was difficult, if not impossible, to determine whether the information received during the Spiritist seances was valid. Since the very existence of the Union depended upon the revelation of accurate information from the Blessed Spirit, it is easy to understand the frustration and anxiety of the President.

The Key was used in this manner: At the beginning of the sessions, the mediums were influenced (induced into trance) by the director of the session and, once in trance, the communications from the spirit would commence. At this point, the President General would secretly question the communicating spirit. The spirit would be asked to identify itself and its reply would be checked against the Key. If the Spirit was one of the spirits of light, then the information the spirit gave could be considered to be genuine and reliable. If not, the session would end immediately. Once the identity of the spirit had been verified, the spirit would then tell the Director of Mediums whether or not the medium was properly predisposed to continue with the session. Once this was determined, the session would begin. The possession of the Key bestowed great power, and the President was severely tested by the spirit before the Key was given. The Minutes of March 5, 1922, details one of the tests:

President: According to thy promise made last year concerning the Key, I am prepared to receive it.
Spirit: Not now.
President: Very well.
Spirit: When can you "influence" for this purpose only?
President: We are at thy orders, sir.
Spirit: Very well, the first Sunday of next month.
President: Very well, sir.
Brother: Now that the Key will be given, I also wish to be relieved, for reasons of "delicadeza" (Spanish for a delicate situation) concerning what occurred with my mother.
Spirit: Yes, we shall counsel those persons, during the day the Key will be given.
President: Therefore, should we call these persons?
Spirit: Yes.
President: Can we tell who these persons are?
Spirit: She will tell you.
President: Who is she?
Spirit: ____, but if she does not come, we shall tell you what must be done. Try to be more serene. Things will be straightened out. You should not have discords after all these years as a Spiritist.
Brother: Sir, when the day comes, I propose that another group of mediums be used instead, to prevent disagreements and quarrels on

the part of the others.
Spirit: Good! Who are the mediums that can come?
President: In my opinion,_____may do, in as much as brother____will have to serve as secretary and will not be able to function with her.
Spirit: Let them come, those of the third group, and then we shall name those who will "influence."
President: Very well, Sir.
Spirit: Go!

On the evening of January 10, 1923, the preparations are finally complete, and the President "influences" the mediums in anticipation of the delivery of the long awaited Key. An elevated Master Spirit begins to communicate:

Spirit: Peace be with you, my beloved brothers and disciples. For quite some time now, I have had to guide you like the Shepherd who guides his sheep into their pasture, because of the fact that it is so difficult to gather all of you together to proceed with such an act as this. Very well, are all the mediums present?
President: Yes, sir.
Spirit: All of them?
President: Yes, sir, the second, third, fourth, and sixth groups, except for the seventh and eighth which we have already tested.
Spirit: Well, how does it seem to you, have you not received any intuitions?
President: Yes, sir, my reservations concerning the Key, thou hast read my mind.
Spirit: Charity, is it not?
President: No, sir.
Spirit: Towards God through Wisdom and Charity?
President: That is our motto, sir.
Spirit: This cannot take place, these mediums are not properly predisposed.
President: Shall we finish with this group then?
Spirit: Yes. Goodbye.

Shortly after the dismissal of the first group of mediums a second group is "influenced."

Spirit: Brother _____ is present. Pray that the Master Spirit comes.
Master Spirit: I am present. Why do you not wish to be mediums of the General Center?
Sister: In my case, it is because I do not know if I have the wisdom for it.
Master Spirit: Do you love me?
Sister: Yes, sir, if thee believes me to be worthy.
Master Spirit: And what about you, brother?

Brother: I am with thee.
Master Spirit: Sister_____, do you remember the Key which was given you during brother_____'s time?
Sister: Yes sir. I do remember.
Master Spirit: And you, brother, are you capable of keeping a secret?
Brother: Yes sir. I shall keep it well.
Master Spirit: Up to the grave?
Brother: Yes sir. I promise thee.
Master Spirit: Very well. In that case, everybody should leave, except for the mediums.
President: If that is the case, is this not the Key which thou gavest me by intuition?
Master Spirit: No.
President: If it is reserved exclusively for the mediums, then I would not be able to guarantee the veracity of the communication to be received.
Master Spirit: For that, you have the capacity, because you will not be the only president to know it.
President: Why, then, have you told me since last year that thee would give me the Key and, due to the difficulties encountered in convening all the mediums, it has not as yet transpired? Said key was to be for my control and management; very necessary in identifying the authenticity of all communications and orders received.
Master Spirit: And do you not have the wisdom to sift (screen) the messages?
President: To sift, (screen) yes, but I want to be able to authenticate them.
Master Spirit: We can not give it to you, but if you so desire you shall be the only one to whom we shall give orders.
President: That is perfectly well, but thou hast said that it would be given to me to prevent doubts.
Master Spirit: Very well. Do not insist.
President: In that case, forget it.
Master Spirit: I certainly think so.
President: I insist precisely because thou hast ordered it so to avoid talks and doubts which may occur.
Master Spirit: But can you not listen to what I am telling you; that this is only temporary because I shall give orders.
President: We are in the time period to receive it.
Master Spirit: The very same.
President: Does this mean that some other group will receive it?
Master Spirit: When they are competent.
President: That is too exhaustive (will take to long.)
Master Spirit: Goodbye. (Master Spirit departs)

The president is disgusted with the evasive position of the Master Spirit

The Spiritual Messengers of Christ

and, after calming down a bit, a third group is "influenced."

Spirit: What is the matter?
President: I am waiting to receive the Key which the Master does not want to give except to the mediums exclusively.
Spirit: Obey, and you shall know the order.
President: It is that I am placed in a bad position, since I was told that I would be given the Key through intuition, and what I would be thinking would be the same thing that would be dictated through apparatus.
Spirit: Who told you so?
President: The Master himself told me in full session.
Spirit: Do you know very well that it is he, himself?
President: At least that is how he manifested. Accordingly, it was so received.
Spirit: Do you not know that your mediums are intuitive ones?
President: I cannot judge over this particularly.
Spirit: You say so, but trust my judgment, and if you want to be disagreeable, then I have nothing more to say.
President: I base my conformity on plain reason.
Spirit: Have I not told you to obey and observe well the orders that we shall give you?
President: Very well. I respect the orders thee gives me.
Spirit: That is why I am telling you. We shall be giving it to you, but not now, because we have to prepare the groups.
President: In that case, can it be done now?
Spirit- Has not the Master told you that this group is temporary?
President: If that is what the Master wishes, I respect his will. When shall you give that order?
Spirit: Right now.
President: Very well.
Spirit: First of all, the mediums should function in the scientific apparatus, the group of _____, and also the group of_____. Do you understand me? That way, nobody has reason to suspect, and there you shall receive the Key. You only. Do you understand me?
President: Yes, sir.
Spirit: Are you agreeable?
President: Yes, sir.

Finally, in the session held on August 25, 1923, the mediums were properly predisposed and the power struggle within the Union was resolved by giving the Director of Mediums a temporary Key, and the President a permanent Key. The communicating spirit had to be cleared twice, and the medium once, before the session commenced. Upon receipt of the Key, the Union Espiritista resolved the greatest threat to its existence and was vested with an authority against which no false spirits could prevail.

In studying the Minutes of this "channeled" organization, the intelligence and administrative skills of the Spiritual Messengers of Christ is evident; as is the morality and sanctity of these dedicated and courageous individuals. While mediumship and Spiritist phenomenon are routinely condemned by all forms of Orthodox Christianity, the Minutes detail the difficulties encountered by Christian mediums to establish an organization in which the love and compassion of the Holy Spirit could find concrete expression in this world. The translation of the Minutes literally opened a window to another world that otherwise would have remained forever steeped in mystery, and forgotten.

In the Minutes of the Union, I finally found the secret tradition that I had been looking for. It answered the question of how the descendants of these disciples of the Holy Spirit could open bodies with their bare hands. It was the experiential immersion into the realm of the Holy Spirit described in the Minutes that laid the foundation for the unprecedented transformation that took place within the members of the Christian Spiritist community. Through their remarkable understanding of and cooperation with the spiritual messengers of Christ, Christian Spiritists opened an intradimensional window. Once opened, they volunteered to cooperate in the missionary efforts of Divine spirits that reside in another dimension of existence. The goal of the mission of the Blessed Spirit is to announce the emergence of a new epoch in the history of the human race...the age of the Holy Spirit.

More than ever before, millions of Christians feel that something very important is missing from Christianity as it is presently being practiced. Archaic religious documents like the Dead Sea Scrolls, and the Nag Hammadi texts of the Gnostic Christians, have generated both intense interest and bitter controversy. Scholars of several organized religions, after studying the Dead Sea Scrolls for thirty years, have refused to openly divulge their findings. Their actions have raised the suspicion that the doctrinal basis of modern Christianity may indeed rest upon *partial truth*. Why else would they have resisted the disclosure of their findings with such vehemence? Whatever the Dead Sea Scrolls may eventually reveal, the Minutes detail the means through which the forces of Christ in the spirit world are *externalizing* their power through specially trained human beings to restore health and deliver a message. The paranormal work of the Holy Spirit may well be the *missing link* between a biblical narrative rich in miracles and modern Christianity.

Chapter Six

Christian Mediumship Training

Once Siegfried had finished his work and returned to Manila, I immersed myself in the newly translated text of the Minutes. As I was collating some of the material one afternoon, the bell rang at my front gate. I walked outside to see an elderly man dressed in a suit, smiling at me. He introduced himself as Reverend Benjamin Pajarillo, of the Christian Spiritist Church. Reverend Pajarillo said he had come to visit at the request of Lino Guinsad. I invited him in and offered him some tea. As we sat and drank our tea, he noticed the Minutes and the stack of the translated texts that were spread out on the table where I'd been working. I told him of my meeting with Brother Ramos, and of my search for a teacher of traditional mediumship training. Lino had told Benjamin about me and also about the Minutes, which he said he would like to see. We finished our tea, and I began to read to him from the translated text.

I told Benjamin that I had not been able to understand many of the terms used in the text. He offered to help me. I was deeply impressed with the ease with which he explained the inner workings of the early Union. As I questioned and he answered, we began to establish a rapport based on an inner affinity we both recognized. After several hours of discussing the texts, Benjamin glanced at his watch, and said it was time for him to leave. There was much I still wanted to discuss with him, and I asked if he would join me for lunch the following day. He graciously agreed. As he was leaving, he gave me his calling card, which read: "The Christian Spiritists of the Philippines-Rev. Benjamin A. Pajarillo-International Minister-National Board of Directors-General Director of Mediums-Spiritual & Distant Healing-Worldwide Healer."

Biblical Proofs of Mediumship

The following day, I prepared lunch for Benjamin and myself. After we had eaten, I asked if he would discuss Christian mediumship training with me. I began by asking him how the term 'medium' had come to be used to describe someone who acted on behalf of the Holy Spirit. He said it had been introduced by Allan Kardec, but that there were many examples in the Bible of mediumship, as it is defined in any dictionary. I asked him to give me some of these references. He thought for a moment and then began with Ezekiel 11:5, in which Ezekiel states, "And the Spirit of the Lord fell upon me, and he said to me, Speak." Benjamin then showed me the reference in Jeremiah 1:4-9, where God says, "Before I formed you in the belly, I knew you; and before you came out of the womb I sanctified you and ordained you a prophet to the nations." Jeremiah then protests that he is a child, and God replies, "Do not say, I am a child; for you shall go to all that I shall send you, and whatever I command you, you shall speak." Jeremiah then states, "Then the Lord put forth His hand and touched my mouth. And the Lord said to me,

Behold, I have put my words in your mouth."

Benjamin assured me that biblical references to God putting His words into the mouths of men were very common. Equally common were Biblical references to virtually every form of spiritualistic phenomenon, including spirit writing, hearing spirits (clairaudience,) seeing spirits (clairvoyance,) spirit communication in dreams, healing with magnetized articles, and many more that had been integrated into Christian Spiritism. *Benjamin pointed out that the Bible describes events that are impossible to explain in spirit-phobic Christian theologies, yet make perfect sense when interpreted in the context of Christian Spiritism.* He sited an example found in II Corinthians 12:2-4, in which the Apostle Paul said, "I knew a man in Christ more than fourteen years ago, but whether I knew him in the body or out of the body, I do not know. God knows; this very one was caught up to the third heaven. And I still know this man, but whether in the body or whether out of the body, I cannot tell. God knows, How that he was caught up to paradise and heard unspeakable words, which is not lawful for a man to utter." Apparently, the Apostle Paul knew someone who resided in another dimension; someone whom he describes as a "man in Christ," a man caught up to the third heaven who hears unspeakable words and who was still known to Paul after fourteen years. While Paul's confession would draw a blank in most circles of Christian orthodoxy, Christian Spiritists interpret this to mean that Paul carried on a fourteen-year relationship with a disembodied spirit who lived "in Christ." The man that Paul knew "in Christ" for fourteen years is considered among Christian Spiritists to be one of the Messengers of Christ, the same group of spirits that brought the Union into existence.

In the introduction of the Doctrina Espiritista, Juan Alvear tells us, "Now, spread all over the world are the new prophets called mediums who receive the word of God through his spirits." He then asks the spirit, "The early evangelists, Apostles, and Saint Paul, are they also mediums?" The spirit answers, "Yes, also the prophets." Benjamin told me that a hierarchical relationship did exist in the spirit world. The spirits of light, who worked under the oversight of the Holy Spirit, used their elevated status to help lower spirits to evolve by teaching them to serve as agents in the Divine plan. The main focus of Christian mediumship training, he explained, was to teach mediums to receive *only* the spirits of light.

In Western culture, the prophet is believed to speak for God, while the medium is thought of as the dwelling place of lower spirits. Jesus cautions his followers, however, that some prophets are false prophets. With that said, I think it just as likely that some mediums are instruments of the Holy Spirit. Even a cursory reading of the Bible reveals the extent of the activity of mediumship in the service of God. Both prophets and mediums act as intermediaries of a personified other, be it Divine spirits, or spirits of the dead. The prophesies of the Bible, from Genesis to Revelation, are widely regarded as transmissions of information that originate with God, and manifest *through* certain chosen individuals who "express the will of God received from another dimension or world." Benjamin pointed out that the terms used to describe human beings through whom Divine forces act are not as important as understanding that in both ancient and modern times, human beings gifted in this manner have been, and continue to be, the most essential element in the revelation and intervention of the will of God on Earth.

A Short History of the Holy Spirit

Benjamin told me that, in due course, he would prepare me to receive the Holy Spirit. He emphasized that I first needed to learn more about the biblical basis of Christian Spiritism. He said that the first thing I needed to know was the spiritual interpretation of the New Testament. While the Holy Spirit is not central to orthodox Christianity, Benjamin made it clear to me from the beginning of my research that the Christian doctrines surrounding the life and teachings of Jesus, and the presence of the Holy Spirit in the biblical narrative, are interwoven to such an extent that *one cannot be understood without the other*. The biblical teachings I received from Benjamin are the essence of Christian Spiritism. Having been raised with a Christ centered interpretation of the bible, I could hardly believe that I had overlooked the story of the Holy Spirit that Benjamin carefully pointed out to me. As I learned the Christian Spiritist theology, my relationship with the bible changed. The bible, for the first time, became coherent to me. The message conveyed through the Christian Spiritist theology was truly good news. Benjamin encouraged me to take notes during our study sessions. From these notes, I have condensed Benjamin's teachings into the following several pages.

Although the Holy Spirit is only referred to three times in the Old Testament (Psalms 51:11 & Isaiah 63:10 &14,) the mission and nature of the Holy Spirit is discussed at length in the New Testament. To give you some idea of the degree of involvement of the Holy Spirit in the biblical narrative of the New Testament, a short history of the Holy Spirit, according to Christian Spiritism, is in order. In the New Testament, the Holy Spirit first appears in the story of the Nativity, or birth of Jesus. In the gospel of Matthew, we are told that Mary was found to be with the child of the Holy Spirit before having had intercourse with Joseph. Joseph was apparently suspicious and was considering divorcing Mary when an angel came to Joseph in a dream and told him, "*he that is to be born of her is of the Holy Spirit.*" (Matt.1:18-20) In the gospel of Luke, we are told that an angel advises Mary of the Divine pregnancy, and Mary asks the angel, "How can this be, for no man has known me?" The angel tells her, "The Holy Spirit will come, and the power of the Highest will rest upon you." (Luke 1:35) In the first mention of the Holy Spirit, the Bible directly infers that Jesus is the Son of the Holy Spirit.

The next reference to the Holy Spirit is found in Jesus' baptism by John the Baptist. The account of the baptism in Matthew says that, "When Jesus was baptized, he immediately went up out of the water; and the heavens were opened to him, and he saw the Spirit of God descending like a dove, and coming upon him; and a voice from heaven said, This is my beloved Son, with whom I am pleased." (Matt.3:16-17) The accounts of the baptism in Mark, Luke, and John all agree with the account in Matthew. John the Baptist tells us, "*he (Jesus) is the one who will baptize with the Holy Spirit.*" (John 1:33) The gospels of Matthew, Mark, and Luke all agree that it was the *Holy Spirit* that carried Jesus off into the wilderness to fast for forty days before being tested by the devil, Satan, or the adversary, depending on whose account we read. After being sired, formally acknowledged, and then subjected to training in ethics and values by the Holy Spirit, we are told in all of the accounts that, "*Jesus returned in the power of the Spirit to Galilee, and the fame about him went out through all the country round about.*" (Luke 4:14)

The Holy Spirit that incarnated in, by, and through the person of Jesus of Nazareth, returned from the temptation in the desert to teach a new message. Jesus taught compassion in the face of repression. His teachings implied that suffering, injustice, and persecution that arose as a result of living a spiritual life would be compensated for in the coming Kingdom of Heaven. To back up his claims, Jesus spent his life demonstrating that *a spiritual power existed that was able to resist and defeat the forces of evil, without becoming evil* in the process. Jesus demonstrated that the spiritual power he embodied was more than adequate to sustain and protect those devoted to a spirit-directed life. He not only demonstrated this power, he taught his Apostles how to receive this power and assist him in his mission of preparing the world for the coming of the Holy Spirit.

As Jesus saw the end of his mission approaching, he promised his followers that the extraordinary power he had demonstrated, the highest and greatest essence of all that is good and perfect, *would remain with his followers.* In the gospel of John, Jesus states, "I will ask of my Father, and he will send you another comforter, to be with you forever. Even the spirit of truth whom the world cannot receive, because it has not seen Him and does not know Him; but you know him because he abides with you and is in you. The comforter, *the Holy Spirit whom my Father will send in my name* will teach you everything and remind you of everything which I tell you." (John 14:16-17 & 26)

Jesus further elaborates the continuation of his mission when he tells his Apostles, "It is better for you that I should go away, for if I do not go away, the comforter will not come to you, but if I should go, I will send Him to you. But when the spirit of truth has come, He will guide you into all the truth, and He will not speak from Himself; but what he hears he will speak; and he will make known to you things which are to come in the future. He will glorify me, because he will take of my own and show it to you. Everything my Father has is mine; this is the reason why I told you that He will take of my own and show it to you." (John 16:12-16) In the final days after the resurrection, Jesus told his followers, "John baptized with water; but *you shall be baptized with the Holy Spirit* not many days hence." The very last thing that Jesus tells his Apostles is, "*When the Holy Spirit comes* upon you, you shall receive power and you shall be witnesses to me both in Jerusalem and in Judea also in the province of Samaria and to the uttermost part of the earth." After making this final statement, the Bible tells us, "When he had spoken these things, he ascended while they were looking at him; a cloud received him and he was hidden from their sight." (Acts 1:5/8-9)

In the next chapter of Acts, the fulfillment of Jesus's prophesies takes place. "Suddenly there came a sound from heaven as of a mighty rushing wind and it filled the house where we were sitting, and there appeared to them tongues which were divided like flames of fire; and they rested upon each of them and *they were all filled with the Holy Spirit*, and they began to speak in various languages, according to whatever the Spirit gave them to speak." (Acts 2:2-4) In the immediate chapters following the Pentecost, the Apostles reveal the parameters of the intervention of the Holy Spirit. It is clear that something extraordinary happened during the Pentecost. The Pentecost marked the beginning of a New Covenant, an intradimensional covenant between human beings and the Holy Spirit. In his sermons, Paul identifies this New Covenant as one written, "not with ink, but with the *Spirit of the living God*; not on tablets of stone, but on tablets of the living heart." Paul tells his followers, "Our strength comes from God who has made us worthy to be ministers of the new covenant; not of the letter, *but of the Spirit*; for the letter of the law punishes with death, but the Spirit gives life." (2 Cor. 3:3-7) The New Covenant challenged not only the autonomy and authority of religious institutions, it also violated the exclusivity of the Jewish community from which it emerged. While many believe that it was Paul who first welcomed the Gentiles (non-Jews) into spiritual fellowship with the predominantly Jewish followers of Jesus, the Bible tells us, "While Simon Peter spoke these words (preached,) the Holy Spirit descended on all those who heard the word. And the Jewish converts who had come with him were seized with amazement because the gift of the *Holy Spirit was poured out on the Gentiles also*." (Acts 10:44-46)

The Jewish converts were shocked and angered when unbaptized Gentiles received the Holy Spirit, and they demanded that Gentile converts be circumcised. Simon Peter replied to them, "God, who knows what is in the heart, has testified concerning them (Gentiles) and has *given them the Holy Spirit just as he did to us*. And he did not discriminate between us and them, because he purified their hearts by faith." (Acts 15:8-10) The New Testament is filled with the accounts of the instruments of the Holy Spirit. They, like Jesus before them, were anti-authoritarian, ignored social propriety if it was a hindrance to their spirit-directed work, and extended their influence through their ability to deliver charismatic sermons, heal, exorcise demons, and initiate these gifts in others. In his understanding of the Holy Spirit, Benjamin believed that the salvation history of Christians was still very much in progress; that both God the Father and Jesus had sent the Holy Spirit to bring the work Jesus had begun to completion. The message of the Christian Spiritists, was that God is alive and present here in the material world in the person of the Holy Spirit.

The People Power Revolution

My growing involvement with Christian Spiritism was juxtaposed with a political situation that was becoming more volatile every day. In the month leading up to the off-year presidential elections that had been called by Ferdinand Marcos, tension had been mounting throughout the Philippines. Benjamin cautioned me to return to Manila, and stay in a hotel close to the American Embassy. I did as he suggested. A week before the elections, the political situation had become so unstable that I avoided leaving the hotel as much as possible. It was clear that the Marcos administration was becoming increasingly desperate, while the opposition was becoming better organized and more aggressive.

These hastily called 'snap' elections pitted President Ferdinand Marcos and his military complex, (which had held absolute power for nearly twenty years,) against Corazon Aquino (the widow of Benigno (Ninoy) Aquino,) the Catholic Church, and most of the academic community. Though nothing was ever proven, it was widely believed that the assassination of Ninoy Aquino, the chief political opponent of the Marcos administration, had been ordered by either Marcos himself, or by someone very close to him. As the elections drew to a close on February 7, 1986, Marcos was 'declared' the winner. Following the election, newspaper headlines reported widespread fraud.

The extent of this fraud included vote-buying, the theft of ballot boxes, hundreds of thousands of phony ballots, and even outright murder in areas believed to be sympathetic to Cory Aquino. The Marcos government, under extreme pressure from the United States, agreed to allow the counting of the votes to be monitored by NAMFREL, an independent monitor, in tandem with the administration's Commission on Elections (COMELEC.) The tally, which was monitored by a team headed by United States Senator Richard Lugar, was found to be a sham, and was reported as such both in the Philippines and abroad.

On my way to breakfast one morning, I saw a newspaper headline that read "Juan Ponce Enrile and Fidel Ramos Defect." I could hardly believe my eyes. Juan Ponce Enrile and Fidel Ramos, who were, respectively, Defense Minister and Chief of the Philippine Constabulary, were both top ranking officials of the Marcos government. On the announcement of their defection, the city of Manila bristled with a strange combination of relief, celebration, and dread. Upon returning to my hotel, I was advised by the staff to remain in the hotel until further notice. I went to my room, turned on the TV and found that all the television networks had gone off the air. The only radio stations that remained on the air were broadcasting feverishly in the Tagalog dialect. In the distance, I could hear the pounding whir of helicopters and walked out onto the balcony. Across Manila Bay, I saw what appeared to be battle ships pulling into the harbor. I called the front desk to ask about the media blackout and was told that most of the staff had already left the hotel. I hung up the phone and now realized how serious my situation had become. I was in the midst of a full scale political revolution.

A war of words raged between the rebel troops, led by Enrile and Ramos, and the Marcos administration. Enrile and Ramos openly encouraged the military to defect from Marcos and join the rebel camp. Civil war seemed inevitable. I was considering leaving the country when I learned that Manila International Airport had been shut down. There would be no incoming or outgoing flights. Enrile initiated the rebellion by plotting a coup which was to take place at Malacanang Palace where Ferdinand and Imelda Marcos lived. Enrile was supported by members of the elite military group known as RAM (Reform the Army Movement.) Fabian Ver, who served as Army Chief of Staff, discovered the coup plot and moved quickly to try to arrest both Enrile and the members of RAM. In the face of mounting danger, Enrile met with RAM soldiers at his home. He told them that the time had come to either fight, or disperse and organize a grassroots revolution against Marcos. When asked which course of action that he thought best, Enrile put on his flak jacket and began handing out Uzis to his soldiers. Enrile then called Fidel Ramos and set up a meeting with him at Camp Aguinaldo.

At a press conference held after the meeting, Ramos and Enrile both announced that they were resigning their posts in the Marcos administration effective immediately. In addition to their own resignations, they called for the resignation of Ferdinand Marcos, and offered their support to Mrs. Aquino, whom they acknowledged to be the duly elected President of the Philippines.

While the press conference was underway, Cardinal Jaime Sin, leader of the Catholic Church in the Philippines, addressed the nation over Radio Veritas. To everyone's astonishment, he announced that he wanted all Filipinos, including priests and nuns, to go to Camp Crame and stage a nonviolent vigil in support of the rebellion led by Enrile and Ramos. As Chief of the Philippine Constabulary, Fidel Ramos had his headquarters at Camp Crame. The now rebel headquarters had previously been the infamous site of the interrogation and torture of opponents of the Marcos administration. Camp Crame was located on one of the main thoroughfares in Quezon City called Epiphanio de los Santos Avenue, and known locally as EDSA. On the Cardinal's prompting, tens of thousands of Filipinos poured onto EDSA.

Marcos mobilized his military forces. A tense situation quickly developed in which government forces tried to advance, only to be forced back by the wall of human bodies that stood in their way. Soon, armored personnel carriers (APC) and other weapons of war rolled down EDSA toward Camp Crame. The APCs took their positions and awaited the order to attack. Meanwhile, tens of thousands of Filipinos, in an astounding display of faith, continued to surround the APCs with their bodies making it impossible for the military forces of the Marcos regime to attack Camp Crame without slaughtering thousands of innocent people. The burgeoning crowds sang hymns while priests and nuns knelt in prayer. The military forces, immobilized in a churning sea of their fellow citizens, held their positions.

Unable to use the infantry, Marcos ordered air strikes to destroy the insurgents at Camp Crame. But by the time these strikes were ordered, hundreds of thousands more Filipinos blockaded the entrance to Camp Crame with their bodies. Catholic nuns and priests were openly conducting masses for the soldiers and imploring them to abandon Marcos and join the people. Though events had gone well up to that point, it was clearly a desperate situation, and the real possibility existed that things could reverse at any moment. Meanwhile, forced to choose between possible court martial and firing squads, and doing the right thing in the eyes of God, mass defections began within the infantry. When the Philippine Air Force arrived, ready to carry out their orders, they saw something that changed their minds. From their helicopters, looking down from thousands of feet above the ground, they saw a *gigantic cross* below them. A cross formed from the bodies of priests, nuns, men, women, and children engaged in nonviolent resistance against weapons of war. Awed by the sight below them, they peacefully landed their helicopters inside the military compound that served as rebel headquarters.

Shortly after the helicopters landed, rebel forces seized control of Channel 4, the government-owned and largest media center in the Philippines. Marcos' forces still controlled Channel 1 and the media battle for the support of the people raged. On the rebel channel, the leaders of the coup simultaneously implored the Marcos' forces to defect while encouraging further mobilization of what had come to be called "People Power" to areas of the city where nonviolent resistance was needed. The excitement and joy at the prospect of a long-awaited freedom poured from the rebel channel, and was perhaps the most moving event I have ever seen on television. On the channel controlled by the Marcos' forces, General Fabian Ver, looking grim and furious, assured the public that everything *was* under control, and equally, that he was ready to shed blood if the rebels did not surrender at once.

Christian Mediumship Training 121

The Cross at Edsa

Having been an avid anti-war activist during the Vietnam War, I felt a deep emotional solidarity with the plight of the Filipinos. I have always believed that the desire for freedom is spiritually motivated. Dictators have always seen the exercise of religious freedom as a threat, and have done whatever they could to destroy or co-opt the free expression of religion. As I watched the rebel controlled television station, I became increasingly fascinated by the "People Power" revolution. I knew I was witnessing a major historical event, the likes of which had never occurred before, except perhaps, in Mahatma Gandhi's nonviolent ouster of British Colonial rule in India. Never before had a housewife struck the chord of resistance and precipitated an all-out revolution. Even more astounding, it was succeeding because of the *nonviolent resistance of the masses*, who immobilized the hostile instruments of war with persuasion, their bodies, and their faith. Rather than merely watch this rare and spiritual event on television, I decided to go to EDSA and participate in it.

On Monday morning, I left my hotel to join the crowds at EDSA. Traveling through Manila, I was immediately struck by how different the reality of the city was from the optimistic reports I had seen on television. Barricades were everywhere. Streets were blocked by overturned buses and very nervous taxi and jeepney drivers were the only ones still driving. I arrived at EDSA at 10:30 a.m., and was immediately overwhelmed by what I saw. EDSA was completely immobilized by fearless, inspired people, who were willing to die to end the dictatorship, and win their freedom. The people who surrounded the soldiers gave them flowers, food, cigarettes, and candies, while pleading and reasoning with them to join the side of peace. Catholic masses were being held in the street, right in front of the APCs, with statues of the Virgin Mary held aloft for everyone to see. The fear and anxiety brought about by the ever-present potential for disaster was diminished by the colorful vendors who cheerfully peddled everything from Cory Aquino souvenirs to fried bananas.

In this absolutely surreal environment, I realized that I was witnessing the direct application of Christ's teachings in the context of a political revolution. Cardinal Jaime Sin was acting as an instrument of divine intervention when he made the decision to attempt the impossible. Christ said, "Don't resist evil, do good to them that curse you, and love your enemies." And here, these devout, freedom-loving people were risking their lives in a final stand to overthrow a third world military dictator by resisting evil, but resisting evil with love and kindness. Actively working to persuade the military forces to join them, they succeeded in transforming evil into good. Christ's admonition to behave in this way had always been shrugged off in the past as merely an ideal, an aspiration. The advice to 'not resist evil' seemed a sure way to allow evil to triumph. Yet, at EDSA, right before my eyes, the exception to the rule unfolded.

The soldiers were visibly unnerved by what they saw. It was clear that the issues at hand transcended politics. It was the final culmination of the struggle for freedom in a people who had known nothing but military domination for nearly five hundred brutal years. In this confrontation between good and evil, the issues were rapidly elevated to ultimate questions that involved the future of the immortal souls of all involved. The troops who had sworn to follow the orders of their leaders without question were faced with the pleadings of tens of thousands of their fellow Filipinos to abandon these forces of darkness that had enslaved them. The soldiers had to decide whether to follow the dictates of a corrupt and ruthless government, or follow the dictates of their own consciences.

The tens of thousands of ordinary Filipinos who surrounded the soldiers and prevented the Marines from attacking Camp Crame, were inspired by a profound longing for and love of freedom that gave them the courage to face death without fear. Overwhelmed by the spiritual resolve and sincerity of the people, the Filipino troops, like the British troops in India before them, decided they would face severe punishment, even death, before they would kill the innocent and face the wrathful judgment of God. I returned from EDSA to my hotel as the sun began to set. The following morning, I watched the presidential inauguration of Ferdinand Marcos on Channel 1 at 8:30 a.m.. At 11:00 a.m., the presidential inauguration of Cory Aquino was broadcast by Channel 4. By Tuesday evening, it was confirmed that Marcos had fled the Philippines. A mass celebration ensued that lasted until the early hours of the morning.

Experiencing what came to be known as "The Miracle at EDSA" deeply reinforced my belief that the Philippines was, indeed, a special place. It was a place where deep, transcendent spiritual forces were at work. I felt it was a blessing to have experienced, firsthand, the political and spiritual event now known as the "People Power" revolution. I do not claim to understand the complexities of the political life of the Filipinos. I will say, however, that whatever opinions one may have about the politics of the years following the People Power Revolution, no one can dispute the unexpected and miraculous nature of the events that ended the dictatorship of Ferdinand Marcos. Despite the political turmoil that followed the overthrow of the Marcos administration, the series of events that forced Marcos to flee can only be described as a miracle. The Philippines were free at last.

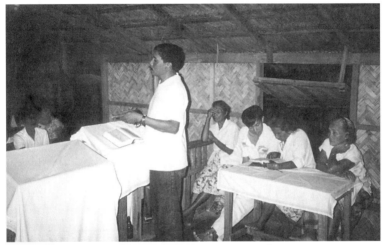

Director of Mediums opens spiritual service.

Espiritism in Lupao

After the revolution, calm returned and I resumed my spiritual training with Benjamin. I questioned him at length about the verbal dialogue between the Holy Spirit and the Christian Spiritist mediums of the Union Espiritista. Fascinated by the spiritual dialogue I had discovered in the Minutes, I wondered whether the intradimensional dialogue still existed. Benjamin assured me that the dialogue with the Blessed Spirit, that had existed in the early Union, was still very much in progress. After months of intensive study of the Minutes, I had learned much about the thought processes of the Blessed Spirit. I was excited by the possibility of interacting with the Blessed Spirit myself. Benjamin sensed my excitement and offered to take me to an upcoming conference of the Christian Spiritist Church, in the rural village of Lupao, Nueva Ecija, so that I could 'speak' with the messenger of the Holy Spirit myself.

In studying the Minutes, I had often tried to imagine what the setting of the sessions was like. I found the prospect of actually attending a traditional Christian Spiritist ceremony to be a rare opportunity. I gratefully accepted his offer. Leaving Baguio City, I traveled for many hours through the rice paddies of Central Luzon, finally arriving in Lupao late in the afternoon. I was surprised to find the Christian Spiritist Church to be the most prominent building in Lupao. I was warmly greeted by the members of the Church and spent several hours with them discussing Christian Spiritism. I was curious about the types of subjects they discussed with the Blessed Spirit, and wanted to know what sort of questions they asked. They told me that, for many years, members of the Christian Spiritist community had been meeting regularly to consult the Blessed Spirit regarding the fine points of biblical doctrine. During these sessions, the Blessed Spirit, speaking through the medium, interpreted the Bible for them in the context of Christian Spiritism. The Blessed Spirit clarified the fine points of the Scriptures and settled doctrinal disputes. The Blessed Spirit also answered questions concerning contemporary events, as the Minutes so clearly illustrate.

Upon Benjamin's arrival, we gathered in the church and the service began. Immediately after the opening ceremonies, the medium was "influenced." She abruptly went into a trance, with her hands holding the outer edges of what Christian Spiritists refer to as an "apparatus." I had read about the use of the apparatus many times in the Minutes, and had wondered what it looked like, and how it operated. The apparatus they used was a primitive looking wooden tripod, upon which sits a movable circular table top. The letters of the alphabet, and the numbers one through ten, are drawn on the surface of the table top. As the medium went deeply into trance, she began to slowly move the circular table. She then began to speak in a normal but subdued tone of voice, in the Ilocano dialect. As she spoke, a man standing next to her wrote down what she said on a pad of paper. When the medium stopped speaking, the man standing next to her turned and wrote several scriptural references on the chalkboard. This was done in exactly the same manner as had been done during the ceremony I'd seen at Marcos Orbito's Interfaith Church. In fact, the only difference between the two was that, during the Interfaith service, the Spirit had communicated through automatic writing; while here, the Spirit communicated through the apparatus.

After the first part of the service, Benjamin formally introduced me. He asked me if there were any questions that I would like to ask the Blessed Spirit. In my conversation with the Christian Spiritists earlier that day, I had been told that there were biblical references to all of the historical events that were part of the Divine plan. In Manila, throughout the military coup and the overthrow of the Marcos government, I had been amazed and inspired by the courage the unarmed Filipinos had displayed in their nonviolent confrontation with the military. Convinced

Christian Mediumship Training

that the revolution had been spirit-directed, I decided to ask if there were any references in the Bible about the "Miracle at E.D.S.A." Benjamin translated my question to the medium and she gave a brief reply. She said so little that I thought at first that she had simply answered in the negative. Benjamin then handed me a piece of paper that had a scriptural reference written on it. It was Isaiah 3:12. I opened my Bible to the verse which read, "The princes shall pluck my people out, and a woman shall rule over them. Oh, my people, your leaders have caused you to err, and disturbed the way of your paths." I stared at the words in amazement. They perfectly expressed what had happened in Manila.

I was impressed, not only with the amazing accuracy of the Christian Spiritist medium, but with the individual members as well. Though the members of the Church in Lupao were very poor, they conducted themselves with the pride of those who live the truth of Christ. I was told that the primary goal in these people's lives was to be able to face God without shame or guilt. To make a commitment like that in a poor country like the Philippines virtually guarantees that your children will wear rags and eat little except rice and dried fish. It was obvious that these people made that commitment joyfully and consciously. It was also clear that these incredibly humble and devout people loved Benjamin and held him in their highest esteem. Following the meeting, we went to a nearby house where I was shown meticulously organized records of spiritual revelations they had received over many years. I asked if they would translate a random sampling of the records, and they agreed. We stayed until far into the night studying the biblical insights the Holy Spirit had revealed to these humble farmers.

The following morning, Benjamin and I left Lupao on what was to become a very informative return trip to Baguio City. As the bus rolled past the green rice paddies and small villages, he told me about his life as a Christian Spiritist. In a country that is 85% Catholic, Benjamin had been a Christian Spiritist all his life, first in the Union and later, with the Christian Spiritists of the Philippines. He had been confirmed as a gifted medium of the Holy Spirit by the age of twelve. Having spent his entire life as a Christian Spiritist, he knew the inside story of the history and development of contemporary Espiritism in intricate detail.

He explained to me that the spiritual practices in the early days of the Union were based implicitly on the teachings of Christ. As the years passed, and the members of the Union were exposed to different types of Spiritist beliefs and practices, many of the members abandoned Christian Spiritism and insisted that the Union become a non-denominational fraternity of mediums. The members who still practiced Christian Spiritism exclusively, became more and more uncomfortable with this situation, until it finally became intolerable for them.

In 1966, this dispute within the Espiritist community led to a schism. This schism was precipitated in part by Allan Kardec's teachings on the life of Jesus. In Kardec's book, *The Gospel as Interpreted by Spiritism*, the virgin birth, crucifixion, and resurrection of Jesus were disputed. Kardec's book had long ignited controversy within Spiritist communities throughout the world. By 1966, several factions existed within the Union. The members of the Union who preferred the Kardecist teachings no longer wanted contemporary mediumship to be defined according to a particular religious orientation. The emerging science of parapsychology seemed, for many, a more appropriate way to explain the mysteries inherent in Spiritism.

Benjamin explained that the wife of the President of the Union was a member of a religious organization known as "Iglesia ni Christo" (The Church of Christ.) The members of Iglesia ni Christo believed in the doctrine of Latter Day Saints. Their particular Latter Day Saint was a Filipino, known as Felix Manalo, who was believed to be a Divine incarnation. According to Benjamin, the President's wife pressured her husband to declare that Jesus was not the only son of God, and to establish that position as a policy of the Union, which he did. The leader of the Christian Spiritists, Brother Eleuterio Terte, objected vehemently to this new policy of the Union. Terte pointed out that the Holy Spirit had instructed them to teach the divinity of Jesus since the beginning of the Union. He insisted that if he were to return to the provinces with a new doctrine that suggested that Jesus was not Divine, he could be stoned, or worse.

In addition to the problems that teaching the new policy would cause, Terte simply did not believe it himself. He finally demanded that the President withdraw from his position. The President refused. Terte resigned and, shortly thereafter, incorporated a new organization he named "The Christian Spiritists of the Philippines, Inc." (CSPI.) About 40% of the members of the Union followed Terte and joined the new organization. Benjamin explained that even if the virgin birth, crucifixion, and resurrection were myths, Jesus' role in the coming of the Holy Spirit provided definitive proof of his divinity. Who, Benjamin asked, but the son of God could have supervised the transference of the Spirit of God into the members of the Body of Christ?

The CSPI also differed from the Union in many other ways. The Union offered none of the Christian sacraments, such as baptism, marriage, or ordination, and allowed many different types of religious texts. The CSPI used only the Bible and offered all of the sacraments of the Christian Church. With the incorporation of CSPI, Christian Spiritism had already integrated everything from the Kardecist teachings believed to be relevant to the understanding of the workings of the Holy Spirit. As I listened to Benjamin, I realized that I had found the contemporary repository of the Christian Spiritist tradition that I had discovered in the Minutes of the Union. Eleuterio Terte had another distinction. In addition to being the leader and founder of the CSPI, he was also known as the first person ever to perform psychic surgery. At long last, a direct connection emerged between psychic surgery and Christian Spiritism.

A Close Encounter

Before moving to Baguio, I had been dating a woman in Manila, and I went to Manila from time to time to see her. While in Manila I stayed in an apartment that I had rented long term. On one of my visits, my girlfriend and I had an argument and she returned to her hometown in Mindanao. I decided to fly to Mindanao to try to patch things up. I was prepared to leave the following morning. At about three o'clock on the afternoon of the day before my departure, the operator at the switchboard of my apartment building called to announce that there was a woman in the lobby to see me. I asked the operator to send her up. Moments later, a woman named Lita Castellano arrived at my door and introduced herself. She was a Christian Spiritist, and a friend of Reverend Pajarillo. I welcomed her in and she told me that she had been sent from Baguio by Benjamin to deliver an urgent message. She handed me a small envelope. I opened it and took out a small note which read:

"As your brother in the name of our Lord Jesus Christ, I wrote you this letter that the Holy Spirit of God abide in your humble servant to give you the following instructions that you will follow: 1) In this critical time, if you go to Mindanao, do not let the girl know that you are in that area. 2) If the reason you are going there is about that girl, forget it. It is very dangerous there in this time." I was stunned. I had told no one of my plans! Even so, Benjamin had somehow learned of the plan, and had arranged for Lita to travel six hours by bus to deliver the note, advising me to cancel the trip. Lita watched me as I read the note, saw my expression and began to laugh. Needless to say, I canceled my trip to Mindanao.

Mediumship Training Begins

Shortly after that encounter, I returned to Baguio to spend Christmas with my friends. Benjamin mentioned during one of our meetings that he felt I was ready to receive mediumship training. He said that we would begin the training in January, after I had been baptized in the South China Sea on the coast of Luzon. He explained that Baptism was a means of sanctification, and when he opened me to the realm of the Spirit, it would protect me from interference by lesser spirits. I was baptized during the second week of January, and the mediumship training began on January 20, 1987. He began our first session by telling me that the Holy Spirit resides within each and every human being. He said that most people experience the presence of the Holy Spirit within themselves as their conscience. (John 14:17) During mediumship training, the medium is taught, one stage at a time, to allow the Blessed Spirit to operate through him or her, until the Spirit of God can function unobstructed through the medium.

Benjamin explained that, since childhood, he had attended regular sessions in which he had been trained (along with a select group of mediums) to allow the Holy Spirit to *externalize* itself through him in different levels of trance. During the training, the Holy Spirit would initiate the operation of spiritual gifts through the medium. Some would write while in trance; others learned to operate the apparatus in trance; others learned to heal in trance; and still others learned to speak in trance. In order to learn to function 'in trance,' it is necessary to undergo extensive training. Such training may take many years, or a few weeks, depending upon the existing predisposition of the medium. Yet, with the aid of a qualified instructor, the medium candidate will eventually learn to function in deep trance. Among the Filipinos, this spiritual opening, which allows someone to function in trance, is called 'nabuksan' (the opening.) The role of the mediumship trainer is to instruct, guide, and monitor the development of the medium until nabuksan takes place. In order to do this, the trainer must be endowed with special gifts of insight and discernment.

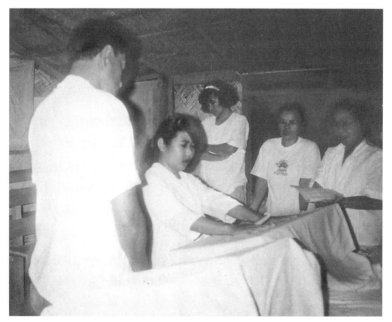

Director of Mediums induces trance in young medium.

Automatic Writing

Benjamin told me that the first stage of engaging the presence of the Holy Spirit within was accomplished through automatic writing. I was surprised to hear this, and asked if he would explain to me what automatic writing had to do with Christian Mediumship. He explained that there are many references in the Bible to hands appearing out of nowhere and revealing the will of God through writing. He gave, as scriptural examples, Exodus 31:18, "And he gave to Moses, when he had made an end to talking with him on Mount Sinai, two tablets of

Christian Mediumship Training

testimony, the stone tablets *written by the finger of God,*" and Daniel 5:5, "In that very hour there *appeared the fingers of a man's hand and wrote* opposite the candlestick upon the plaster of the wall of the king's palace, and the king saw the palm of the man's hand that wrote." Benjamin further explained that the spiritual gifts of speaking and interpreting in tongues could actually be understood as "any method through which the revelations of the Holy Spirit are delivered and interpreted," and that automatic writing was one of those methods.

After explaining the scriptural basis of automatic writing, Benjamin then asked me to sit down at a table that he had prepared for the training session. In spite of the biblical references and Benjamin's assurances, I was still having trouble accepting the concept that automatic writing was somehow related to the Holy Spirit, and was skeptical about my ability as an automatic writer. As I sat there at the table with the pen in my right hand and my left hand positioned on top of the sheet of paper, as I had been instructed, Benjamin moved around behind me and placed his hands on my back near my left shoulder blade. He began to apply pressure with his hands, and said in a barely audible tone of voice, "Come now, O Holy Spirit, and fill the heart of thine faithful. Kindle in him the fire of your love. Send forth thy Divine wisdom and cause the ARK of thy might to dwell on we, who faithfully and wholeheartedly, trust in thee." I suddenly felt as if I was dreaming and my head fell forward as semi-consciousness overcame me. In this state, I became dimly aware that my right hand was moving and writing on its own, almost totally disconnected from my normal cognitive processes. This semi-conscious state lasted for about fifteen minutes at which time Benjamin restored me to my normal level of awareness by placing his hands on my forehead.

Induction of trance is complete.

As I sat there, stunned, Benjamin asked me to read the message that the Holy Spirit had sent to me. I picked up the sheet of paper, and instantly noticed that the message was written in a cursive handwriting style. I have always written by printing. It took me a while to make out what the message said, but finally I was able to read it to him. The content of the message was as follows:

"When will we be together again, O brother of the eternal life. I will be always until the end of time and even unto the new life of the faithful. Give me your undying promise to glorify me in all your words and works. See the light of grace that is your challenge. Breathe and know that we shall never die. Breathe and feel the presence of the Holy Spirit. Even as I live in you, so also will you live in me, if you will but follow my commandments.

Blessed Spirit delivers sermon through medium.

Open your heart to the mission of these, your brothers and sisters, that live forever in me. Let the Holy instructions come forth with a loud and living testimony to the peace that has no beginning or end.

The spiritual forces of the eternal covenant are with you always, as we have always been since the original spark of the Holy fire that purifies and cleanses those with the spiritual seed within themselves."

After I finished reading the message, Benjamin smiled and commented that for my first message, I had done very well. On that note, we ended the first session and Benjamin advised me to rest and offer a prayer of thanks to God for the message. He then told me that we would continue with the mediumship training the following day.

We met the following afternoon at two o'clock, and Benjamin

"influenced" me in the same manner he had done at the first session. The same thing happened all over again. After completing the second session, he asked me once again to read the message. The message was written in a far more legible handwriting than the one I had received the day before. Benjamin commented that this development indicated progress in the first stage of the incorporation of the Holy Spirit within. The second message read:

"We greet you, brother, with gladness. We have waited long for your return to the Love and Peace of Christ. The path of your life has been full of the tensions and illusions of this world. But fear not, brother, for the way of your life has now been joined with the promise of our Lord.

Continue in the path that you now see unfolding before you and many great works will be accomplished for the glory of God. Be ever mindful of your responsibilities and bear them with joy, because the work that you do is in the service of the King of Kings and the Lord of Lords.

The Blessed Spirit delivers sermon through Reverend Pajarillo.

You must visit with your family and help them to understand the true teachings of our Lord. Forgive all the wrongs that have been done to you and go forth with the spirit of forgiveness as your light.

Pray often asking for forgiveness and abandon any activities that would lead you into error."

Benjamin indicated that I was making rapid progress and I felt very blessed and grateful for the assistance he had given to me. He said we would resume the training on the following day, at the same time. Once again, he suggested that I rest and offer another prayer of thanks to God; which I did. The following afternoon Benjamin "influenced" me again and my hand wrote the following message:

"Greetings, our brother in Christ. We are pleased with your efforts. Be careful in your propagation of Truth. Many will plot against you and

try to turn the ignorant against you. Do not resist them or argue with them. Continue your works and pray often. Your silence will be your armor, for evil unchallenged will turn on itself and destroy itself.

The path of Christ is filled with obstacles and temptations, but you will succeed in your efforts if you closely follow the commandments of our Lord.

Live your life so that none may find fault with you. Purify yourself and prepare for the struggle that you will endure in carrying out the work of your redemption.

Peace be with you, brother, and know that we are always with you as you know we have always been. Your life has been spared many times through our Lord's grace. The life in you is not your own, it belongs to God."

I was awed by these words. After receiving the message, Benjamin told me that I had completed the first phase of mediumship training. From that point on, I would function as a writing, or "psychographic," medium. He then informed me that, following a three-day break, we would begin the second phase of mediumship training, which was clairvoyance training. Benjamin explained that clairvoyance, in the context of Christian Spiritism, was the means by which the discernment of the true spirit was accomplished. (I Cor. 12:10) As a writing medium I have learned to open myself to the Blessed Spirit as I write for insight into the hidden meanings that the messengers of the Holy Spirit wish to communicate here in the material world. Whenever I reach a difficult juncture in writing, I concentrate, suspend my thoughts, and ultimately receive the information I need to continue.

Scribes record the revelations received from the Holy Spirit.

Clairvoyance Training

Before the clairvoyance training could begin, several preparations had to be made. Benjamin asked me to purchase a white bed sheet and also a brandy snifter (a globe-shaped goblet) made of clear glass. He

Christian Mediumship Training

proceeded to tack the sheet to the wall in front of me. He filled the snifter with water, and placed it on the table directly between me and the sheet. I commented that the water-filled glass looked like a crystal ball. He replied that the Blessed Spirit had given them instructions to use a water-filled glass in clairvoyance training because the bible recorded that "the Spirit of God moved upon the face of the water." (Genesis 1:2) I was instructed to gaze at the sheet and the water-filled snifter at the same time, without staring at either of them. I attempted to do as he instructed, at first with difficulty, but eventually, I came to see shifting patterns of color, in the reflective water of the snifter and on the sheet.

Healers concentrate to God in preparation for healing session.

At the end of the first clairvoyance session, I felt that I had not been able to attain the desired state of mind. Even though I had, indeed, seen shifting colors, I attributed them to retinal fatigue. Benjamin sensed my disappointment and told me to be patient. He emphasized that, in this phase of the training, he was going to induce a much deeper level of trance than automatic writing required, and therefore, it was necessary that I be resolutely predisposed. The next day, we proceeded with the session as we had the day before. I felt much calmer and more at peace than I had felt in the previous session. Benjamin quietly walked up behind me and placed one of his hands on the top of my head and then placed his other hand on the back of my neck at the base of my skull. He began to apply pressure on the back of my neck and suddenly I lost consciousness.

I regained 'consciousness' in a desert landscape standing in front of what appeared to be a mountain. In this out-of-body experience, I adjusted to the visionary landscape, which seemed three-dimensional and entirely real. As the details of this parallel world came into focus, I saw a man standing on top of a boulder at the base of the mountain. He was dressed in a long, brown, coarse cloth robe and sandals and looked like a monk of the early Christian church. As I concentrated my attention on him, he began speaking to me. Even though his lips were moving and his facial movements expressive, I could not hear anything he said. I tried desperately to read his lips as he continued to speak. I couldn't help but feel that in my inability to hear his words, I was missing something very important. As I struggled with a certain degree of anxiety, I suddenly sensed that I was receiving his nonverbal communication and that his conversation was too complex to be communicated in ordinary words. Filled with light and indescribable peace, I realized that I had received a profound spiritual revelation and felt blessed to be in the presence of this radiant, powerful being.

The Holy Spirit descends upon the healers.

I returned from this visionary experience to find Benjamin standing beside me, smiling broadly. Before I could speak, he told me that the man I had seen in the vision was one of the angels of God from New Jerusalem, and that he and another angel I had not seen, had placed a golden halo one foot over my head, and a seal over my forehead that could be seen only by those possessed of the ability to discern the true spirit. Benjamin then congratulated me, and told me that I was now confirmed as a medium and clairvoyant of the Christian Spiritist Church. He commented that, in most cases, mediumship training could be a long and arduous process, but, in my case, the process had occurred very quickly. Benjamin told me that my past experiences had predisposed me to function as a medium of the Holy Spirit. He told me that the Holy Spirit had been assisting me throughout my life; and in my case, the training served as a formal acknowledgment of a pre-existing condition. He pointed out to me that if the Holy Spirit had not been guiding me, I would never have gotten as far in my research as I had.

In my capacity as an initiated medium of the Holy Spirit, I was told that I was to receive my true name, one that was recorded in a spiritual dimension that the Christian Spiritists called 'New Jerusalem.' Benjamin said that the scriptural references to the new name I was to receive were found in the Book of Revelation, verses 2:17 and 3:12, and in Isaiah 56:5. The first reference states, "He who has ears let him hear what the spirit says to the churches: to him who overcomes, I will give him a white stone, and on the stone a *new name written*, which no man knows except he who receives it." (2:17) The second reference states, "He who overcomes I will make a pillar in the temple of my God, and he shall not go out again; and I will write upon him the name of my God and the name of the New Jerusalem which comes down out of heaven from my God; and I will write upon him my *new name.*" (3:12) The reference in Isaiah states, "I will give to them in my house and within my walls a place and a name better than sons and daughters; I will give them an *everlasting name* that shall not be cut off."

Young healers prepare to dispense Magnetic Fluid.

Benjamin told me that one of the requirements of his position as the General Director of Mediums was the ability to spiritually transport himself out of his body, and travel in that state of consciousness. He demonstrated this ability most often in his capacity as a divine and distant healer. He told me that, every night between midnight and 2:00 a.m., he left his body and traveled to the homes of his patients. In addition to visiting the homes of his patients, he would occasionally travel in spirit to New Jerusalem. To complete the final stage of my training as a medium, Benjamin said he would travel in spirit to New Jerusalem, learn my eternal name and bring it back to me as the confirmation of my status as a medium of the Holy Spirit. On January 29th, 1987, I received my eternal name.

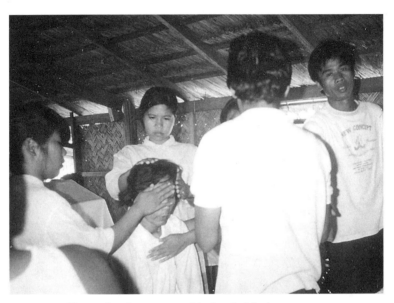

Young healers proceed to heal elderly woman.

At this stage of my training, Benjamin told me that receiving empowerment as a medium of the Holy Spirit was *a means to an end, rather than an end in itself.* According to Benjamin, spiritual attainment, rather than being the culmination of anything, was in fact, the preparation for the spiritual work that an instrument of the Holy Spirit is destined to do. Having modeled their spiritual work on the healing ministry of Jesus, the Christian Spiritists exercised new mediums in the same way that Jesus trained his Apostles: by having them perform healing missions among the poor, the sick, and the afflicted. I told Benjamin that, in addition to the training I had already received, I was ready and willing to undertake whatever else I could do to further develop my abilities as a spirit-directed healing medium. Benjamin suggested that I accompany him into the rural provinces to help him in his missionary work, which I readily agreed to do. He then explained to me that he had completed his work as my teacher. He emphasized that, in the future, the Holy Spirit would be my mediumship trainer and mentor. Understanding and performing my role in the work of the Holy Spirit would depend solely upon my ability to discern the lessons and messages I received on a day-to-day basis.

Christian Mediumship Training 137

Healing Missions

Benjamin invited me to participate in some healing missions that he was planning in the remote provinces of Aurora and Quezon. These provinces, located in Northern Luzon, were still loyal to Marcos. Anarchy reigned in these areas. Communist insurgents, who had risen in opposition to the Marcos administration, as well as whole battalions of the Philippine Army who had defected and set up their own command posts in open defiance of the political leadership of the Aquino government, controlled vast areas of the countryside. Both the communists and the military criticized the Aquino government as being a puppet of American interests, and backed by the U.S. military. Anti-American sentiment was strong in the regions Benjamin chose to undertake the healing missions, and I had mixed feelings about placing myself at risk. I voiced my concerns, but he assured me that I need not worry. He said that as long as I was with him, I would be safe.

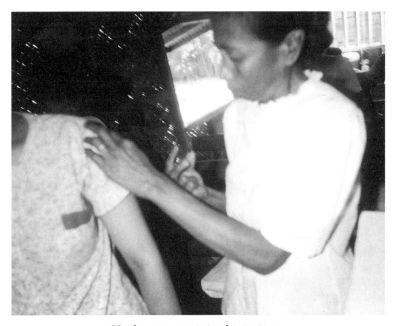

Healer gives spiritual injection.

He explained that insurgencies existed in the Philippines because of the exploitation of the poor. While he was not politically-oriented, he believed that it was the mission of Christians to help the poor in all situations. Once again, he assured me that we would have nothing to fear among the insurgents. One of the members of the Christian Spiritist Church told me that many of these insurgents regarded Benjamin as a 'holy man.' They often asked for his blessing, in case they were killed in combat. It was a source of humor among Christian Spiritists that very few of the Filipino Communists were willing to take the chance of going to hell in the event that Marx and Lenin were wrong and God, in fact, did exist!

There is nothing easy about conducting healing missions in undeveloped areas of the Philippines. We would travel in jeepneys for hours on endless, bumpy, dusty roads, to finally arrive in areas where abject poverty prevailed. The conditions were so desperate that merely turning on a fan to keep the mosquitoes at bay while I slept at night upset my hosts. The fifty cents' worth of electricity it took to run the fan overnight could buy enough rice for two days, and while my hosts felt duty bound to pay for the electricity, they knew they could not afford it. Even though I made it clear that I was willing to pay for the electricity, Benjamin asked if I would try to ignore the inconvenience. He explained that the Filipinos were very proud and were ashamed of their poverty. I complied with his request and consequently....got very little sleep.

Young couple come to spiritual service for marital counseling and healers hold open Bible over them as minister asks God to resolve their dilemma.

In central Luzon, I was shocked to learn that the wages a laborer received for ten hours of backbreaking work in the rice fields was equivalent to one dollar and twenty-five cents. Nevertheless, upon our arrival, the barangay captains, who served as the mayors and welcoming committees of the small towns we visited, would take us to their 'guest quarters' where we slept and ate our meals. After the evening meal, the community gathered together and Benjamin introduced me as a medium/healer of the Christian Spiritist Church. He told everyone that we had come to offer our services to them. The only white missionaries that these rural Filipinos had ever seen were missionaries of Western religions. I was the first white American these Filipinos had ever seen who was a Christian Spiritist healing missionary. As a result, I was held in high esteem. As Benjamin had assured me, I found I had nothing to fear.

Couple receive magnetic healing from spirit-filled healers.

The first healing mission we conducted together was in a coastal village in the province of La Union, in Northern Luzon. The village leader was an elderly Filipino woman who warmly received us and provided us with a delicious meal of fresh seafood and vegetables. Afterwards, she told me that her daughter had been suffering from migraine headaches for a number of years; that she had tried everything she could to heal her, but had failed. She then asked me if I could heal her. Naturally, I told her I would try my best. The next morning, we began the healing service with Benjamin leading us all in prayer. Benjamin had told me that I had to change my attitude when I was healing. For many years prior to the mediumship training, I had practiced various healing methods with much success. During those years, I had learned to depend solely on myself. I believed that my success in healing was based on my own personal skills and experience.

Benjamin emphasized to me that *all success in healing is based on the intervention of the Holy Spirit,* and that I had to learn to be mindful of the role the Holy Spirit played each time I healed. I asked Benjamin if there were any special prayers I should say before healing. He replied that the most effective thing I could ask for is that the will of God be done. I was instructed to concentrate, suspend my thoughts, and allow the light of God to enter my body and operate *through* me, rather than inhibit the power of the spirit by harboring the misconception that I was doing the healing. I, like the patients I worked on, had to learn to place my full trust in God and work in as selfless a manner as possible.

The daughter of the elderly woman was the first in line to be healed. She told me that she had suffered a migraine the night before and, though it had subsided, her head still hurt. I placed my hands on her head and silently asked the Holy Spirit to have mercy on this poor woman and heal her. As I prayed for her, I experienced a sensation of coldness come over my body while, simultaneously, I felt a tingling sensation in my hands. Almost immediately, she burst into tears and said that the pain had completely left her. She was overcome with emotion, as was her delighted mother. Benjamin and I continued in our healing work until all thirty-two people who had come for healing had been worked on. As my healing work proceeded, I noticed that the sensations I felt varied from person to person.

Reverend Pajarillo prepares to baptize new converts
the morning after the spiritual service.

I could not help but feel limited by solely using prayer and laying on of hands. I felt that I could have successfully treated ailments that had not responded to prayer and laying on of hands with other healing methods I had used for years. Of the people we worked on, all seemed to show improvement in varying degrees. After we finished, Benjamin told the patients that they needed to dedicate themselves to God and strive to lead a moral life. He assured them that God would continue to bless them and keep them healed. As Benjamin and I rested, I reviewed the events of the day and realized that the healing of the elderly woman's daughter had set the pace for the rest of the day. The healing had happened so suddenly that I hardly had time to assess the nuances involved. Yet, I knew that whatever had transpired, she no longer suffered and I was grateful for that. The dramatic healing that took place within her also had another effect. Her healing established my credibility as an instrument of the Holy Spirit in the eyes of the rest of the patients. After breakfast the next morning, the elderly woman thanked Benjamin and me and invited us to return to her village. We agreed to return in ten days.

As we travelled inland from the coast into the interior of Luzon, I asked Benjamin if he felt that I should stop using my previous methods of healing entirely and concentrate all my efforts on prayer and laying on of hands. He repeated once again that all success in healing is brought about by the intervention of the Holy Spirit. He stressed that the means by which the Holy Spirit is brought into the healing process is of primary importance, while the mode of healing or the technique one uses is secondary. He explained that praying for the light of God to enter one's body, and then directing the light into the body of the patient through prayer and laying on of hands, is emphasized as a means of establishing oneself as an instrument of the source of healing power.

From Benjamin's point of view, spinal manipulation was limited as a technique in and of itself. He pointed out that however effective any single technique might be, no single healing method will consistently cure all ailments. Spinal adjustments will sometimes produce a total cure, other times it will provide only temporary relief. It is well known that experimental drugs often achieve a high percentage of cure at first, while doctors are optimistic about their potential. As the doctor's faith in the drug diminishes, cure rates plummet. In sum, the efficacy of any given therapeutic method is subject to fluctuate according to the degree of power invested in it. As the parameters of one's belief expands, the power that belief invests in therapeutic interactions increases.

Benjamin believed there was a spiritual prerequisite central to the optimal effectiveness of all therapeutic interaction. According to him, to treat patients most effectively, one first needed to pray and concentrate that the will of God be done. Secondly, one called the Holy Spirit to intervene in the task at hand, allowing the light of God to come and operate through both healer and patient. The healer must then discern the source of the problem and the proper course of treatment, which often comes in a spontaneous insight. Expanding the parameters of belief to include the possibility of Divine intervention in healing transforms the healing act. Seeing oneself as an *instrument* of the healing power of the Divine removes the limitations inherent in the shifting sands of dualistic thought. Through understanding and mastering these spiritual prerequisites as the *primary* means of healing, and fully integrating them into personal interaction with a patient, *any and all forms of medicine can be instantly transformed into spirit-directed medicine.*

During the following ten days, Benjamin and I did three more healing missions, all with excellent results. We did a mission in Benjamin's hometown of Dingalan, in Aurora province, among people who had known him his entire life. On the way to Dingalan, we were stopped at a roadblock manned by Communist insurgents. Following that, we were stopped at another roadblock manned by soldiers of the Philippine Army. We were granted safe passage by both. Benjamin was revered as a spiritual leader among the people of Dingalan. They held ongoing Christian Spiritist services for three days in his honor. During this time, he presided over the services and delivered inspired spiritual revelations, while in trance, which were duly recorded by the scribes at the center. On the third day, we held healing services while the entire congregation sang spiritual hymns as invocations of the Holy Spirit. During the healing service, the room was filled with magnetic healers and Christian Spiritists who freely dispensed magnetic fluid from the Holy Spirit into all who came for healing.

New converts are baptized in the Pacific Ocean.

Many of the patients who came were the wives and children of Communist insurgents, who wore crosses made from spent bullet casings. In Dingalan, I saw, once again, that the most effective way to generate the proper environment for spirit-directed healing was to have groups of like-minded people cooperate in bringing forth the spiritual power that underlies the healing process. The three days of spiritual services culminated with a mass baptism ceremony in the Pacific Ocean.

On our trip back to La Union, Reverend Pajarillo explained to me that attending Christian Spiritist worship services was an essential

Christian Mediumship Training

element in becoming an instrument of spirit-directed healing. The worship services provided an opportunity for groups of Christian Spiritists to become filled with the power of the Holy Spirit. During these services the presence of the Holy Spirit increased to levels that I had not experienced anywhere else in the Philippines. As the spirit-directed teachings proceeded, the group became increasingly animated. Towards the end of the services, the Holy Spirit was fully present.

Christian Spiritist worship services are a mass invocation of the Divine light of the Holy Spirit. Reverend Pajarillo assured me that a lot more was going on in those services than the eye could perceive. During the services, the Spirit Protector and the elevated Spirits could evaluate the development of the members. More importantly, the Protector often decided to help certain members. Acquiring one's own Spirit Protector was a great blessing. Everyone in the villages, Christian Spiritist or otherwise, understood what was going on in the services, and came en masse to be healed when the services concluded.

Reverend Pajarillo and Reverend Esther Bacani bid me farewell.

On the tenth day, we returned to La Union where our mission had begun. I was astounded to find nearly one hundred people waiting for us. The daughter of the elderly woman was ecstatic to see us, and reported that her headaches had not returned. The level of enthusiasm bordered on hysteria. In the days since we had left, many patients had fully recovered from their ailments and, because of their testimony, sixty more people came to receive healing. During the healing services the next day, the Holy Spirit operated very powerfully through Benjamin and me, and succeeded in producing fifteen dramatic cures, and many less dramatic but powerful healings.

After the healing service in La Union, Benjamin and I returned to Baguio. Several days after that, we met for breakfast and spoke at length about the healing mission. At one point in our conversation, Benjamin asked me what I had discerned from the workings of the Holy Spirit during the healing missions.

In my mind, I silently reviewed the events of the past ten days. I told Benjamin that it seemed each successful healing had strengthened the faith of those who received it. This increase of faith multiplied not only the frequency of cure, but also deeply inspired those who merely observed. As faith and trust in God increased in the participants, the externalization of the power of the Holy Spirit filled everyone present, setting the stage for even more profound manifestations. Borrowing a term from physics, I described this exponential increase of faith through healing as a spiritual chain reaction.

Benjamin asked me to explain what a chain reaction was. I finally came up with the words "a spiritual domino effect." Deep in thought, Benjamin repeated the words "domino effect." At last, he smiled broadly and told me that I had listened well. He then said that "through the spiritual domino effect, the Holy Spirit was setting the stage for a profound transformation of human life." I asked him to explain. He hesitated for a moment and then said that the advent of the Holy Spirit was already well underway and that the greatest obstacle to the Coming of the Holy Spirit was an entrenched religious bureaucracy that has dominated and controlled Western civilization for hundreds of years. Benjamin said that the spell that organized religion had woven with a combination of torture and charity, hellfire and salvation, would be broken from within the Church. He then described how the mass possession of entire congregations would take place. Rather than a Rapture wherein the members of the body of Christ are taken off the earth, they will experience the transcendent peace and wonder of the Holy Spirit, yet remain here on earth...transformed. In this transformed state, they will receive the knowledge and conversation of the Spirit of Truth. As I listened to Benjamin, I knew that he spoke from experience.

Chapter Seven

The Enigma of Psychic Surgery

The Enigma of Psychic Surgery

*I*n the previous chapters, I have drawn from a wide range of sources to document the cultural history of the spiritual tradition from which psychic surgery emerged. In the Philippines, psychic surgery is not seen as a scam by those who use it in a *spiritual context*, as most healers do. Psychic surgery is deeply woven into the fabric of Filipino culture and exists as an indigenous expression of the miraculous potential for the restoration of health. I think it's safe to say that anyone who believes in the existence of God, believes, in one way or another, that God can intervene into the affairs of human beings, and do so in a way that is unmistakable proof of God's existence. Thus, if God exists, then the potential for the manifestation of the Divine must also exist. This belief is the motivation behind prayer, pilgrimage, and sacred ritual. For many, it is also the motivation to seek out a spiritual means for the restoration of health. Human beings have always longed for tangible proof that God exists, and when word gets around that this proof is available, people flock to see and experience the phenomenon. Jesus apparently knew this and demonstrated that, through Divine healing, the intervention of the miraculous power of God could be realized.

Psychic Surgery and the Mass Media

In presenting the Filipino beliefs and practices from which psychic surgery has emerged, I hope that I have illustrated the depth of misunderstanding that exists between psychic surgery as it is portrayed by the media, and the religious origins of the phenomenon in the Philippines. Mention psychic surgery in the United States and the reaction will inevitably be derisive; someone will immediately recall the expose of psychic surgery that aired on the television program "Unsolved Mysteries." For ten years now, the producers have been replaying the segment on the psychic surgeon, Gary Magno, and his wife Terry, and will probably be airing it on into the future. The media has consistently presented psychic surgery as criminal activity perpetuated by impostors posing as surgeons who enrich themselves, while offering false hope to the sick and afflicted.

The narrator tersely reports that the Magnos have exploited the sick by pretending to offer miraculous surgical operations. Then, he admits that the woman, reportedly exploited by the healers, disowned her own son after learning that he had gone to the police and turned the Magnos in. The commentator goes on to say that the woman never spoke to her son again except to tell him that, in her opinion, he was responsible for the deaths of hundreds of people, for whom, treatment by the Magnos was no longer possible. The program ends with photos of Gary and Terry, and the revelation that they have fled the country and are fugitives from justice. This is the typical portrayal by the American media of psychic surgery. Media images are limited to those of psychic surgeons allegedly caught practicing medicine without a license, trapped in police sting operations with sleight-of-hand props, or in other equally sordid circumstances.

In addition to the media barrage of negative publicity, the public is given the complete assurance of James Randi, the self-appointed debunker of psychic phenomena, that psychic surgery is a sleight-of-hand simulation of surgery. Being a sleight-of-hand expert himself, Randi explains that through a skillful manipulation of animal tissue and blood, the *illusion* of an operation can be produced. To illustrate his point, he performs his own psychic surgery operation using sleight-of-hand techniques and rests his case. In his book *Faith Healers,* Randi exposes the abuses of faith healing among American evangelical and Pentecostal Christians. Though much of his criticism may be valid, he then draws a comparison between the most corrupt faith healers, and Jesus' healing ministry described in the biblical narrative of the New Testament. After indicting Jesus as the original fake healer, Randi then admits that he has found no "compelling" reason to believe in God. As I have established in previous chapters, the healing practices of the Filipinos, psychic surgery included, are an extension of their religious beliefs. Taken out of context, the religious practices of even the most widely accepted orthodox religions can be portrayed as the attempts of clergy to 'con' the gullible 'true believers' out of their money. Are thin white wafers and grape juice 'really' transformed into the flesh and blood of Jesus when they are offered in communion? Can this transformation be proven scientifically? Should communion be banned or criminalized, and charges filed against priests, if it can be proved that no transformation actually takes place? Like Randi, I suspect the claims and motives of know-it-all true believers, but I am equally suspicious of the motives of atheist scientists who feel that declaring war on the well documented power of the imagination in healing is somehow in our best interest.

As self appointed iconoclasts of healing mediated by faith, so-called skeptics insist that genuine psychic phenomenon doesn't exist. All psychic and spiritual healers are portrayed as charlatans desperately attempting to compete with scientific medicine. Skeptics neglect to mention the fact that many of the healing methods they have attacked in the past, have now been proven in rigorous scientific studies. With the growing body of scientific evidence that establishes the therapeutic value of prayer (Dossey,) laying on of hands (Therapeutic Touch-Kreiger,) and religiosity in general (Benson,) the skeptics are either badly misinformed, or harbor other reasons for trying to infer that because there is corruption among *some* Western faith healers, that all faith healing is a sham.

I have often wondered where the advocates of medical science are when the foremost proponents of scientific medicine are caught red handed and convicted of criminal violation of antitrust laws. Why weren't we warned, for example, that the American Medical Association (AMA) deliberately tried to destroy the Chiropractic profession? Why doesn't Randi go on national television and give us an example of the fraudulent and underhanded tactics the AMA used to discredit Chiropractors? Where were the champions of medical ethics when, for many years, the journal of the AMA sold advertising space to the tobacco industry, with full knowledge that tobacco was a health hazard? Even going so far as having medical doctors endorse cigarette filters, using their prestige to mislead the public into believing that cigarettes were 'safe' to smoke.

Why are the failures of scientific medicine such closely guarded secrets? It was recently reported that 100,000 Americans die each year from the side effects of correctly prescribed drugs. A million more are seriously injured but survive the side effects of correctly prescribed drugs. This study didn't include the death rate of incorrectly prescribed drugs. Who is in charge of testing these toxic prescription drugs? Why are so many toxic drugs allowed to be 'tested' on the public? For a counterpoint to the ethical posturing of scientific medicine, read John Robbins' book *Reclaiming Our Health-Exploding the Medical Myth and Embracing the Source of True Healing*. Perhaps, if Randi and others like him were more objective, they might give equal time to uncovering and exposing the extent of ethical corruption in *all* forms of medical practice, scientific as well as unconventional. The fact that they don't should raise questions concerning the integrity of their findings.

The Destructive Effects of Biased Science

To the best of my knowledge, I have never seen any studies done on the reason why so many people *benefit* from psychic surgery. I have seen a number of scientific researchers dismiss the often dramatic healing effects of psychic surgery, simply because they were unable to prove, under controlled clinical conditions, that psychic surgery is the equivalent of conventional surgery. In every instance, the failure of psychic surgery to produce a cure has been loudly indicted as proof that the procedure is fraudulent. Yet, whenever psychic surgery produces a spontaneous restoration of health or dramatically improves a condition that has been medically diagnosed as terminal, scientists and debunkers become strangely silent. I believe that this tendency to emphasize the failure, and disregard the success of unconventional healing, reflects a long standing agenda to discredit 'all' unconventional therapies in the guise of scientific inquiry. The so-called Committee on Quackery, formed by the AMA with the stated purpose of protecting the public from unethical doctors and healers, was used instead to undermine and eliminate competition and preserve their medical monopoly. Throughout my extensive research into psychic surgery, I have found that the number of people who benefited from the healing far exceeded those who did not.

I have taken the beneficial, health-restoring aspects of psychic surgery very seriously and have followed the pragmatic guideline that if someone is healed, there has to be a reason. For every effect, there must be a cause. It simply doesn't make sense that a person can be healed of a terminal illness through deceit. *Fake* healing is an oxymoron. If someone is truly healed, then the healing method must be given credence. I find the tendency of some medical researchers to dismiss spontaneous remission, and other types of cures that do not conform to their theories, as anecdotal or irrelevant, to be intellectually dishonest and misleading. There must be an explanation for the spontaneous remission of diseases healed by psychic surgery. This explanation should be vigorously pursued.

The intentional denigration of unconventional forms of healing is a serious disservice to those who fail to respond to conventional treatment. In my work with the Filipino healers, I have seen people cured from all sorts of terrible illnesses. They undergo what I can only describe as a spiritual conversion experience as a result of having been healed. The transformations in patients I have witnessed are truly remarkable. In order to sustain these overwhelming conversion experiences, however, the experience *must* be supported. I have found that the dilemma that Mark Olmstead faced is faced by the majority of people who are healed through unconventional methods. The staff at the healing centers, and even the healers themselves, offer very little in the way of support to help patients to assimilate the phenomenal experience of (what patients perceive as) Divine intervention in their lives. In the aftermath of these spiritual experiences, patients are physically fragile and emotionally vulnerable. The only place that the patients have to turn are to other patients, whose perceptions of their own healing experiences vary so greatly that they seem to be speaking in tongues.

This dilemma only worsens when the healed patient returns home. The conversion experience that comes from being given a new lease on life compels the person who has been healed to want to go out and shout the good news to the world. Many do so only to find that no one believes them. It is very difficult to truly believe that you have been touched by the very hand of God, and then realize that when you share it with anyone, they stare at you in silence, or worse. When faced with social censure and criticism, it becomes impossible to sustain the joy and enthusiasm that can support complete recovery. Having to constantly defend their personal experience against the "conventional wisdom," the healed person rapidly loses patience and becomes frustrated, adamant, and insistent.

At this point, they may find that even their most intimate friends think they have lost their minds. In many cases, I have seen illness return in those who had been healed, simply because the disbelief and the pressure from their friends and relatives is so overwhelming. They are finally convinced that they are wrong, that they hadn't actually been healed at all. When their illnesses return, they are viewed as pathetic victims of fraud and false hope. Their deaths are blamed on the fact that they abandoned conventional medical treatment and the healer is castigated. In my experience, however, I believe that another factor is responsible for these tragedies.

These tragedies occur because *there is no acceptable explanation to support the experience of those who have been healed.* The reason why no acceptable explanations exist is that the medical profession has done its best to undermine and discredit any theories of medicine or methods of treatment that they are unable to profit from. A new generation of doctors are attempting to reform the medical profession, and I applaud their efforts. The research taking place at the Office of Alternative Medicine at the National Institutes of Health is encouraging. Dr. Andrew Weil's efforts to create a new 'integrated' medical system are nothing short of revolutionary. Despite their efforts, however, the lie that unconventional methods of treatment have no basis in fact, and that anyone who chooses unconventional methods of treatment is irrational, gullible, and deserving of ridicule is still in force. As long as this lie is allowed to underpin the 'conventional wisdom,' people who could recover in a supportive environment, will continue to die.

Psychic Surgery and Parapsychology

Long before I arrived in the Philippines, researchers were breathlessly searching for acceptable explanations of psychic surgery. As vice president of the Philippine Healer's Circle, I had the opportunity to meet many of the scientists, parapsychologists, journalists, doctors, and other researchers who came to the Philippines to research and, hopefully, to solve the mystery of psychic surgery. The Healer's Circle sponsored five International Healing Conferences, of which I attended three. These conferences brought together healers from virtually every corner of the earth and gave them the opportunity to meet and share ideas and techniques. The Healing Conferences were timed to coincide with Alex Orbito's birthday, so they were also extravagant social events. In addition to being the most well-known and widely traveled of the psychic surgeons, Alex is also the most socially accomplished and diplomatic. Although he has spent most of his life healing the sick, Alex considers his mission to be much greater than that. He has also strived, at great expense to himself, to bring together healers from around the globe in an attempt to understand the techniques and beliefs involved in spiritual healing. More importantly, he has worked tirelessly to lay the foundation for the legitimization of spiritual and faith healing throughout the world.

One of the best researched and documented studies I've come across was conducted by an Austrian writer named Gert Chesi. In his book, *Faith Healers in the Philippines*, he describes his study of only certifiably incurable patients taken to the Philippines to undergo psychic surgery. As a result of the treatments, 30% of the patients lived well past the expected time of their demise. Even with these dramatic results, however, when Chesi sought to determine whether the operations were genuinely paranormal events or merely sleight-of-hand, he was confronted with a maze of contradictions. Both the parapsychologists and the scientists were hoping that psychic surgery could be proven to conform to their various scientific theories. The range of these scientific hypotheses were so extensive that, even if they had been proven, the result would have been a scientific maze of contradictions.

Parapsychologists have long been frustrated in their attempts to *prove* the paranormal. Parapsychological researchers long for phenomena that fulfill concrete, practical objectives in the material world, while originating in and operating from paranormal dimensions. In psychic surgery, parapsychologists saw the answer to their prayers: a paranormal means to a specifically tangible end. In a hasty rush to judgment, the parapsychologists made a big mistake. They convinced themselves that psychic surgery could be proven to be equal to, or even a replacement for, conventional surgery. The belief that psychic surgery could somehow be demonstrated to be equivalent to conventional surgery led them down a long, winding path to an unhappy conclusion. Certain that they had finally found definitive proof of the paranormal, the parapsychologists and researchers of the paranormal invited medical doctors and surgeons to the Philippines to "prove" that psychic surgery was not only paranormal, but an alternative to conventional surgery as well.

In their haste to link psychic surgery to Western science, early researchers of psychic surgery completely ignored the cultural background of the phenomenon as it was understood by Filipinos. Though psychic surgery had emerged from the religious practices of Filipino Espiritism, the parapsychologists believed it to be a paranormal ability possessed exclusively by certain individuals. The only mention of the existence and work of the Union Espiritista were fleeting references in the literary works of a few researchers. To the dismay of parapsychologists, the scientists who came to the Philippines were quick to point out that, aside from superficial resemblances to "real" surgery, psychic surgery was not, and would never be, compatible with conventional medicine. To compound the plight of the parapsychologists, the scientists immediately suspected that psychic surgeons were not actually *opening the body* and declared that, at least part of the time, psychic surgery was merely an illusion produced by sleight-of-hand. Their solution was to scientifically test the blood and tissue samples taken from actual "operations" to determine whether the samples matched those of the patients. If the blood matched the blood type of the patient, and the tissue was proven to be of human origin, the healer would be acknowledged as "genuine."

The parapsychologists faced an awkward dilemma. If they ignored the possibility that sleight-of-hand was being used by the healers, they ran the risk of being ridiculed as victims or even co-perpetrators of fraud. If they acknowledged that fakery was used to mimic surgery, they were forced to separate the impostors from the genuine healers. Realizing that sleight-of-hand was indeed widely used and not wanting to be labeled as supporters of quackery, the parapsychologists began to distance themselves from the healers. They retreated to the position that while fakery did exist, genuine psychic surgery was also a reality. By the time that I arrived in the Philippines in 1983, the majority of psychic surgery research had been done to define psychic surgery in terms of black or white; either reject it entirely or insist that it be included in the conventional practice of medicine.

In the mid-1980's, virtually every researcher I met in the Philippines strictly limited the scope of their inquiries to the nature of the operations. Debate raged over two main issues: (1) Were psychic surgeons actually opening the body with their bare hands, or were they merely performing sleight-of-hand and (2) Were the tissue and blood samples of animal or human origin? A number of studies were conducted on these questions in virtually every country the psychic surgeons visited. For every test that confirmed the tissue and blood were of human origin and matched the blood types of the patient, another found the samples to be of animal origin. For the Germans, Australians, Americans, and Japanese who tested these samples of blood and tissue, the results of these tests merely led to a stalemate and ultimately proved nothing.

In the midst of the controversy, the psychic surgeons never hesitated to tell anyone that it was the Holy Spirit that made psychic surgery possible. The antireligious bias of most of the researchers was so pronounced that I was accused of suffering from a "retrocognitive disorder" for merely mentioning that the Filipinos might have derived their healing abilities from their religious practices. In spite of the desperate and often comical attempts of parapsychologists to explain psychic surgery, I could see they were rapidly losing ground. The fact that some of the Filipino healers were caught using sleight-of-hand thoroughly eclipsed the well documented proof that "genuine" psychic surgery did exist. Scientists and skeptics had a field day trashing psychic surgery. The message they conveyed to the western world was that psychic surgery was totally fraudulent, and without any redeeming value. The parapsychologists, after investing years and considerable sums of money in their research efforts, chose to drop the subject of psychic surgery. In the absence of any further discourse or study, the majority of Westerners assumed the "mystery" of Filipino psychic surgery had proven to be a just another hoax, with no redeeming value.

During Alex Orbito's first visit to Hawai'i, we strictly controlled the environment, eliminating any possibility of fraud. The results of the healing mission were so impressive that I readily accepted that Alex was genuinely performing paranormal healing, and that psychic surgery was real. When I arrived in the Philippines, I was surprised to find myself surrounded by both skeptics and believers. After what I had personally experienced in Hawai'i, I found it hard to believe the accusations of skeptics. The majority of detractors denounced the healers for purely personal reasons. Adding to the confusion, the healers were extremely competitive among themselves, often criticizing and denouncing each other. In counterpoint to the argument regarding the nature of psychic surgery, one group of foreign patients after another kept arriving from around the world, and leaving satisfied.

Psychic Surgery Lessons

At Alex's Center in Cubao, there were always a few healers who claimed that they could teach anyone with sufficient spiritual ability to perform psychic surgery. There were two in particular who insisted that the ability to perform psychic surgery was a *learned skill*. I was especially interested in one of them, who was training a young Filipino at the time. I asked him why Alex would not discuss the operations except to say that it was the work of the Holy Spirit. He laughed and said that Alex wouldn't teach psychic surgery because he feared a glut of psychic surgeons entering the field would result in lost revenues.

This fellow assured me that it was he, not Alex, that the Holy Spirit had appointed as my teacher. I attended several Espiritist sessions at this healer's house, and though I liked him personally, it was obvious that he was very jealous of Alex. He criticized him incessantly which became very irritating for me. It also became clear that this healer had a drinking problem. One day, he invited me to his house to see a demonstration of his student's newly acquired power to perform psychic surgery. I went, and watched, as his student extracted the head of a worn out toothbrush from a woman's abdomen. When I asked him how the head of a used toothbrush could have ended up in the woman's abdomen, he replied that the woman had been cursed by a witch and the toothbrush head was the form that the curse had taken when removed. Needless to say, his explanation seemed rather farfetched, and I was not very impressed with what I saw. I decided that this was not the healer who would teach me psychic surgery.

For every psychic surgeon who claimed they could teach foreigners to become psychic surgeons, there were ten foreigners who desperately wanted to become one. This set the stage for some of the most surreal student/teacher relationships that have ever existed. In one case that I was personally involved in, an American doctor came to the Philippines intent on becoming a psychic surgeon. He had achieved a great deal in his life and committed himself to becoming a psychic surgeon with a resolve that bordered on obsession. He discovered early on that psychic surgeons were in need of money and made it clear that he would richly reward anyone who would train him to become a psychic surgeon. A year and a half later, after having gone through a number of willing teachers, and well over one hundred thousand dollars, he told me that, in his opinion, all psychic surgery was sleight-of-hand. During one of our many conversations on the subject, I told him about the psychic surgeon and his student who had extracted the head of a toothbrush. While my intention in telling the doctor about the psychic surgeon was to warn him in advance, the doctor's eyes lit up and he insisted that I introduce him. Reluctantly, I did as he requested.

A few weeks later the doctor called and asked me to have lunch with him. We met, and he discussed his situation. The psychic surgeon told him that the ability to perform psychic surgery depended on the intervention of spirits through the healer. He then told the doctor that, as a psychic surgeon, he had the ability to petition the spirits to intercede for the doctor. He told the doctor that he was willing to do so for a fee of only eleven hundred dollars. The doctor paid the money and was assured that, in three days time, he would wake up with the power to perform psychic surgery.

Three days passed, and the doctor was still unable to do anything out of the ordinary. He angrily confronted the healer, who said that the spirit was testing him. The healer told the doctor to be patient. He then offered to send his student to the hotel where the doctor was staying and put him directly in touch with the spirit that would enable him to perform psychic surgery. The doctor met with the student and was told that the spirits that made psychic surgery possible were actually low earthbound spirits. After telling him that, the student offered to send the low spirit into the doctor's body. The novice psychic surgeon then proceeded to sit in a Yogic position on the floor, and asked the doctor to sit and stare into his eyes. The doctor was shocked and asked the student to leave. The eleven hundred dollars was never returned. This sort of scam mentality pervaded the world of psychic surgery. Anyone who stayed around for long was bound to see these blatant contradictions and lose faith.

The Corruption of Psychic Surgery

Christian Spiritists believe that as the power of the Holy Spirit increases on earth, unevolved people who have no interest in spiritual matters will find themselves the unwitting instruments of paranormal healing and other forms of spiritist interventions. There was plenty of evidence of this phenomena in the community of healers in the Philippines. It was explained to me that the Holy Spirit was intervening through unevolved, materialistic individuals, and healing through them, in order to awaken them and their acquaintances to the spiritual dimension of life. *What better way to save sinners than to produce genuine miracles through them?* I met a number of people who had been awakened to healing in this way. I found that most of them believed that in their new roles as healers, God had given them the means of redemption for their former transgressions. Most were sincere and thankful, and took their healing missions seriously. It was apparent that these spiritist interventions through the unevolved did sow seeds of enlightenment in some who went on to become good and ethical healers.

In spite of the good this produced, however, it also served as a means of entry into a very lucrative profession for scam artists, crooks, and others who saw psychic surgery as a dream come true. By merely *pretending* to be an aspiring healer, it was possible to infiltrate legitimate healing organizations and use their newly acquired status to gain access to the flood of foreign patients. By 1983, the problem had grown to the extent that pseudo-psychic surgeons with well organized support groups were impersonating famous Filipino healers! These unscrupulous phonies undermined the mission of the Christian Spiritists and created doubt in the validity of the phenomenon. Reverend Benjamin Pajarillo referred to these renegade psychic surgeons as "liar healers."

As would be expected, the aspiring "liar healers" generated a great deal of concern within the community of legitimate healers. These pretenders thrived on the foreign patients who arrived daily at the airports in Manila and Baguio City, where taxi drivers stood ready to transport them to the psychic surgeons of their choice. In many cases, rather than taking the patients to the real psychic surgeons, the taxi drivers took them to impostors who proceeded to "operate" on them, charge exorbitant fees, and, then send them on their way. The taxi drivers received generous commissions for their participation in the scams. I spoke with several unfortunate patients who had fallen prey to fraudulent psychic surgeons. After learning of the liar healers, I advised any prospective patients to avoid healers who lacked a strong background in Christian Spiritism, and suggested that they obtain a photograph of the healer they wanted to see before they arrived in the Philippines.

In addition to the uncertainty and confusion that had been generated by unevolved, materialistic "liar healers" who had infiltrated the authentic healing community, the question about the use of sleight-of-hand, even among highly ethical and spiritually-motivated healers, was one that had to be addressed. My relationship to Benjamin up to that point had been as a student of Christian Spiritism. Believing as I did that all psychic surgery was a spirit-directed phenomenon that became possible after extensive training as a medium of the Holy Spirit, I had never really discussed the subject of sleight-of-hand psychic surgery with Benjamin. As a medium-in-training, I found the study of Christian Spiritism and spirit-directed healing missions in the provinces to be just as fascinating as psychic surgery. Benjamin told me that very few of the mediums who become instruments of the Holy Spirit end up becoming psychic surgeons. It was clear that he was frustrated by what he knew psychic surgery to be, and what it had become. He told me that the Christian Spiritists were actively discouraging promising mediums from pursuing psychic surgery. He expressed deep concern that the commercialization of psychic surgery was corrupting the values of the young mediums and leading them astray.

Psychic Surgery as a Spiritual Sacrament

Reverend Pajarillo explained to me that spirit-directed psychic surgery had originally been a *sacrament* of Christian Spiritists. Christian Spiritists understood the value of spiritual healing as a means of religious conversion and spiritual transformation, and used psychic surgery in that context exclusively. Benjamin discussed the sacramental use of psychic surgery with me on several occasions. The restoration of health is a real, measurable experience. To receive the gift of restored health, restored life, directly from God, is a profound and transformational event. Spirit-directed restoration of health can become a *bonding* experience with God when it takes place in a supportive environment. Christian Spiritists were adept at providing the social context in which healed individuals could process their transcendental experiences. Psychic surgery was merely the spark that could, in some cases, ignite the flame of self-transcendence. But the Christian Spiritists made it very clear to me that unleashing these powerful forces out of context could be very detrimental.

Benjamin explained that with the unwitting collaboration of foreign parapsychological researchers and scientists, factions within the Filipino healing community had succeeded in redefining psychic surgery. Rather than the work of the Holy Spirit through natural mediums trained in Christian Spiritism, psychic surgery had become a mysterious parapsychological/quasi-medical event. The antireligious bias of scientists played right into the hands of Filipinos who had a vested interest in obscuring the true origins of psychic surgery. By the time I came to the Philippines, the cover-up had succeeded in marginalizing and driving the Christian Spiritists into obscurity. With so much money at stake, some 'healers' even resorted to threats and intimidation to prevent the Christian Spiritists from revealing the true origins and context of psychic surgery. Benjamin was deeply saddened by these developments.

In the new definition of psychic surgery, custom made for Westerners, the ability to open and close bodies with bare hands was portrayed as a spiritual gift granted exclusively to a select few. Presenting psychic surgery in this way conferred a godlike status on individual healers. This new definition completely avoided any mention of the role of Christian Spiritism or the mediumship training that was central to the development of a broad spectrum of spiritual gifts, which included psychic surgery. Everything that Benjamin told me lent further credence to the stated belief of the critics of psychic surgery: that many of the psychic surgeons were impostors.

Benjamin acknowledged that much of what I had seen the psychic surgeons do were skillfully constructed performances carried out by masters of sleight-of-hand. I was stunned to hear my worst fears confirmed, especially by someone I held in such high esteem. I protested that if that were the case, how could the often miraculous cures I witnessed be explained? Benjamin then explained that sleight-of-hand psychic surgery, as well as spirit-directed psychic surgery, *both produced miraculous healing phenomena*!

Sleight-of-Hand Psychic Surgery

I found his admission to be very discomforting. I asked him why healers would resort to trickery? His answer surprised me. He said that sleight-of-hand psychic surgery was, in fact, a very effective healing method and should not be regarded as trickery. Although spirit-directed psychic surgery and sleight-of-hand worked on two very different levels, Benjamin insisted that both methods were extremely powerful in their own right. He emphasized that the sincere intent to help others is a tacit invitation to the Blessed Spirit to intervene regardless of religious affiliation, faith, or spiritual belief. Once again, Benjamin stressed his point that the essential requirement for successful healing did not lie in the *healing method*, but in the ability of the healer to allow for the intervention of the Holy Spirit into the *healing act*. I asked him how anyone could possibly determine who the 'real' healers were if sleight-of-hand could produce healing miracles? He replied that a 'real' healer is one who restores health.

As I sat and listened to Benjamin, an inner turmoil raged within me. I loved Benjamin, and I knew instinctively that he was telling the truth. Still, no matter how much I tried, I could not avoid falling into the same trap the scientists had fallen into. That is, the narrow judgmental parameters of modern Western medical ethics which demand that any form of treatment involving deception is fraudulent. In the years I had spent researching unorthodox medical practices, I had never considered Chinese medicine, BioKinesiology, or any other mode of treatment that I studied, to be deceptive in any way. Obscure perhaps, or misunderstood, but not deceptive. Sleight-of-hand psychic surgery forced me to question the Western belief that all therapies that involve deception are fraudulent; and therefore, unethical. After years of witnessing the curative power of psychic surgery, I was forced to consider the possibility that, in certain cases, deception could indeed be therapeutic. I was beginning to realize that therapeutic interventions could not be limited to the simplistic dualism of being either "fake" or "real." I saw that psychological factors within the patient could render "real" therapies useless while deriving dramatic results from "fake" therapies. The power of the mind leveled the playing field of medicine, transforming duality into relativity, black and white into shades of gray.

Still, the fact that sleight-of-hand psychic surgery might not be fraudulent or unethical was so far out of the comfort zone of Western medical ethics that I knew it would never be accepted. A compassionate attitude did not justify the use of deception in healing practice, or did it? In spite of all the wonderful healing I had seen, I was overcome with depression and guilt over these developments. In my naive acceptance of psychic surgery as a genuine paranormal phenomena, I was completely unprepared for the possibility that many of the profound restorations of health I had witnessed were the result of sleight-of-hand simulations of surgical operations. Viewed from the perspective of fraud-wary Westerners, I had, in spite of my best intentions, fallen prey to a scam and was guilty of promoting quackery. Had I unwittingly used my powers of persuasion to mislead a number of my dearest friends? The enigma suddenly became the horns of a very serious dilemma.

I considered apologizing to everyone I had made psychic surgery available to. I found myself in the odd situation of trying to determine what to say to those who had been healed. It seemed to me that it would be a disservice to tell someone who had been healed that their healing was brought about by trickery. I was torn by the fact that if I told the truth to those who had been healed, they might lose faith and relapse. But if I withheld the truth, I was perpetuating a fraud. I did tell a number of people about my discovery and was shocked to find that *no one believed me!* None of those who had been healed believed that the very dramatic transformations in their health could have resulted from anything other than a genuine paranormal intervention. Although I had no interest in becoming a psychic surgeon, I was accused of turning against the psychic surgeons because of my failure to become one.

What bothered me most was the fact that I was forced to doubt myself. I could no longer trust my own judgment which had always served me so well. My purpose in life suddenly shifted from what I had thought was a Divine mission, to a nightmare. What I had witnessed defied every conventional ethic about healing. I had seen the healing power of psychic surgery with my own eyes. As far as I was concerned, the preponderance of evidence confirmed the effectiveness of psychic surgery. Suddenly, I had to reevaluate all that I had seen and experienced. I questioned some of the other healers about the use of sleight-of-hand. While openly admitting that sleight-of-hand was used in some of the operations, I got the distinct impression that they, like Benjamin, were perfectly comfortable with what they were doing and considered the sleight-of-hand operations to be of great value. I was certain that a great deal of the healing I had seen was genuine. Nevertheless, questions remained. How could sleight-of-hand produce the results I had witnessed? I had listened to the inspired testimonies of *hundreds* of patients, any of whom, in retrospect, could have received sleight-of-hand operations. Yet, these patients had experienced recovery of their health, not only in subjective terms (felt better, no pain, etc.) but in objective terms as well (returned to work, resumed normal lives.)

Even among those Filipino healers whom I considered to be the most spiritually evolved, the criticism they offered was directed more at the way the money derived from the healing was used, than the nature of the operations. The Christian Spiritists felt that the best use of the proceeds from psychic surgery was to expand the work of the Church. When I brought up the issue of the fees to the more well-to-do healers, they made it clear that the fees they charged helped to set the stage for success in their healing work. When I asked them what that meant, they explained that materialistic patients failed to value things that they received for free, and that paying substantial amounts of money for spiritual healing services raised their expectations of receiving the best possible treatment. High expectations, I was told, more often than not, were followed by successful treatments. I believed that they were right, and frankly, I wanted the healers to become rich and successful.

I often wondered why some people harbor such hostility towards spiritually-oriented individuals who become financially successful; while matter-of-factly accepting the financial success of those who amass great fortunes by manufacturing and selling weapons of mass destruction or producing products that destroy the environment. Among the Filipinos, class envy alone served as motivation to criticize the successful. I had personally seen how the psychic surgeons (rich or poor) used their assets to do good works. Still, I was haunted by the paradox that however much the Filipino healers felt it was proper to use sleight-of-hand in their healing work, I had to explain their behavior to a rabidly skeptical American public who very definitely felt that what the healers were doing amounted to fraud. This was true, regardless of the results.

Conversely, I had no doubt that much of what the healers did was not done with sleight-of-hand. These were complex issues that I could not discuss with the Filipinos because of my limited command of their language. I desperately needed to find out why spiritually gifted healers willingly used a technique that was sure to destroy their credibility, thereby casting doubt and suspicion on everything that they did or said. Benjamin understood my dilemma and suggested that we resume our healing missions in the provinces. Torn between the matter of fact acceptance of sleight-of-hand operations by the healers, and the medical ethics of Western society, I resumed my healing missions in the provinces with the Christian Spiritists. In the relative calm of the provinces, I began to think the unthinkable. Could the Filipinos possibly know something that Western science had *overlooked*? I decided to put aside my western mind set and take another look at a very controversial method of healing.

The Archaic Origins of Therapeutic Sleight-of-Hand

Benjamin carefully explained to me that, in Western society, sleight-of-hand is seen as the basis of parlor games that involve pulling rabbits out of hats and performing card tricks. Because we define sleight-of-hand in this context only, we tend to perceive it solely as a form of illusion and trickery. Yet, if we discovered an innovative and unique purpose for sleight-of-hand, one that could extend the lives of incurable patients to well past the expected dates of their demise, we would be foolish not to use it. I learned that the Filipino mananambal used sleight-of-hand in a therapeutic context for centuries before Christian Spiritism existed. Initially, it was employed as a means of exorcism. During a rite of exorcism, the mananambal would call out the possessing entity. The ceremony would intensify until finally the mananambal would grab the head of the possessed person and dramatically extract a live cockroach from the person's ear; then, immediately kill the cockroach. The stunned patient would suddenly show signs of recovery and his relatives would breathe a sigh of relief. The spell was broken.

Only the mananambal knew that the live cockroach had been *palmed* in his hand all along, and that nothing 'supernatural' had occurred except *the restoration of sanity to a man who had been insane only minutes before.* Judging from the results, the mananambal concluded that the sudden and seemingly miraculous restoration of health by sleight-of-hand, or any other means, had to be a miracle from God. I should point out that, while science judges the validity of a concept or practice on how well it conforms to the scientific model of inquiry, a shaman judges the validity of the same factors *solely from the outcome.* Among Filipinos, if health is restored, then the method, however unconventional, is acknowledged as valid.

The therapeutic use of sleight-of-hand has ancient roots among the Filipinos. In 1565, Pedro Chirino describes the earliest reference to the therapeutic use of sleight-of-hand in the Philippines. Chirino tells us, "He (the sorcerer) placed one end of a hollow bamboo upon the affected part while through the other end he sucked up the air; then, he let fall some pebbles from his mouth pretending that they had been extracted from the affected spot." Chirino goes on to tell us, "In times of sickness, these men were at their best, because in times of sickness they (the patients) were ready to venerate anyone who could give or at least promise to obtain a remedy for them." Another early reference to the therapeutic use of sleight-of-hand in the Philippines was recorded by an English explorer named Cavendish. In 1588 he states, "The priests of these tribes were known as Catalona in the north, and Babailan in the Visayas. They were the sorcerers or medicine men, and rude beyond measure was their art in curing, consisting generally of the *imaginary extraction* of pebbles, leaves, or pieces of cane from the afflicted part." (italics mine)

The mananambal have long known that if you extract a symbolic object from the body of a sick patient in a convincing manner, the disease, (for reasons unknown to the healers,) often disappears. The disease presumably goes into the extracted object. Wherever it goes, the most important issue is that of the restored health of the patient. From this fundamental understanding, the mananambal experimented with this phenomenon. Though first used for curing psychological problems, the mananambal had long suspected that the same principal could be applied to physical ailments as well. Sleight-of-hand psychic surgery was the final result of the evolution of the archaic healing method described by Cavendish and Chirino. It was designed to not only look like a surgical intervention, but to sound like one...everything but feel like one. The operations were performed with little or no pain, and left no scars. Eventually, the psychic surgeons learned to master the dynamics and nonverbal cues that predispose the patient to begin healing in advance of the operation itself. It is important to understand that the psychic surgeons never considered what they were doing to be deceitful or dishonest in any way.

They believe that through interactive rituals like sleight-of-hand psychic surgery, they predispose their patients to heightened emotional activity. As I discussed in Chapter 3, this heightened emotional activity causes a particular form of bisa that exists as a gaseous vapor in the blood to condense. When this bisa condenses, it becomes a potent force for either healing or causing illness, with the main factor determining the outcome being the *attitude* of the healer. Any form of healing that involves heightened emotional activity involves this bisa. It can also be condensed by merely being in the presence of certain individuals who possess psychic power. Far from being a form of fakery, sleight-of-hand psychic surgery is the natural outcome of the traditional wisdom of the ancestors of the psychic surgeons, and has been practiced in Filipino culture for centuries.

What we Westerners know as suggestive therapeutics, placebo cure, and hypnosis, are recognized in shamanic cultures as processes through which miracles may be ritually induced. The rituals vary widely throughout the world, but the result is the same: the seemingly miraculous restoration of health. I believe that the understanding of what we call hypnosis and the placebo effect *may* have been the basis for the development of shamanic systems of healing ritual from the earliest stages of human existence. Tribal shamans may well have developed and structured their healing rituals around their knowledge of the mysterious phenomenon we call hypnosis, and the placebo mechanism potentiated through various religious beliefs and practices. In the Philippines, this is certainly the case.

In any culture where poverty is widespread, and modern medical care is not available, other methods are developed to compensate. In these situations, healers are forced to rely solely on their ability to manipulate the mind set and expectations of their patients in order to activate the healing processes that lie dormant within the patient. If they fail, the patient dies. Under these circumstances, healers have paid close attention to the nuances of the processes at work. In underdeveloped parts of the world, what we term mind/body medicine is an ancient and effective alternative to scientific medicine.

I realized, after much confusion, that spirit-directed psychic surgery and sleight-of-hand psychic surgery had developed independent of each other. Sleight-of-hand psychic surgery was *not* merely a 'fake' simulation of 'genuine' psychic surgery that the healer used when his powers waned. Sleight-of-hand psychic surgery is the outcome of shamanic healing practices that have been successfully applied in the Philippines for hundreds, perhaps even thousands of years. Spirit-directed psychic surgery, on the other hand, is a recent development. Sleight-of-hand simulations of surgery are also practiced among the Tibetans, Native Americans, and many other cultures.

Chapter Eight

Psychic Surgery and Placebo Research

In reviewing the studies done by many of the early researchers of psychic surgery, I discovered that Stanley Krippner, George Meek, and Andrija Puharich all suggested that the placebo effect could possibly have played a role in the healing phenomena they had witnessed. They also suggested that an in-depth study was needed on the correlations between psychic surgery and placebo cure. Having discovered the truth about sleight-of-hand psychic surgery, I was compelled to follow their advice and conduct the study. As I began to study placebo cure in earnest, I was surprised to find very little information available. I did, however, find references to a new model of healing that was emerging in the West, called mind/body medicine. In Norman Cousins' book *Human Options*, written in 1981, I was immediately drawn to his theory that human beliefs set physiological processes in motion via an internal, belief-mediated healing system. The parallel between the forces at work in Cousins' theory, and the shamanic processes I have described, seemed undeniable.

Norman Cousins' theory, that the power of one's personal belief system interacts with the immune system in ways that activate physiological processes in the body, was the first step in what is now a widely accepted field of scientific research. It seems reasonable to believe that if Cousins' theory is correct, the same process *had to apply to the dynamic spiritual beliefs of like-minded groups of people*. Cousins' theory certainly seemed to have been borne out in my healing missions with Benjamin. The *spiritual domino effect* I explained earlier could well be the collective outcome of the belief-mediated healing system Cousins describes in the context of the individual. The theory that our belief system is the primary pathway that translates expectations into either immune function or dysfunction is certainly an idea whose time has come.

It was not until 1989 that I finally found a source of information about placebo cure that satisfied my study requirements. In an article in Critique Magazine, I read about a study being conducted by Brendan O'Regan at the Institute of Noetic Sciences in California. I ordered a copy of the study and found, to my amazement, that a great deal of research had been conducted by medical professionals in the United States, specifically on the subject of *placebo surgery*. The research focused upon the surgical procedure for angina pectoris and was prompted by a disagreement among medical doctors about the effectiveness of the surgical procedure in use at the time of the study. Angina Pectoris is a medical condition in which one suffers from heart pain caused by insufficient blood flow to the heart muscle. In the 1950's, a new surgical procedure was developed that redirected blood into the heart muscle by tying off the mammary artery. Surgeons who believed in the effectiveness of the procedure reported that it worked in up to 75% of cases; while the surgeons who were skeptical of the procedure reported much less success. The skeptical physicians proposed a study.

In the study, the doctors decided that three out of five patients would receive the prescribed surgery, while two would be placed under anesthesia and merely be given a surface incision in the area where the operation would normally occur. After making a surface incision, the incision would be sutured and the patient awakened. To the amazement of the doctors, most of the patients who received placebo operations reported no further symptoms of angina pectoris. In O'Regan's study he reported that Dr. Henry Beecher reviewed two double blind studies conducted in 1961 which convincingly demonstrated that the actual operation produced *no greater benefit* than placebo surgery (in which only surface incisions were made.) In another study by Dr. Leonard Cobb and his associates, placebo surgery once again proved to be *as effective* as the real thing. Dr. Cobb reported that 43% of the patients who received placebo operations reported both subjective and objective improvement, while only 32% of the patients who received the actual operation showed the same degree of improvement! It was quite a revelation that the American medical profession had proven, in rigidly controlled, scientific studies, that if a person merely *believes* he or she has received an operation, in many cases they will enjoy full recovery! If the 'placebo effect' can produce these results in pseudo-operations performed by Western doctors, is it not logical to assume that similar results might be expected when psychic surgeons perform a placebo operation?

The placebo procedures reviewed by Dr. Beecher in the 1960's have never been repeated. It is now considered unethical to administer anesthesia and make incisions in patients merely for experimental purposes. Since the 1950's, however, other experiments have been conducted on the placebo effect of treatment procedures. Most have been done with machines that can be turned on and off without the patient's knowledge; thus, making it easy to conduct placebo studies on the therapeutic effects of the machines. For example, a study was conducted on the effects of pulsed magnetic-field therapy on broken bones. Using subjects whose fractures had failed to heal for at least fifty-two weeks, *five out of nine* patients treated with working machines were treated successfully, while *five out of seven* who were treated with 'dummy' machines were also treated successfully. Placebo effects have also been noted in studies conducted for the treatment of gall bladder and kidney stones, as well as for treatment of urological disorders, such as urgency and incontinence.

To summarize: it has been scientifically established that the mere form (metaphor) of surgical procedures as well as other treatments produce the same results as the actual procedures in a certain percentage of patients. This finding certainly seems to support the therapeutic potential of sleight-of-hand psychic surgery. After reviewing the extensive studies done on the placebo effect, I realized a double standard existed.

Belief-Mediated Healing

I came to realize that the term "placebo effect" was a catch-all phrase used to describe the great mysterious power of *belief-mediated activation of physiological processes.* The flip side of Norman Cousins' belief-based healing system is also well known to Western science. The reverse placebo effect is sufficiently powerful to cause hair to fall out in patients who simply *believe* that they have taken a chemotherapy drug. The Latin term for this effect is called the "nocebo" effect, which translates 'I don't please,' while the Latin term "placebo" means "I shall please." O'Regan illustrates this with an example which was published in the "*World Journal of Surgery.*" In this study conducted in 1983, one control group was given chemotherapy drugs, while the other group was given sugar pills. Thirty percent of the control group given sugar pills lost their hair. Using this example to illustrate the mind/body dynamic, O'Regan points out that the physical loss of hair could not possibly occur unless *physiological mediating pathways* exist that are capable of translating beliefs into physiological processes.

In George Meek's excellent book, "*Healers and the Healing Process,*" he quotes Dr. Adolph Grunbaum, who points to the history of Western medicine itself as the history of the placebo effect, up until the discovery of antibiotics. Prior to the 20th century, many of the medications dispensed by physicians were poisonous and harmful. But they also produced beneficial results, as long as the patient had sufficient belief in the doctor and the doctor had sufficient belief in the medication. While most people, and even most doctors who haven't studied the subject, consider placebos to be extremely limited in their application, placebos have been proven to treat a wide range of medical conditions which include, cardiovascular and heart disorders (angina and hypertension,) cancer, rheumatoid and degenerative arthritis, gastrointestinal disorders such as peptic ulcers and nausea, migraine headaches, coughs, allergies, radiation sickness, acne, multiple sclerosis, diabetes, organic brain disorders such as Parkinson's disease, pain, and psychiatric syndromes such as depression, anxiety, and to a lesser extent, schizophrenia.

In studying the phenomenal results as well as the astounding variety of placebo-induced healing, it is apparent that the American medical profession has long been aware of its own version of "psychic healing." *The administration of placebos is the primary means through which healing is self-induced in the United States even though it is not acknowledged or understood as such.* In testing new pharmaceutical drugs, scientists have always assumed that they were dealing with precise laws of cause and effect. If the drug is effective, then the results should be predictable. In testing these drugs, however, psychological factors often muddy the test results. Like a ghost in the machine, the human mind can produce a therapeutic result from a sugar pill while showing no reaction to the 'real' drug. In the testing of drugs, the 'real' drug is often not the one that restores health.

This power of the human mind has long frustrated scientific efforts to sort out 'real' from 'imaginary' medications. The degree to which the placebo effect is evident in scientific studies has been referred to as a 'nuisance variable.' Underlying this concept of the placebo is the assumption that the therapeutic effects of the placebo are not real, merely an indication of the degree of interference of the power of suggestion. Scientists want to believe that physical and psychological factors can be compartmentalized. To acknowledge that psychological factors can produce a therapeutic effect from a sugar pill is to acknowledge mind over matter. This denial of the power of the mind underscores the huge difference between 'faith healers,' who openly and shamelessly exploit the phenomenon, and doctors who simply cannot seem to formulate a means through which placebos can be used without subjecting themselves to ridicule or loss of control.

O'Regan quotes Drs. White, Tursky, and Schwartz from their book *Placebos: Theory, Research, Mechanisms*, "If some placebo phenomenon currently being dismissed as nuisance variables are understandable as clinically significant psychobiological processes, a more comprehensive model of clinical practice may be rationalized. This more complete model may be expected to have a salutary effect upon patient care. On the other hand, the pragmatic limits of placebo phenomenon must be determined if patients' needs are to be realistically addressed, while avoiding the excesses of quackery." In the same book, O'Regan quotes Drs. Sherman Ross and L.W. Bucklew saying, "apparently, some disciplines or at least some of its practitioners, fear that the recognition of placebo effects and the powerful influence a placebo can have, detracts from their power, authority, and expertise, and ultimately serves as a source of embarrassment."

O'Regan included a study conducted at the New Mexico School of Medicine, in which Drs. James Goodwin, Jean Goodwin, and Albert Vogel reported "a disturbing pattern of misunderstanding about placebo effects among physicians and nurses in New Mexico, and placebo misuse more often than not." They found "physicians and nurses used placebos only rarely, and when they did, it tended to be because they were having trouble with a particular patient." To quote O'Regan, "Among the reasons they discovered for the use of placebos were: 1) To prove a patient wrong about the 'reality' of his or her pain, 2) To pacify undeserving patients, 3) In cases where specific treatments were failing and physicians were faced with their inability to help the patients, and 4) In cases where the staff was simply frustrated by the patient. Why did these patterns of misunderstanding and misuse exist? Goodwin and his colleagues observed that few of the therapists could remember any formal training concerning placebo effects. "Better education," they concluded, "might result in more effective placebo use."

The Ethics of Placebo Use

Philosophically, the debate concerning the medical ethics involved in the use of placebos has revolved around two very different perspectives: the deontological and the utilitarian. To quote O'Regan, "The deontological perspective argues that deception of any sort is immoral and not to be used. Assuming that the use of placebos invariably involves deception, they argue that placebos are therefore inadmissible in principle in medical practice. Those who adopt a utilitarian viewpoint, by contrast, do not invoke absolute principles of the sort used by the deontologists. Rather, they attempt to weigh the benefits of placebo use against the costs involved, including the danger that the use of deception will undermine the trust on which the physician-patient relationship is based."

Studies have been conducted in which a third position has also emerged. In these studies, the patients were told they were to receive placebos, yet a placebo effect *still* occurred. O'Regan concludes by saying, "This fact suggests that there may be a clinical role for the nondeceptive use of placebos."

In spite of the continuing controversy concerning the medical use of belief-mediated healing, things are beginning to change. Research has definitely and definitively led to a new understanding of the mind/body connection. The questions scientists are presently asking are no longer confined to speculations about whether placebo cure is real or not, but rather what the specific mediating pathways are that activate those systems in the body responsible for the seemingly miraculous self-healing phenomenon. In other words, *medical research designed to isolate the inner mechanisms of the placebo effect and develop clinical models to use the placebo effect in medical practice is currently underway.* An overwhelming amount of confirming evidence has forced medical researchers to take the phenomenon seriously, and such significant evidence clearly has far reaching implications. Having acknowledged that cures produced by placebos are as "real" as any produced by conventional medicine, scientists must now reconsider the therapeutic value of belief-mediated healing as derived from *nonscientific cultures.*

As I reviewed the research into the medical studies of belief-mediated healing, several things became apparent. I found that the attitudes and practices recommended for physicians to obtain the optimum placebo effect were already employed by Christian Spiritist healers, as well as the psychic surgeons. Western science is just beginning to comprehend the principles that have been in use by indigenous healers throughout the world for centuries. Norman Cousins stated in *Human Options,* "An understanding of the way the placebo works may be one of the most significant developments in medicine in the twentieth century." From my own research, I know that the means by which belief-mediated healing occurs is already understood by other cultures. I have also come to believe that the sleight-of-hand method of psychic surgery may prove to be one of the *advanced refinements of how the placebo mechanism is activated.*

The Common Ground

Having reviewed studies on the subjects of both placebo cure and sleight-of-hand psychic surgery, I found (as the early researchers of psychic surgery suspected) that there *are* elements common to both. These factors are:

1) Surgery, real or imagined, has a proven placebo effect as demonstrated by the placebo studies done on angina pectoris surgery.

2) Psychic surgery acts as an active placebo. As I have noted, the great majority of patients who receive psychic surgery *believe* the operation to be real. This aspect of belief further facilitates the activation of the immune system. An example of this is found in the fact that, although antibiotics are ineffective against viruses, many patients will experience rapid relief from viral infections after taking antibiotics.

3) Expectations shape physiological response. As I have pointed out, the patients of psychic surgeons are often exposed to the testimonies of people who have been healed. As a consequence, many patients are *expecting* a miracle. In a study conducted in Sweden, in 1963, patients were given placebos they were told were depressants. As a result, their pulse rates, systolic and diastolic blood pressures, and reaction times all decreased; and they felt sleepy. When given placebos that supposedly contained stimulants, their pulse rates, blood pressures, and reaction times all increased, as did feelings of alertness and happiness. These dramatic results all occurred based on the patients' expected response to depressants and stimulants.

4) Group size affects placebo response. In the Philippines and elsewhere, healers generally perform their work among crowds. In group situations, the expectations that shape physiological response are significantly amplified and, as a result, are realized far more often than in one-on-one situations.

5) In many cases, even if the patients know that they are receiving a placebo, they will still have a placebo effect. I have seen this happen many times.

Bisa and the Placebo Mechanism

I now understand that the reluctance of the Christian Spiritists to condemn sleight-of-hand psychic surgery was based on the same discoveries that modern scientific research has yielded. Though the Filipinos possessed advanced methods of demonstrating the effectiveness of belief-mediated healing, they were unable to describe the complicated phenomena in scientific terms. Western experiments in placebo surgery are mostly regarded as a scientific anomaly and a mystery, while placebo surgery, used in the context of spiritual healing is condemned as a criminal offense. This ethical schizophrenia has characterized a double standard that has existed for far too long. We have much to learn from the Filipinos. The Filipino belief that a gaseous vapor exists in the blood that condenses, following heightened emotional activity, into a potent source for either healing or harming the patient, can be seen as an explanation of the placebo/nocebo effect.

The mysterious placebo/nocebo effect is directly influenced by the *attitudes* of those administering the placebos. Therefore, if the Filipinos are correct, influencing the belief system in ways that produce a heightened emotional response may be the key to activating the placebo effect. Psychic surgery, as it is practiced by the Filipinos, suggests that it is the *method of placebo delivery* that translates beliefs into the heightened emotional response that condenses the gaseous vapor, bisa, into a potent therapeutic force. As the arbiter of ultimate beliefs, religion plays an important role in the delivery of placebos and belief-mediated phenomena. Of the five elements that psychic surgery and placebo cure have in common, two are also present at religious gatherings. The fact that expectation and group size shapes physiological response suggests that religious belief is an ideal *mind set*, and religious gatherings an ideal *setting* for the self-induction of healing. Delivered in the context of Christian Spiritism, one can reasonably expect the power of the placebo effect to increase to extraordinary levels.

If human belief is the spark that activates the inherent potential of the immune system, then we may consider religious beliefs and rituals to be the bellows that fan that spark into heightened emotion. Based on the cure rate attributed to the placebo effect, I feel it is reasonable to conclude that even in the much maligned practice of psychic surgery based solely on sleight-of-hand, at least 35% of the patients will recover from their ailments.

In this, lies the answer to my original question regarding the positive response of patients to sleight-of-hand psychic surgery. Many of these patients will experience recovery that can only be described as miraculous. Once again, psychic surgery integrates four major factors and one minor factor discovered in the scientific research of placebo cure. In a study done in 1996, at the Scripps Clinic and Research Foundation in La Jolla, California, investigators reported that placebos were found to be twice as powerful as previously thought. In their study of more than six thousand people being treated for asthma, ulcers, and herpes, placebos had some effect *two-thirds* of the time. Another study done at the University of Washington, Seattle, has also confirmed that the placebo effect is *twice* as effective than originally believed.

There has been speculation that the cure rate reported in placebo studies done in the 1950s was intentionally underestimated in order to avoid lending official credence to a subject that was discomforting to scientists and doctors alike. I predict that, as public awareness increases in these matters, alternative therapies will produce better and better results. The time is fast approaching when the therapeutic use of sleight-of-hand may be reevaluated in the light of preexisting studies done by no less than our own modern and highly sophisticated medical establishment.

The Mind and the Immune System

In his pioneering work entitled, *The Psychobiology of Mind/Body Healing*, Earnest L. Rossi tells us, "the means by which healing is self-induced involves physiological mediating pathways through which information is transduced through the cerebral cortex via the neurotransmitters to the hypothalamus which releases endorphins and various other neuropeptides. These chemicals then circulate through the blood, central nervous system, and lymphatic system. These systems, in turn, transduce chemical information via the immunological system, which is strengthened resulting in the restoration of health." In addition to Rossi's work, research scientist, Candace Pert, has conducted studies in which neurotransmitters are 'tagged' and monitored through the body. She reports that she has identified a specific neurotransmitter that *may* mediate the placebo effect. She calls it neuropeptide T. Dr. Pert found that the placebo response is heightened in patients with elevated levels of neuropeptide T.

Dr. Pert's research raises a number of questions. Could arbitrary levels of neuropeptide T in patients account for the mixed results achieved by the placebo experimenters and psychic surgeons? Is there a mind/body connection that exists between the production of neuropeptide T and deeply held religious beliefs? I will venture a guess that "yes" is the answer to both of these questions. Inquiries into the inner mechanisms of the mind/body dynamic have led to the emergence of a new field of science known as psychoneuroimmunology (PNI,) which studies how the mind (psycho) interacts with the immune system (immunology) via the nervous system (neuro.) Yet, though an abundance of evidence exists that supports Norman Cousins' theory of belief-mediated healing, all of the physiological reactions that lead to healing are secondary in the transformation of *belief* into chemical process. The most important factor is still the belief system, and its power is derived from those *beliefs* that are held to be true.

One can only wonder what the results might have been in the 1961 angina pectoris study, if the doctors who conducted the study were thought to be committing a crime for which they could be prosecuted. Or, if the patients had been told upon awakening that they had only received a surface incision.....that no operation had actually been performed. Let us suppose that Randi and the skeptics were vehemently opposed to the study and told the patients the "*truth.*" I seriously doubt that the results from the original study would have been quite so impressive. Though some patients will respond positively to placebos even when told that they are to receive one, I believe *most* patients will respond more favorably if they are *not* told in advance.

This is especially true if they are told by people who do not believe in the placebo effect. The successful therapeutic value of placebos appear to be potentiated by the *positive* beliefs of both the patient and the doctor. In the case of the therapeutic use of sleight-of-hand, the secrecy that surrounds the procedure is *not* maintained with ulterior motives, as many skeptics have charged. Secrecy is such an important factor in obtaining optimal placebo response from a patient, that even the *doctors* involved in the scientific experiments are *not allowed to know* which patients are receiving placebos to avoid contaminating the experiments with doubts and negative expectations.

When I showed Benjamin the research I had done on placebo cure and the results attributed to placebos in the West, he commented that whenever the Blessed Spirit wants to bring something to the attention of intellectuals and atheists, they will produce strange anomalies in otherwise ordinary procedures. These anomalies lead to research, and eventually to a deeper understanding of the processes at work. It is a well known fact that many new medical procedures initially have an impressive cure rate. This initial success seems to depend *entirely* on the attitudes of the doctors who believe in them. As long as the doctors who use unproven medical procedures are enthusiastic and optimistic about the treatment, they report greater success. If the new therapies are ultimately shown to be ineffective, the former high cure rate drops, and the procedures are subsequently discarded.

Benjamin predicted that the current research into mind/body medicine will ultimately result in the revelation of a *spiritual science,* underlying the roles of belief and faith. I described to Benjamin the past and present-day resistance by the conservative elements in conventional science to mind/body medicine. Benjamin replied that the Blessed Spirit will continue to produce increasingly profound phenomenon until the researchers finally "get" the message. Benjamin also predicted that, in addition to the role of the belief and faith of the patient in healing, the role of faith and belief on the part of the doctor would also be reevaluated and better understood. In studying the effect of the belief system vis-a-vis the placebo cure, the role of the doctor's beliefs and how they synergize with those of the patient to initiate *belief-mediated biological processes,* is now being closely examined.

The Role of the Imagination in Healing

In the last chapter, I discussed how objects that appear to have been extracted from a patient's body may allow a psychological transference of the disease out of the body of the patient and, presumably, into the extracted object. This process of psychological transference is evident in many aspects of the placebo mechanism. In terms of psychological transference, how can we explain the loss of hair brought about by a sugar pill that is presumed to be a chemotherapy agent? What I learned from the Filipinos suggests that *when a series of events take place that conform to the vividly imagined anticipation of an expected outcome, the subconscious mind produces a virtual reality that the conscious mind translates into the desired state.* This is why movies make us happy, or sad, and cause us to react with fear or confidence to imaginary scenarios portrayed by actresses and actors. Individual reactions to the virtual realities produced by the subconscious mind vary according to imaginative capacity. It is not just imagination, however, it is a juxtaposition of imaginative capacity with a series of events that conform to our anticipation of an expected outcome that sets the stage for the realization of the expected outcome. One of the best examples of this is found in Earnest Rossi's book, *The Psychobiology of Mind-Body Healing.* Rossi relates the case history of a patient that he refers to as the "Likable Mr. Wright." Mr. Wright was in the final stages of lymphatic cancer with "huge tumor masses the size of oranges in the neck, axillas, groin, chest, and abdomen. His spleen and liver were enormous, and between one and two liters of milky fluid had to be drawn from his chest every other day." Though his doctors thought him untreatable, Wright believed against all odds that a new drug would be found, and that it would cure him. The series of events that he imagined began to take shape. He learned that the clinic where he was receiving treatment had been chosen to evaluate the new cancer drug, Krebiozen. Though Wright was not eligible to participate in the program, he begged his doctor to include him.

Finally, the doctor relented and gave Wright his first injection on a Friday. When the physician returned to the clinic the following Monday, he found Wright "walking around the ward, chatting happily with the nurses." The doctor then found that of all his test subjects, only Wright had shown improvement. The doctor also observed that Wright's tumor masses had "melted like snowballs on a hot stove, and over the weekend had shrunk to half their original size." Within ten days of the first treatment, Wright was discharged from his "deathbed."

After being discharged, Wright continued to follow the progress of the evaluation of the "miracle" drug that had saved his life in medical journals and newspapers. The continuing study, however, found the drug to be totally ineffective. Disheartened by the negative test results, Wright lost faith in the drug and quickly *relapsed* to his original condition. Wright's doctor decided to "play the quack," as he describes it. The doctor told Wright that the newspapers had been mistaken about Krebiozen, and that a new, superrefined, double-strength supply was due to arrive the following day. Wright was ecstatic. The doctor delayed treatment with the "new" batch until Wright's "anticipation of salvation had reached a tremendous pitch." The doctor then proceeded to give Wright an injection of *water*. Following the placebo injection, Wright's second recovery was even more dramatic than the first. Once again, the tumors melted, his chest fluid vanished, and he resumed life as he had before. For two months, he continued to receive injections of water and remained symptom-free. The newspapers continued to follow the progress of the Krebiozen tests. Ultimately, the AMA announced that the drug was worthless in the treatment of cancer. Shortly after learning that, Wright suffered a second relapse, was readmitted to the hospital, and died in less than two days.

Rossi concludes that it was Wright's "total belief in the efficacy of the worthless drug" that brought about the remarkable transformation. What I find most interesting about the story is the astonishing manner in which Wright's *imagination* reversed the final stages of terminal cancer, in a hospital, under the direct supervision of his doctor! His imagination had the power to cause prominent tumors to *disappear.* Westerners tend to regard imagination as a faculty of mind that has little or no relationship to physical reality. When a child wakes up in the night crying from a bad dream, they are reassured that the dream is only imaginary. The term imaginary is used to describe events that are confined solely to the mind.

At its best, imagination is believed to play an important role in the creative processes of artists, musicians, and writers. At its worst, imagination is a source of delusional pathology. Mental institutions are full of people who hear imaginary voices, see imaginary people; even imagine they themselves to be Napoleon, or Jesus. Contemporary scientific studies suggest that the imagination is the driving force behind the placebo effect, spontaneous remission of illness and disease, and even psychic surgery. When I first read how Wright's tumors had "melted like snowballs on a hot stove" to half their original size over a weekend, I knew that Wright's recovery, and the recovery of many of the patients of psychic surgeons, shared a common denominator.

Wright's miraculous recovery from cancer seems to stem from two things. First, is his belief in the ability of science to produce wonder drugs; second, was the fact that the hospital where he was staying had been chosen to test what might have been the very wonder drug he had imagined. Wright clearly regarded the conjunction of his vividly imagined expectations with the official testing of a potential wonder drug at the very hospital where he was staying as definitive confirmation of his most cherished hopes and desires. This remarkable conjunction of events could only mean one thing, his life would be spared. Despite the fact that the drug was totally ineffective, and the doctor decided to substitute water injections in place of the drug, Wright responded to the *fraudulent* treatment *not only positively but miraculously.*

The expectations of the patients of the psychic surgeons differ in many ways from those of Mr. Wright. For example, most of the patients of psychic surgeons have already exhausted the possibilities of conventional medical treatment, with no results. In the absence of a scientific cure, the patient begins to investigate alternative healing, discovering an entire subculture in open rebellion against the medical establishment. As they learn of the vast array of alternative healing options, their faith is restored along with their expectations of recovery.

Finally, the patient experiences a synchronicity of events that convinces them that they have found the answer to their prayers. This is often facilitated by a chance meeting with someone who has recovered from the same disease that they themselves are suffering from. The testimonies of patients who have recovered their health against all odds is fertile ground for the imagination and quickly become part of the interior landscape of the imagination. Once the vividly imagined expectations are in place, the only thing that remains is an *event* that connects the constellation of imagined expectations to a specific person and place.

In Jeanne Achterberg's enlightening book, *Imagery In Healing-Shamanism and Modern Medicine*, she traces the theme of the role of the imagination in healing from our earliest history on into the present. She relates Alexis Carrel's study of the Lourdes healing shrine in France. In his study, Carrel noticed that a pattern was present in all of the documented cures at Lourdes. The cures were characterized by an "acute pain," followed by a "sudden sensation of having been cured." Following the sensation, the "wounds tended to heal in a normal way, except at a very fast rate." Carrel concluded that, "The miracle appeared to be chiefly characterized by an extreme acceleration of the normal processes of organic repair."

In Brazil, where psychic surgeons use crude surgical instruments, the incisions also heal "in a normal way, except at an accelerated rate." These similarities suggest that this acceleration of the "normal processes of organic repair" is the physical outcome of enhanced imaginative expectation. Though much research remains to be done on the role of the imagination in healing, it is clear that there are untapped reserves of phenomenal potential within human beings. The power of the imagination appears to be directly affected, for better or worse, by the opinions of those in whom we place our trust and belief.

Psychokinetic Interference in Imagined Expectation

In a study done in England, the placebo effect of individual doctor's personalities was evaluated. It was discovered that procedures performed by optimistic surgeons had significantly better results than those performed by surgeons who were pessimistic or skeptical. These studies proved rather conclusively that the effect of personality is measurable and is a definite factor in the outcome of surgical procedures. Current placebo research indicates that when the doctor does not know whether or not he is administering a placebo, the placebo response is significantly increased. In other words, if the doctor who is administering a placebo *knows* that he is giving you a placebo, and is skeptical about the results, the doctor's mental skepticism can actually *block* the effect of the placebo *in the patient*.

This strange fact supports the belief shared by Filipino psychic surgeons in regard to attempting to demonstrate and prove their healing abilities to skeptics. Psychic surgeons have been expected to replicate the same results *consistently* in clinically controlled conditions, that are presided over by people who have a vested interest in disproving them. Many scientific studies of psychic surgery have been ended abruptly by the healer informing the participants that he or she has lost their power because of (what they believe to be) the negative thoughts or beliefs of the observers.

When a Filipino healer tells a researcher that a hostile, negative, or cynical attitude will obstruct, and even nullify, the ability to heal, the skeptic interprets this to mean that the healer is a fraud. Serious scientific research, however, has demonstrated that the success or failure of medications, operations, and placebos are definitely influenced by a mysterious interaction between the *subjective beliefs of the physician* and the patient. In the terminology of parapsychology, this ability of the mind to influence matter and, in this case, biology, is known as psychokinesis. A growing body of evidence exists that supports the healers' claims that the psychokinetic effects of the beliefs of both physicians and healers serve to either inhibit or enhance biological reactions in the patient. Christian Spiritists explain the phenomena from the perspective of the intervention of spirits who possess and manifest the same intent as the human beings they influence. Whatever the case, if the mental skepticism and overt prejudices of a physician or scientist can nullify the effects of active drugs in placebo studies, is it not possible that the therapeutic effects of psychic surgery would be equally affected?

The validity of all scientific research revolves around the belief that conditions can be established that allow for objective, unbiased research to take place. Though this objective evaluation of evidence is taken for granted, other studies, which I will discuss, suggest that ideological biases and personal prejudices on the part of research scientists have contaminated studies to such an extent, that the accuracy of vast areas of scientific research have been called into question. If the personal prejudices and emotional biases of the researchers cannot be eliminated from the research process, we may expect the results to conform to the expectations of the researchers. What has come into question in recent years is whether or not *it is even possible* to prevent the emotions and personal prejudices of researchers from contaminating their scientific research.

Breach of the Double-Blind Research Protocol

Probably the most sophisticated method that has been developed to insure objectivity in scientific research is the double-blind study. This protocol was designed to keep participants who administered the drugs and those who received the drugs, completely unaware of their roles in the experiment. Yet, even in double-blind studies, the psychokinetic effect of the beliefs and prejudices of experimenters continued to assert themselves. One double-blind study was designed so that the doctors who were to participate, were chosen with regard to their particular attitudes about the drug to be tested. Conversely, the patients involved were unaware they were even in a study. The doctors distributed the pills to the patients without knowing which patients were receiving placebos and which were receiving active drugs. Though both doctors were completely unaware as to which patients had received the active drug, the clinical results showed that the patients of the doctor who was convinced of the *drug's effectiveness* responded positively, while the patients of the doctor who was *skeptical about the drug* had no response. This study demonstrates that the beliefs of the physician acts to potentiate the effects of an *active* drug in a patient, even when the identity of the patient is unknown. In some mysterious way, both doctors appeared to have unconsciously "infused' their beliefs into the pills, which were then communicated to total strangers by merely ingesting them. This experiment was repeated three more times at different clinics, with identical results being replicated two out of the three times.

"Thus, in three out of four studies, it appears that the effectiveness of the drug over the placebo directly correlated with the physician's beliefs and attitudes toward it, and that the beliefs of the prescribing physician can somehow penetrate the double-blind conditions of the experiment and shape the action of the drug." (Dossey, 1993) This study, and others like it, indicate that objective scientific research may not even exist. The limited scientific research done on unconventional healing may well reflect only the self-fulfilling conclusions of prejudiced experimenters, instead of the actual strengths and weaknesses of the specific healing methods. The scientist who conducted the above study concluded that, "*As a general rule, the double-blind cannot any longer be assumed to guarantee the exclusion of the nonspecific effects of the treatment, especially when the actual treatment has a weak or variable effect.*" (Jerry Solfvin, 1984) These studies have raised the possibility that the conclusions of the scientific community in regard to unconventional healing may be *meaningless*. Until it is possible to eliminate the emotional biases and personal prejudices of the experimenters from the scientific method, we will have to depend on our own experience as the litmus test of what is real and what is not.

Several excellent books have been written on the health-enhancing effects of religious belief and spiritual commitment. Two books I have found to be especially inspiring, and highly recommend, are *Timeless Healing* by Dr. Herbert Benson, and *Healing Words* by Dr. Larry Dossey. The thing I found most striking in both books is that the Filipino Christian Spiritists understand, and have long since put into practice, a great deal of what both of these erudite physicians recommend. All of the healing practices of the Filipino Christian Spiritist healers have evolved within a highly disciplined system of spiritual healing, incorporating the most enlightened use of the placebo effect within the context of the Healing Ministry of the Holy Spirit.

In summary, I want to stress that the thoroughly documented

research I have reviewed regarding the placebo effects of real or imagined surgery, compels us to reconsider much of what we have been led to believe in the past. The supposition that there is anything criminal, fraudulent, fake, or irrelevant about the use of placebo delivery systems such as sleight-of-hand psychic surgery is false. Our own medical system has confirmed the value of placebo surgery. As such, we can no longer portray the use of placebos by Western physicians as valid medical procedures while condemning others to prison for using placebos in highly-evolved healing practices. In the United States, legal harassment of Filipino Christian Spiritists for healing by any means is tantamount to religious persecution. I advise all those who heal within a religious context to educate themselves about their rights in regard to the freedom of religion.

Westerners have much to gain by establishing a dialogue with the Filipino healers. This should be based on mutual respect and our shared interest in understanding the phenomenon of belief-mediated, self-induced healing. Acknowledging and reevaluating sleight-of-hand psychic surgery as a legitimate mind/body therapeutic system will one day level the playing field and remove the double standard that still stands.

I realized early on that it would not be possible to write a credible book on psychic surgery without thoroughly examining the subject of sleight-of-hand psychic surgery. From my first encounter with psychic surgery, I didn't doubt for a moment that all I had witnessed was "*real.*" I was able to observe the effects of psychic surgery on an endless procession of foreign patients and saw that many of them were being healed. My belief in the reality of psychic surgery was based entirely on the *results* it produced. The fact that patients arrived daily at Alex's Center from around the world certainly suggested that many thousands of people besides myself also believed that psychic surgery was real.

After years of enduring the televised sleight-of-hand demonstrations of James Randi, the scientific importance of Filipino healing finally began to emerge like a lotus from the mud. Medical research in the past ten years has shed a very different light on sleight-of-hand psychic surgery. I was astounded to find that in the context of contemporary science, even the most reviled aspect of the Filipino healing phenomenon was finally making sense. As I reviewed Western scientific research into the dynamics of mind/body healing, I breathed a sigh of relief. I have debated whether I should even include this information about sleight-of-hand psychic surgery. I decided to include it because I believe it is important to clarify that there is a basis in *science* for the *miraculous* restoration of health.

The role of the imagination in healing....the connection between the belief system and the immune system....the power of suggestion....can and often do combine to produce a vast acceleration of the healing process. If current momentum in mind/body research continues, science will soon find itself in a landscape well understood by people now considered by science to be primitive, archaic, and superstitious. Our progress will depend on our ability to communicate with these people. There are vast reservoirs of knowledge waiting to be discovered, but we must learn how to ask the right questions. Having gone to great lengths to explain Filipino placebo surgery in the light of science, I want to make it clear that, far from being at the heart of the enigma, it is merely an interesting stratum in the multidimensional constellation of Christian Spiritist healing. Psychic surgery has a basis not only in science, but also in the progressive revelation of the Holy Spirit.

Chapter Nine

Spirit-Directed Psychic Surgery

Spirit-Directed Psychic Surgery

*T*he detractors of psychic surgery as a paranormal event, rested their case with the televised demonstrations of James Randi performing sleight-of-hand operations to mock the Filipinos. The opponents of psychic surgery insisted that the sleight-of-hand operations were part of a criminal conspiracy to impersonate surgeons, practice medicine without a license, and grow wealthy at the expense of the public. The very term "psychic surgery," invented by Harold Sherman, suggested that the Filipinos were performing illegal surgical operations while posing as legitimate medical doctors. The legal prosecution of the psychic surgeons followed hearings by the United States Federal Trade Commission (FTC,) and the United States Senate Subcommittee on Health and Long-Term Care.

In these hearings, the FTC heard the testimonies of 48 witnesses and reviewed 134 exhibits. According to the witnesses, the Filipino healers had defrauded their patients by palming small plastic bags which contained blood and tissue....the equivalent of stage props used in magic acts....and then producing these props in skillfully executed sleight-of-hand simulations of surgery. Working from the premise that the Filipino healers were impersonating surgeons, and practicing medicine illegally, the police began to set up sting operations and entrap the psychic surgeons at work. In 1986, Gary and Terry Magno were arrested in Phoenix, Arizona, for the fraudulent practice of medicine. They posted bail, and fled back to the Philippines. In 1987, Jose Bugarin was arrested in Sacramento, California, for cancer quackery, and the illegal practice of medicine, and was sentenced to nine months in prison. In 1989, Placido Palitayan was arrested in Oregon for the illegal practice of medicine. As recently as 1991, immigration officials arrested Terry Lynn Magno in the Philippines, and deported her back to the United States to face charges of "17 counts of fraud and one of conspiracy in connection with the practice of psychic surgery in Arizona."

The damning evidence in all of these cases and exhibits were the sleight-of-hand props that, as I have explained, are distant cousins of the placebos used in Western medical practice. In the FTC hearings, witnesses who claimed to have been trained by the psychic surgeons described how the placebo props were made, hidden, and used in the context of placebo surgery. Expecting to learn how to open the body with their bare hands, and knowing nothing of the placebo effect or the powerful effects of imagery in healing, the witnesses were apparently disappointed to learn that the psychic surgeons were using a form of placebo surgery. The fact that the healers used placebos was interpreted as fraud by both supporters and detractors of psychic surgery. The aura of suspicion and paranoia that surrounded the work of psychic surgeons in the wake of negative media publicity changed the expectations of those who sponsored and attended healing missions. These expectations changed from joyful anticipation of the miraculous, to fear of arrest and imprisonment, of not only the healers, but the patients as well. Those, like myself, who had looked beyond the operations and understood the religious orientation and spiritual practices of the healers, were aware that the demonization of the Filipino healers was, in fact, religious persecution.

In the previous chapter, I have discussed the phenomenon of placebo surgery and its place in our evolving understanding of the role of the belief system as a mediator of bio-immunological processes. I believe that the arguments used to justify the demonization and legal prosecution of the Filipino healers are examples of the exploitation of public ignorance by detractors who probably knew the truth. I have never known a psychic surgeon to impersonate a medical doctor. Once again, the psychic surgeons *never* pretended to be doctors of medical science. It is understandable, however, that the healers would be thought of as doctors. Lacking the language skills to explain the nuances of their backgrounds, they were misunderstood both by their patients and the authorities. The only claim the detractors of the Filipino healers have been correct about, is that the results obtained through placebo surgery are not paranormal. Based on scientific evidence, we may conclude that there is *nothing paranormal* about either Western or Filipino placebo surgery.

Up to this point, I have discussed psychic surgery from a scientific perspective. I have explained why I believe that, even if psychic surgery is used solely as a therapeutic application of sleight-of-hand, it can be a powerful tool in the practice of mind/body medicine. Now, I would like to explore another aspect of psychic surgery: the spiritual dimension. While placebo surgery and the therapeutic application of sleight-of-hand can be explained within the emerging science of mind-body medicine, there is a dimension to the practice of psychic surgery that is truly a mystery. This form of psychic surgery is what I refer to as spirit-directed psychic surgery. When I use the term mystery, I mean it in its deepest sense. I found what I consider to be the best description of a true sacred mystery in Larry Dossey's excellent book, *Healing Words*. Dossey explains, "By mystery, I do not mean temporary ignorance that will later be swept away by additional information, or questions that will someday be resolved by future research. I mean mystery in the strongest possible sense, something unknowable, *something essentially beyond human understanding.*" (Italics mine)

The Spiritual Dimension of Psychic Surgery

Spirit-directed psychic surgery exists independent of any of the methods used to engage the belief system that are currently being researched and developed into clinical models of mind/body medicine. Spirit-directed interventions do *not* involve sleight-of-hand, and often occur in the *absence* of faith or belief. While belief-mediated healing therapies are designed to interact with the imaginative capacity of the belief system, spirit-directed healing speaks to a deeper, hence, mysterious level. This type of healing addresses issues that involve the spiritual growth of human beings. Spirit-directed healing almost always provokes deep introspection and self-examination in those who receive it. Those who narrowly escape death, by any means, tend to make major changes in their lives following recovery. For those who escape death as a result of the direct intervention of God through spirit-directed psychic surgery, their lives are often permanently transformed. In order to better understand spirit-directed psychic surgery, we must look to the cultures from which the most prominent examples of this phenomenon have emerged. Spirit-directed psychic surgery developed simultaneously in Brazil and the Philippines. In both cases, the phenomena emerged from Christian Spiritist communities.

As Juan Alvear pointed out, when the forces of Christ in the spirit world manifested in the midst of the Filipino Christian Spiritists, they manifested as *medicine* that flowed from the spirit world through the mediums, to establish Christian Spiritism by *conversion through healing*. It was through healing that they developed and learned to apply the insights they gained from both the Bible and Allan Kardec's writings. What were these insights? All Christian Spiritists knew about the spiritualism movement. They knew that spirits could move tables and other heavy objects and influence the material world in a very physical manner. *The Book of Mediums* contains a detailed explanation, provided by spirits, that explains how the Blessed Spirit enters into and manipulates solid objects, such as a human body, through the bodies of mediums. These teachings of the spirits via Allan Kardec provided insight into the inner mechanisms of spiritual healing. The following are the tenets of the Kardecist philosophy:

Fundamentals of the Spiritist Doctrine

Allan Kardec was told by the spirits that:

1) The entire invisible world is inhabited by spirits, and that human beings are constantly surrounded by them.

2) Not only are we surrounded by spirit beings, but we are also actively influenced by these spirits who constantly intervene in and influence events in the physical world.

3) The spirits are the souls of those who had lived on Earth and other worlds who, upon death, became spirits.

4) There are many different levels of development that comprise the hierarchy of spirits that inhabit the invisible world. Some of these are perfected spirits who exist to help and uplift mankind; some are unevolved spirits who continue to demonstrate the ignorance they possessed during their human incarnations.

5) All spirits possess free will, evolve, and will achieve perfection according to the amount of effort and determination they put forth.

6) The temperament of any particular spirit is measured in proportion to the amount of good or evil it has done during its life on Earth or elsewhere. Perfect bliss and peace characterize those spirits who have arrived at the supreme degree of perfection.

7) Under the right conditions, all spirits can manifest themselves to the living, and communicate with the living through human beings who possess the faculty of mediumship. The character of any particular spirit can readily be discerned by the type of information they communicate. In essence, good spirits offer good counsel and everything about them attests to their elevated status. Less evolved spirits are deceptive and demonstrate ignorance and imperfection.

The spirits taught Kardec that the principle of life resided in what they called the "*universal fluid* which permeates all of creation," and that the universal fluid was the primary means through which spirit manifestation was achieved. Before the spirit could manifest, the universal fluid had to be condensed into what Kardec termed the *perispirit* by the will of the spirit. The perispirit was defined by Kardec as *the semi-material envelope through which the spirit could penetrate and manipulate matter*. The condensation of the universal fluid into the perispirit provided the link through which the spirit could attach itself to and penetrate the medium's body via the magnetic fluid that emanated from the perispirit of the medium. Once this connection was made, the spirit took over and the healing from that point on was directed "by the will of the spirit." In order for the spirit to manifest, the properly predisposed medium had to invoke the spirit, conjoining his or her magnetic fluid with that of the spirit. If the magnetic fluid of the medium and the universal fluid of the spirit harmonized, the spirit could incarnate.

In the *Doctrina*, Juan Alvear clarified the teachings of Kardec in a series of questions that he asked the Blessed Spirit. Concerning the nature of the interaction between the spirit and the medium/healer, Alvear asks the spirit, "If the medium is an intermediary between the world of spirit and people, and also a magnetizer, does the medium rely on his own strength in the use of fluids and magnetism?" What is the role of the spirit in the manifest abilities of the medium?" The spirit answers, "It may be true that the power of strength from fluids is in a person, but the power is added to by the help of the spirit that the healer may call in the name of God. In the event that you use the fluid with the idea of curing or *intend to cure*, and you call on a good spirit who loves you and your sick patient, the spirit will add to your strength and strengthen your will. He will direct your fluid to the sick part and provide the power that is needed to heal."

In the following question, Alvear focuses on what the proper conditions are for miraculous healing to occur. He first asks, "What is the status of the magnetizer who does not believe that there is a spirit?" The spirit responds, "The spirits do not mind whether the healer believes in them as long as the *intention of the healer is good. All persons who aspire to do good will attract the help of the good spirits.* Likewise, if the desire and intentions are negative, they will draw the same." At this point, Alvear had learned that the ability to heal does not necessarily require a conscious understanding of the forces involved. He then asks, "If a healer with strong magnetic fluid and the help of the Blessed Spirit are joined together, what will be the result?" The spirit responds, "When this occurs, this will bring about the healing which is miraculous." Alvear then asks, "If that is the case, is the miraculous healing a result of the healing fluid of the medium, or is it only the power of the spirit that heals?" The spirit answers, "It is the combined efforts of both the medium and the spirit which bring about the healing that is miraculous. The mediums who have the power to attract the help of the Blessed Spirit are the real mediums." Alvear closes the session by asking, "Can these powers be transferred to another person?" The Spirit answers, "The power cannot be transferred *but it can be taught and learned.*"

The Magnetic Fluid of the Holy Spirit

Since God is described as Spirit in the bible, He is regarded by Christian Spiritists as the epitome of all things spiritual, and the supreme authority in both the spiritual and material worlds. Below God are the Angels, and elevated Spirits of deceased human beings that follow the Angels. At the bottom of the spiritual hierarchy are the unredeemed souls and the elementals. In the bible, the Holy Spirit is described in terms of being '*poured*' forth into the material world. The Pentecost is described as the '*outpouring*' of the Holy Spirit. God tells the prophet Joel that He will "*pour*" out his Spirit upon all flesh." Likewise, Allan Kardec describes the subtle essences that connect the Spirit to human beings in liquid terms. He calls these substances *fluids*.

Kardec taught that even though Spirits did not possess fluids in and of themselves, they could draw from and direct what he called the '*universal fluid.*' He describes the universal fluid as the "pervasive universal element." Though the Spirits can 'condense' the universal fluid, they rely on a physical medium to intervene in the material world. While the Spirits draw solely from the universal fluid, the medium possesses another type of fluid known as '*terrestrial fluid.*' Terrestrial or animalized fluid, as the name suggests, is derived from earthly sources. Terrestrial fluids include mineral fluids, vegetable fluids, and animal fluids. Terrestrial fluid, a product of the earth, is believed to be magnetic in nature. The healing power of human beings possessing sufficient amounts of terrestrial fluid, while powerful in and of themselves, is greatly expanded through the intervention of Divine Spirits.

Throughout the biblical narrative, when someone receives God's Spirit, they are said to be '*filled*' with the Spirit. The connecting link between the medium and the Spirit, the link that enables the Spirit to '*fill*' the medium with the condensed universal fluid, is called the '*perispirit.*' The word perispirit is derived from the Greek words, peri (round-circular) and spiritus (spirit.) It is used to describe the fluidic envelope that links the incarnated spirit to the fleshly body. After death, the perispirit becomes the body of the spirit. It is the link between the spirit world and the material world. In the living, the perispirit is a receptor site through which we communicate with the Spirit. The Spirit and the medium connect through the perispirit. When the terrestrial fluid of the medium and the condensed universal fluid of the Spirit connect, their fluids combine. Once they combine, the Spirit enters the body of the medium.

The conjoining of the fluids of Spirit and human beings is fraught with obstacles. An affinity must exist between the Spirit and the medium that will enable them to unite as one being. If the medium is improperly predisposed to receive the Spirit, the fluids will combine imperfectly and the spirit cannot enter into the medium. Even when the medium and Spirit are in accord, the mere presence of the 'wrong' people can obstruct the intervention of the Spirit. When they *do* combine, however, the combined fluid, under the control of the Spirit can direct the perispirit to penetrate animate and inanimate objects, and infuse an artificial and momentary life into them. It is this momentary infusion of magnetic fluid that produces the movements in inanimate objects that were so widely reported during the 1800's.

Inner Mechanisms of Spiritual Psychic Surgery

We have now arrived at an understanding of what Christian Spiritists consider the inner mechanisms of spirit-directed psychic surgery to be. The medium prepares to receive the Blessed Spirit and then, after prayer and concentration, asks God to send the spirit. The Blessed Spirit heeds the call and condenses the universal fluid into its semi-material envelope....the perispirit. Once the perispirit is sufficiently charged and the medium is properly predisposed, the Blessed Spirit combines this condensed universal fluid with the terrestrial magnetic fluid that emanates from the healer, and conjoins itself with the body of the medium/healer which it penetrates. The body of the medium/healer is used to direct the combined fluids into the body of the patient. Lastly, the Blessed Spirit vitalizes the afflicted patient with additional magnetic fluid which the spirit produces by the exertion of its will. This impulsion of magnetic fluid, willed by the Blessed Spirit, is directed through the body of the healer into the patient. In many cases, Spirits facilitate spiritual healing by joining together and condensing fluid that the healing Spirit can use.

As for the ability to open the body, Christian Spiritists believe that once the Blessed Spirit had directed a sufficient amount of combined magnetic fluid to the area of the body to be opened, the magnetized area takes on a life of its own. Distinct from the rest of the body, it now spontaneously obeys the force communicated to it by the spirit. *In other words, it opens.* In her book *Going Within*, Shirley MacLaine describes placing her hand inside the open abdomen of her friend under the guidance of Alex Orbito. As Alex guides her hand inside her friend's open abdomen, she describes the dissociative nature of her experience in this way, "It was as though my hand had a mind and spirit of its own, unconnected to my brain." The magnetized area that is under the control of the Blessed Spirit includes both *the area to be opened and the hands of the healer*. Reverend Pajarillo said that once the healing Spirit was in synchrony with the medium, other elevated spirits would link up with the possessing spirit and lend their support in condensing concentrated amounts of universal fluid. This conjoined effort of elevated spirits is the basis of spirit-directed psychic surgery.

Eleuterio Terte

The First Psychic Surgeon

Although archaic forms of sleight-of-hand psychic surgery had existed in the Philippines for centuries, spirit-directed psychic surgery began with Eleuterio Terte. In the course of our travels, Reverend Pajarillo introduced me to Arsenia de la Cruz, the daughter of Eleuterio Terte. One afternoon, at her home in Baguio City, we discussed the life and work of her father. Terte was born in 1905, in San Fabian, Pangasinan. His parents were deeply involved members of the Union Espiritista. Despite his religious upbringing, Terte showed no interest in spiritual matters. In 1927, he nearly died from a terrible illness. During the course of his illness, he had a dream. Close to death and suffering from a high fever, two angels appeared to him and offered to heal him, on the condition that he would, in turn, heal others. He agreed to become a healer and, upon recovering from his illness he was baptized and initiated into the community of Christian Spiritists. During his baptism service, the presiding medium revealed that Terte had been chosen by God to heal through magnetic healing and laying on of hands. Following his initiation into the church, Terte's reputation as a healer spread and soon his renowned healing ability brought hundreds of patients to his small village.

The Japanese invasion of the Philippines forced Terte to abandon healing work and join the resistance as a supply sergeant. As the war grew more intense, Terte formed his own guerrilla unit. Terte was captured many times and suffered terrible cruelties at the hands of the Japanese. He always managed, however, to escape and continue the struggle. After the war ended, Terte fell ill once again and the two angels appeared once more and told him to resume his healing work. The angels also promised to teach him *a new method of spiritual healing*, what we now know as psychic surgery. Though he used a knife in his initial operations, he soon discovered that he could operate with his bare hands.

Terte's fame as a healer came to the attention of two American reporters in 1957. In 1958, Ron Ormond and Ormond McGill published *Into the Strange Unknown*, the first book about psychic surgery ever written in English. Being the first Western journalists to encounter psychic surgery, Ormond and McGill provide gripping descriptions of Terte's healing power when it was at its peak. After the publication of Ormond and McGill's book, Terte's fame spread. He went on to establish the Christian Spiritists of the Philippines Inc. (CPSI) and was a mentor and friend of Benjamin Pajarillo for many years. The professed purpose of the CSPI, as outlined in it's statutes, was to, "*establish a nonsectarian brotherhood of mankind, by mankind, and for mankind with malice towards none and charity to all; to send and establish missions to all parts of our country and abroad if necessary and possible, whenever and wherever needed; to propagate the teachings of Jesus Christ, whereby love of God and love of neighbors should be preached, thereby germinating the moral rejuvenation and spiritual uplift of mankind; to cure all kinds of illness in the name of our Lord Jesus Christ and also to drive away all evil spirits in whatever form they may exist.*"

Various Forms of Spirit-Directed Healing

The following examples of spirit-directed healing were derived in part from studies that took place long before I arrived in the Philippines.

Spirit-Directed Psychic Surgery

Since I wasn't present during the early studies, I can only report what I have learned from others. Over the years, as psychic surgery has become commercialized and the scrutiny of skeptics and detractors has increased, the intensity and frequency of spirit-directed psychic surgery has decreased. In the 1960's and 1970's, the spirit-directed phenomenon in the Philippines and elsewhere were taken very seriously and were researched with the best equipment available by highly qualified and well funded individuals. These researchers reported that they had not only witnessed genuine psychic surgery, but had also documented the veracity of the phenomenon with sophisticated equipment. I have reviewed their studies and chosen what I consider to be examples of the healing phenomenon that best characterizes true spirit-directed healing.

Spirit-directed healing encompasses far more than psychic surgery. In Brazil, an illiterate peasant, Jose De Freitas, later known simply as Arigo, claimed to be guided while in trance by the spirit of a long-deceased German physician who identified himself as Dr. Alphonso Fritz. Other than two years in a parochial school, Arigo had received no formal education. He admitted to the psychic researcher, Andrija Puharich, that he had quit school because he did not have the aptitude to continue. Before beginning his healing work, Arigo had been a field hand, a miner, and a clerk in a social security office. In spite of his lack of any kind of formal training in medicine, however, Arigo was able, while in trance, to treat as many as three hundred patients in a single day. He diagnosed and treated ailments with what appears to be a combination of spirit-directed surgical interventions and spiritually revealed scientific medicine. Arigo was never known to charge anyone for his healing work.

In an extensive study funded by Henry Belk, a team of six American medical doctors, which included Dr. Henry (Andrija) Puharich, went to Brazil to document Arigo's healing work. In addition to the doctors, the study group included a professor of Portuguese, a filmmaker, a still camera specialist, a sound engineer, and the full range of equipment necessary for complete documentation. The medical equipment included a portable x-ray machine, EKG, EEG, bacteriological slides, stains, cultures, an x-ray viewing box, blood typing equipment, and everything else needed to make the study as comprehensive as possible. When the study ended prematurely because of interference by the Brazilian media, a great deal had already been documented.

Puharich reported that, while in trance, Arigo had proven his ability to diagnose the condition of the patients by simply looking at them. Henry Belk, who has an extensive record of the study of Arigo in his archives, allowed me to review the data. Puharich reported that Arigo successfully diagnosed the conditions of nearly a thousand patients, ninety-five percent of which were found to be totally accurate. While in trance, Arigo not only diagnosed illness, but also identified the conditions in *correct medical terminology*. When questioned about his diagnostic ability, Arigo told Puharich that he simply listened to a voice in his right ear and repeated what it said. He identified the voice as "Dr. Fritz." In addition to his diagnostic skills, Arigo demonstrated, again while in trance, an extensive knowledge of pharmacology, which included a knowledge of pharmacological molecular matching techniques that would normally be known only by someone versed in scientific medicine.

Puharich's study documented that Arigo's abilities went far beyond his scientific mediumism. In addition to his amazing diagnostic skill, he also treated ailments in a very unconventional manner. Arigo performed hundreds of operations with knives, scissors, and other similar instruments which, in many cases, he borrowed from his patients as they stood in line. Using these crude pocket knives and scissors, he quickly performed surgical operations on one patient after another. During these operations, patients experienced no pain, no postoperative infection or shock, and incisions healed more quickly than normal. What's more, these operations were performed without sterilizing any of the crude instruments which Arigo used to operate. Arigo even performed eye surgeries in which he would plunge the blade of a pocket knife deeply into his patient's eye sockets and aggressively probe the eye socket, all while the patients passively sat in a chair without anesthesia or pain.

Puharich himself received an operation for a lipoma on his arm which Arigo quickly removed without pain. Suspecting that Arigo was abnormal in some way, and that his abnormality might explain his skills, Puharich thoroughly tested Arigo's physiological abilities. As medical standards go, he was found to be perfectly normal. Puharich also attested to Arigo's ability to treat incurable illnesses. Arigo was very successful in treating cancer by using a combination of conventional chemotherapy drugs, and his spirit-directed surgery. In prescribing chemotherapy drugs, Arigo would write down what Dr. Fritz spoke in his right ear in a nearly illegible script, which only his assistant Altimiro could decipher and transcribe.

At Alex Orbito's birthday party in 1985, Dr. Lee Pulos showed his slide show of the Brazilian psychic surgeon known only as Maria. Like Arigo, Maria used household scissors as her primary surgical instruments. She would make deep incisions, as long as ten inches with the scissors. Yet, it was apparent that Maria's patients suffered no pain, even though they were not anesthetized. Everyone present was astounded by the slides. Dr. Pulos explained to us that the incisions Maria made would heal without suturing within three to seven days. Several of the slides showed Pulos' hand inside the incision that Maria had made in the patient's chest where the ribs and the muscles were plainly visible. Assembled at Alex's party were a number of scientific and parapsychological researchers. It was clear there was no ambiguity as to whether or not the Brazilian psychic surgeons were actually opening the body. It was the first time that I had seen a group of researchers all agree on what they were seeing.

In the discussion that followed the slide show, the ten-inch scars that remained after the operations dominated the conversation. Some members of the group asked Alex why the operations performed by the Filipinos did not leave scars. Alex replied that the reason the Brazilian healers left scars, and the Filipinos didn't, was because the Brazilians were the mediums of lower, disincarnate spirits, like Dr. Fritz. The Filipinos, he said, were the mediums of the Holy Spirit.

At first, it seemed that Alex was merely being defensive. As I learned more about Brazilian Espiritism, however, I found that there were major differences in the indigenization of Espiritism in the Philippines and Brazil. Lee Pulos' slide show was my first experience of contemporary Brazilian psychic surgery, and it was a revelation. After having reviewed the study on Arigo's healing abilities, I wondered to what extent psychic surgery still existed in Brazil. The fact that it continued to be practiced there added a new dimension to the mystery of psychic surgery, and served to further undermine the accusations of its detractors. Perhaps James Randi will come forth and volunteer a sleight-of-hand simulation of *Brazilian* psychic surgery.

A Short History of Spirit-Directed Healing In Brazil

Spiritualism arrived in Brazil with the Portuguese exiles from the Napoleonic Wars. While Spiritism developed within a Christian mind set in the Philippines, spiritist healing in Brazil was introduced through homeopathic doctors. The early practitioners of homeopathic medicine in Brazil dispensed their remedies to the afflicted poor free of charge. These homeopathic doctors used magnetic healing in conjunction with their remedies. Samuel Hahnemann, the German founder of homeopathy, encouraged the use of magnetic healing as a means of increasing the effect of homeopathic remedies. Like the Filipinos, Brazilian spiritists rejected the sensational aspects of spiritualism, preferring to structure their healing work within the Christian principles expressed in their motto "God, Christ, and Charity." The first private spiritist group in Brazil was founded shortly after 1848. By 1853, the Brazilian spiritists had established their own intradimensional dialogue with the Blessed Spirit.

As in the Philippines, the arrival in Brazil of Allan Kardec's *The Book of Spirits*, in 1858, ignited the zeal of the spiritist community. Critics of Spiritism published an article that ridiculed and mocked the beliefs of the homeopathic doctors. This article was rebutted by four distinguished doctors. The rebuttal publicized Spiritism among Brazilians and led to many conversions, as well as the formation of many new spiritist groups. The first spiritist magazine, published in Brazil in 1869, was called *The Echo From Beyond The Grave*. The first spiritist group in Brazil was incorporated in 1873, and was named Group Confucius, in honor of a prominent spirit guide that communicated with the spiritists.

Spiritism in Brazil was established to provide spiritual healing and assistance to the poor. The healers organized their activities around the distribution of homeopathic remedies, which they freely dispensed to those in need. The specific prescriptions needed to cure the sick were "received" from the spirits by medium-healers, and then dispensed to the patients on a per case basis. In a country where Kardecist Spiritism was introduced by doctors, and championed by the elite, homeopathic remedies used in conjunction with magnetic healing were....and still are....the primary means used to mediate the healing power of the spirit. Brazilian Spiritism appears to have been conceived within an alternative medical model, consistent with the views and practices of its founders. Though the diagnoses are "prescribed" by the spirit, the medicine is administered in the form of milk sugar tablets or water.

Homeopathic remedies have been tested by the National Institutes of Health in Silver Springs, Maryland, and proven to have a distinct therapeutic effect in and of themselves. In addition to the scientific basis of the efficacy of the remedies, they also have unusual properties that Brazilian Spiritists interpret as proof that the therapeutic effect of the remedies are spirit-directed. Hahnemann found that small amounts of plants could be used to treat the same symptoms they produced. For example, the plant Nux Vomica, if ingested in large amounts, will cause nausea and vomiting. If someone, however, is suffering from nausea brought about from alcohol consumption, a small amount of Nux Vomica, prepared with a special method, will successfully treat the condition.

Homeopathic remedies are prepared through a process of progressively diluting and succussing (shaking) the amount of the active ingredient with a neutral substance. As the active ingredient is diluted and succussed, its concentrations become smaller and smaller. So small, in fact, that at a certain stage of homeopathic dilution and succussion, *none* of the active ingredient can be scientifically detected. Yet, even though none of the active ingredient can be detected, the effects of the preparation become increasingly *stronger*. How can this be possible? Brazilian Spiritists believe that as remedies are diluted, and less and less of the material presence of the active ingredient can be found, the remedies eventually reach a state of juxtaposition between the spirit world and the material world. Having reached that point, the fluids of the person preparing the remedies combine with the fluids of the elevated healing spirits who infuse the combined fluid into the remedy.

There are a greater number of spiritists in Brazil than anywhere else in the world. By conservative estimates there are more than 4,000,000 spiritists in Brazil. Brazilian spiritists are referred to as Kardecists. Filipino Christian Spiritists, by contrast, have about 55,000 practicing members. The reason for the widely divergent numbers is found in the size of the countries and the fact that, historically, Spiritism in Brazil was introduced by the upper classes and spread from the top of society down, while Spiritism in the Philippines was introduced by a

Spirit-Directed Psychic Surgery

former revolutionary and developed in constant opposition to the Catholic church and the Filipino medical profession.

In the two cultures that have taken the messages of the spirits seriously and founded organizations to facilitate an intradimensional dialogue with the spirit world there are, however, far more similarities than there are differences. The fact that psychic surgery emerged among the spiritist populations of countries as geographically separated as the Philippines and Brazil, suggests that there are religious traditions and philosophies that speak directly to transcendent spiritual forces. These powerful forces are universal, and apparently ready and willing to counsel the problems and heal the afflictions of human beings. The training I received from Reverend Benjamin Pajarillo and the Christian Spiritists has given me access to *another world*. Even though I emerged from my training as a writing medium, my ability to heal has increased substantially as well. While the elevated spiritual forces at work among the healing mediums of Brazil and the Philippines have been indigenized in very different cultural environments, I am certain that they are one and the same.

The paranormal healing abilities of Arigo and Maria are not in the same category as placebo healing. If Arigo's description of "hearing" the voice of Dr. Fritz in his right ear is accurate, then we must accept the possibility that spirit-directed healing is a reality. How else are we to explain an illiterate peasant who periodically possesses a highly developed understanding of chemistry, particularly as it pertains to chemotherapy treatment and molecular matching techniques necessary in the treatment of disease with pharmaceutical agents? That this same man could violate every known principle of anesthesia and antisepsis while performing operations...that left deep, visible incisions...is a mystery of the most profound order. The fact that Arigo was only able to perform paranormal healing while under the influence of the spirit Doctor Fritz became the basis of his legal defense when he pleaded innocent after being arrested, charged, and tried for practicing medicine without a license. Though he pleaded innocent, he was found guilty and sent to prison for the crime of being a willing instrument of God's grace. While in prison, Arigo, with the cooperation of the warden, continued to heal.

At present, psychic surgery is still being practiced in Brazil, just as Arigo practiced it in the 1960's. A spiritist healer and psychic surgeon, Joao Teixeira de Faria, is renowned for his amazing healing power. At his healing center in Central Brazil, as many as 90 mediums voluntarily gather to meditate in preparation for the healing sessions. These mediums meditate throughout the sessions, which often last for up to 12 hours. The concentrated magnetic fluid generated by the mediums empowers Joao to serve as the instrument of 30 different spirit doctors. As a result, multiple 'invisible' operations often occur in the large crowds waiting to be operated on, while he operates on others. As he works, Joao watches the crowd and directs his assistants to take those who receive invisible operations to his clean and comfortable recovery room. Joao not only refuses payment...even donations...for his work, he actually feeds the thousands of people who come to his center...for free.

Spiritual Injections

While psychic surgery has received the most publicity, it is only one of several types of spirit-directed healing that have been developed within the Christian Spiritist community. In my travels in the provinces, I was able to observe a number of other forms of spirit-directed healing. Among the most interesting of these is what is known as spiritual injections. While conducting healing missions with Benjamin Pajarillo, I witnessed and received a number of these 'injections' from healers. The spiritual injection appears to be a metaphor for an injection with a hypodermic needle. In preparation for a spiritual injection, the healer will hold his or her hand in the same position that would be used if they were holding an actual hypodermic needle. There is, however, no visible needle. The *invisible* needle is then plunged into the upper arm just below the shoulder and the invisible contents 'injected' in the same way a hypodermic injection is given. In roughly half of the spiritual injections I received, I was amazed to discover a tiny hole in my arm, which bled following the extraction of the invisible 'needle.' The blood was sometimes visible for eight to ten minutes. In one spiritual injection I received, no blood appeared, but a persistent sinus problem that had bothered me for days suddenly disappeared.

One of several studies that have been done on spiritual injections was conducted in the Philippines in 1972. The study included nine healers, a team of scientists, and a professional camera crew. Spiritual injections were made without touching the bodies of the seven European participants. All participants reported sensations in the areas where the invisible needles entered their bodies, which they described as feeling like "actual needles" or "electric shock." Three of the seven Europeans experienced bleeding at the point of entry. It was noted that the spiritual injections had left tiny holes in their arms which bled. Blood samples were taken and analyzed. During the same study, one of the scientists placed a piece of paper under his shirt sleeve which was examined after the spiritual injection. It was found to have three small holes where the injection had been made. The Europeans were baffled to find that the blood samples from their arms was *not* human blood. The mysterious nonhuman blood would have cast doubt on the entire study if not for the professional movie camera that had recorded the spiritual injections frame by frame. Close examination of the film proved that the healers *never touched* the bodies of the participants at any time prior to or after the injection.

Incisions at a Distance

The undisputed master of spirit-directed incisions made without physically touching the body was Juan Blanche. In the second chapter, I described my experiences with Juan and how he made an incision in my leg with a pass of Mark's hand, from a distance of about two feet. George Meek studied Blanche's incisions made at a distance for four years. Meek reported that the cuts often appeared without "any contact or previous treatment of the skin, where the skin burst open the moment the movement occurred in the air." Meek further tested Blanche's apparent ability to open the body from a distance by placing pieces of plastic film over the areas where Blanche was going to make an incision. In one test, Blanche made the incision from a distance. Upon examining the film, Meek found that the film had remained untouched on the surface facing away from the skin of the patient. Closer examination revealed a clearly visible scratch on the *underside* of the film that paralleled the incision that had appeared on the patient's arm. In another test, Meek placed a piece of film over the area which was to be cut. Blanche, after completing his first attempt to make the incision, announced to Meek that he had not been successful. Meek removed the film and observed that neither the skin nor the film had been cut. After replacing the film, Blanche tried again using Meek's left index finger to make the incision. Upon examination, Meek found that the second try had produced a "clean cut," and that the "*cut in the film and the cut in the skin were of the same length.*"

Materializing and Dematerializing Cotton Wool

Another well-documented form of spirit-directed healing in the Philippines involved materialization and dematerialization. Josephine Sison was a gifted spiritist healer who practiced her healing ministry in the province of Pangasinan. She healed thousands of people during her lifetime with a method that was truly unique. She was able to "stuff" large masses of cotton wool *through* the skin into the body, where it would disappear and remain until she was ready to remove it. She was able to do this without making any form of incision. Sometimes she would leave the cotton wool in the body and other times she would remove it. Whether the cotton wool she inserted into the body was left in the body permanently or removed immediately, it was believed to absorb the disease once in place inside the body. Sometimes, the cotton wool would be in the body for extended lengths of time and would be bloody when removed. Other times, it showed very little sign of having absorbed blood. Alex Orbito would also 'stuff' cotton into his patients, on occasion, in the same way Josephine did. Sometimes one healer would 'stuff' the cotton wool into a patient's body, and another healer would remove it days or weeks later. As amazing as this method of healing sounds, whether the cotton was left in the body or removed immediately, it appeared to be very effective in curing the health problems of thousands of patients who received the treatment.

Josephine allowed close scrutiny of her work, and many studies of her healing work were conducted. During these studies, she was extensively tested for fraud and was never found to be using deception. One of her 'operations' was filmed using high-intensity lighting with 16mm color film. When George Meek examined the film frame by frame he said he could see the "*cotton actually disappearing between her fingers*" and noted, "it does not appear to physically pass through the patient's skin." In another study, a team of Swiss researchers persuaded Josephine to use special cotton wool that was treated with a weak radioactive dye. After inserting the cotton wool into the patient's body, the scientists were able to locate the exact position of the cotton wool with the help of a Geiger counter. The same Swiss team filmed the study with cameras that recorded the insertion of the cotton wool in increments of 1/25th of a second. The film also showed the cotton wool disappearing.

Healing at a Distance

Last, but not least, is the form of spirit-directed healing that Christian Spiritists refer to as "distant" healing. Benjamin Pajarillo was one of the best distant healers. I asked Benjamin how he was able to heal at a distance. He explained that he left his body every night between midnight and two a.m., and traveled in his spiritual body to the homes of his patients. I was fortunate to have been able to do follow up studies on several of these patients. He encouraged me to have people contact him by telephone, or to send their contact information to him by mail. I followed his suggestion and several people reported excellent results from Benjamin's distant healing. One woman reported being cured of a life-threatening case of phlebitis. In another instance, the parents of a nine-year-old boy suffering from a brain tumor, contacted me.

The child's parents had previously tried a variety of holistic therapies, with no positive results. After contacting Benjamin, he told them to set aside an hour at a precise time each day. During that hour they were instructed to pray with the child and read specific verses of Scripture. After three weeks of following his instructions, they took the child for a regularly-scheduled medical checkup and discovered, to their amazement, that the size of the tumor was dramatically reduced. The last time I heard from them, their child had improved enough to resume his schooling.

Mediumship and Compassionate Service

The laws that govern the various methods of spirit-directed healing are no mystery in the spiritist communities in which they developed. Spirit-directed healing in the Philippines and Brazil are the outcome of applying the spiritual wisdom of the Spiritist Doctrine in the context of the teachings of Jesus. The belief that there are compassionate spiritual forces that exist for the benefit of humanity is common to all religions. While most people are content to passively believe that these Divine forces exist, Christian Spiritism offers us the means to communicate and cooperate with these compassionate spiritual forces. The Blessed Spirit has explained the process used to communicate through those who are its instruments in very lucid terms. Allan Kardec was the first Westerner to articulate the means through which spirit intervention was accomplished. In spite of the concerted attempts to demonize and discredit all forms of Spiritism, and instill fear and distrust towards the Blessed Spirit, the true nature of the elevated Spirits is evident in the work they do and the people they choose as their instruments.

Christian Spiritism is Christianity as an "awakening" religion. In both the Philippines and Brazil, the Holy Spirit is celebrated as the living core of a Divine mission organized around spiritual healing. The goal that the development of spiritual gifts is oriented toward, is awakening to an active role in the work of the spirit. The phenomenon of spirit-directed psychic surgery is as dependent on the healer as it is on the spiritual forces that work through the healer. The training that Christian Spiritists emphasize, such as concentration, meditation, self-hypnosis, and progressive mediumistic cognition, prepare and empower the psyche to allow the transfer of dynamic spiritual forces into their patients. As a willing instrument of the Holy Spirit, there are no limits to what a person can accomplish.

The children of Christian Spiritists grow up knowing that the Holy Spirit speaks to their fathers and mothers through holy mediums. Having intuitive bible scholars and spiritual healers as role models, inspires goals that reach so far beyond the norm as to be difficult to envision. Filipino psychic surgeons were raised in that world. It is one where their fellow healers meditated in complete silence for long periods in caves in order to fine tune themselves to the spiritual dimension of existence. It is a world they gained access to as a result of their ancestors success in decoding the cryptic instructions that Jesus left in the Bible regarding the Holy Spirit. The fact that the paranormal abilities I have described only take place in the presence of evolved mediums suggests that human potential takes giant leaps forward in cultures which value and develop mediumship as a means of compassionate service to humanity.

Faith is considered by many to be the measure of the ability to heal and be healed. Yet, the term 'faith' seems inadequate to describe the dynamic inner power that is derived from seeing and experiencing the miraculous day after day, year after year. Faith in the miraculous is a personal matter and, in most cases, even believers have to be convinced. Once the preponderance of experience, either objective, subjective, or both, verifies the object of one's faith, internal psychological processes begin to realign themselves to a new constellation of possibilities. For most people, this realignment involves admitting the flaws in one's beliefs, and turning, in faith, to an alternative belief system that is perceived to be superior. Most people never question the values they are taught until they are forced by dire necessity to do so. It is very difficult to abandon deeply held beliefs...even when they fail. Many of the foreign patients I met at Alex Orbito's clinic found themselves incapable of crossing the threshold between skepticism or doubt, and faith. Even in the face of death, many continue to negate the possibility of the one thing that could save them. When, however, this psychological alignment to the real possibility of the miraculous is accomplished, one begins to perceive the hand of God in everything. I once asked Benjamin what he believed the role of faith to be in healing. He replied that it was helpful, but not necessary, for the patient to have faith. He then said that it was far more important that the healer have faith than the patient.

The experience of the healer is unique. Though the inexperienced healer enters healing work with faith, it is gradually superseded by the knowledge of the inner workings of the Holy Spirit. Ultimately, the experienced healer comes to accept the intervention of the Holy Spirit as a certified fact. After personally witnessing the miraculous restoration of health hundreds or thousands of times, the healer comes to *expect* the miraculous every time he or she heals. This expectation emerges as the logical outcome of faith that has been extensively confirmed in pragmatic terms. What begins as the vividly imagined expectations of a healer soon translates into the means through which powerful spiritual forces can enter the material world. Among Filipino Christian Spiritists, this deep and pragmatic expectation of the miraculous leads to a profound transformation in the perception and ability of the healer.

The transformation that takes place is characterized by the healer entering an active role in the work of the Holy Spirit. The constant and ongoing success achieved through continual immersion in spiritual work, transforms the healer into a living circuit of Divine power. Elevated healing spirits interact with the bodies of the sick and afflicted through the healer. Though a spirit-directed psychic surgeon appears to be operating on a specific area of the body, many patients have received powerful healing on numerous levels simultaneously. As I have already discussed, the attitude and beliefs of the healer plays an important role in the symbiosis between healer and patient. A doctor who has doubts about the effectiveness of a medication may convey that belief so powerfully that it may obstruct and even cancel the effect of pharmaceutical medicine in a patient. If a negative expectation is disempowering, is it not likely that an equal and opposite effect might be expected in the presence of healers who are physical embodiments of the highest and best expectations that any patient can wish for? In India, just being in the presence of holy men and women is believed to bestow supernatural blessings. How much more so will we be blessed by a holy man or woman who is also a healer?

Spirit-Directed Psychic Surgery

We have already seen how Mr. Wright's faith in a miracle drug caused his tumors to melt away in what could be described as an extreme example of mind-over-matter. Spirit-directed healers who participate directly in the recovery of hundreds of people like Mr. Wright transcend belief and expectation and finally acquire knowledge of God. This knowledge, and the immediacy of God's presence in these people, is communicated to their patients. The patient sometimes responds to this unconscious communication by healing in ways that appear to be miraculous. In spirit-directed healing, the bond between healer and patient becomes a direct opening...a channel...through which the spirit heals.

The question of the ultimate purpose of these spiritual forces that have chosen to intervene in the affairs of human beings is still a mystery. The Filipino Christian Spiritists were given the task of creating an organization through which the Spiritual Messengers of Christ could lay the groundwork for the coming of the Holy Spirit. While most Christians expect the return of Jesus in the flesh, at some point in the future, Christian Spiritists teach that the coming of the Holy Spirit is already in progress. Are the "Second Coming" of Jesus, and the coming of the Holy Spirit, one and the same thing? If not, how do they differ? For what ultimate purpose has the Blessed Spirit, the Comforter, the Spirit of the Pentecost manifested its presence in our contemporary world through the paranormal healing work of the Filipinos and the Brazilians? In the chapter that follows, I will attempt to shed some light on the nature of their mission here on earth.

Chapter Ten

The Coming of the Holy Spirit

The Coming of the Holy Spirit

*S*hortly after meeting Reverend Pajarillo, he told me that Divine spirits were using psychic surgery and other methods of paranormal healing, to bring broader issues to light. He explained that the revelation of these hidden issues was central to the mission of Christian Spiritism. The Union had been established to prepare the world for the Coming of the Holy Spirit. In the Doctrina, Alvear went further, however, announcing that the Holy Spirit had arrived. As my understanding grew, I began to realize that the message the Blessed Spirit wanted to communicate was that the Holy Spirit has indeed come, but our belief systems were based on inaccurate preconceptions and were preventing us from recognizing the dawning of a new epoch of human evolution. When psychic surgery was first discovered, dynamic results, both therapeutically and visually, were widely reported. From 1965 through 1975, the studies I described in the last chapter produced well documented evidence that psychic surgery was 'real.' These results led early researchers of spirit-directed phenomena to assume that psychic surgery would be easy to document and "prove" scientifically.

During the early seventies, psychic surgery continued to produce amazing results. Then something very odd happened. As psychic surgery drew more and more attention, and came under the increasingly focused attacks of powerful opponents, the healing efficacy of psychic surgery began to diminish. Skeptics, of course, insisted that psychic surgery had been a sham all along, and that their scrutiny had merely exposed the obvious. Psychic surgeons complained that the negativity of their opponents, and the increasing danger they faced in practicing psychic surgery, was straining the essential link to the Blessed Spirit that made genuine psychic surgery possible. In the majority of scientific studies after 1980, psychic surgery either failed to produce the desired therapeutic results, involved easily detectable sleight-of-hand, or both. I and many others had the unusual experience of watching a psychic surgeon perform an operation that was genuine in every respect. Then minutes later, the same psychic surgeon would botch a sleight-of-hand operation so badly that a child could detect it. This maddening inconsistency seemed to be a mockery of believers and detractors alike and confused and frustrated everyone who saw it.

I asked Reverend Pajarillo if he could explain the inconsistency. He told me that no one had been able to establish definitive proof that the operations were genuine because psychic surgery was only a pawn in the larger strategy of the Holy Spirit. His emphasized that *definitive proof of psychic surgery did not serve the purpose of the spiritual forces that were using spirit-directed phenomena to prepare the human race for a profound new understanding.* Through their intradimensional dialogue with the Holy Spirit, the Christian Spiritists learned that a new stage of spiritual evolution had dawned. As early as 1909, Juan Alvear announced the dawning of the age of the Holy Spirit in the *Doctrina Espiritista,*.

According to Benjamin, the activities of psychic surgeons, for better or for worse, served a hidden agenda; that is, to bring the attention of the world to the Filipino healers and lead humanity to the *realization that the age of the Holy Spirit is in progress.*

In the *Doctrina*, Alvear explains that the Spiritualism movement was the first in a series of three spiritist interventions designed to reform and, ultimately, transform the Christian religion. The second spiritist intervention took place in France where Allan Kardec received the Spiritist Doctrine from elevated spirits through trance mediums, which he published in *The Spirit's Book* and *The Medium's Book*. The third spiritist intervention is described by Juan Alvear as "the founding of schools of moral evangelism which arose from the knowledge of the Holy Spirit." From these schools came "the true Spiritism in formal mediums followed by the emergence of conferences and evangelical sessions." Once again, awakening the world to the presence of the Holy Spirit is central to the mission of Filipino Christian Spiritism.

After spending years divining the origins of psychic surgery, I found that the religious practices of Christian Spiritists were, in fact, the source from which they drew their power. It was the intervention of Divine healing spirits that enabled them to function in paranormal capacities. Though it manifests in a much different context, genuine psychic surgery is to Christian Spiritism what stigmata is to Catholics; a paranormal manifestation of intense religious conviction and practice. In direct contradiction of the beliefs of spirit-phobic Western Christians, the religious practices of Christian Spiritists are based exclusively on a positive and beneficial relationship with disembodied spirits who serve humanity under the direct tutelage of the Holy Spirit.

In the poverty of the rural Philippines, I found overwhelming evidence of an unprecedented role of both the Holy Spirit and spirit-directed healing in the lives of Christian Spiritists. Among the provincial Filipinos, I discovered a form of Christianity that has proceeded from the direct revelation of the Holy Spirit. After centuries of religious persecution, and against all odds, a Christian community in which the Holy Spirit plays a defining role has emerged. Having realized that the paranormal healing ability of the Christian Spiritists was derived from their religious practices, I immersed myself in Christian theology and biblical study to gain a clear understanding of their beliefs, and how they differed from those of Western Christians. There are several theological subjects in particular that are common both to Western Christian theology and Christian Spiritism that I feel warrant discussion. First, however, I will discuss our religious history.

Questioning the Accuracy of Religious History

In our modern world, we have all seen how successfully history can be rewritten to accommodate the vanity and assuage the guilt of those who end up on top. The official revisioning of history is a common occurrence. Was America really *discovered* in the sense that we discover new planets, or was it taken by force from its former inhabitants? Is Tibet really a province of China, or have the Chinese invaded an independent nation? Bowing to the pressures of victorious conquerors, organized religions, and dictators, the historians of the world have often had no choice but to distort and rewrite history. The history of religion is no exception. The bible has been rewritten a number of times, and interpreted in many different directions. In spite of the obvious plurality of interpretations of Christian doctrine that exist, *human* vanity and egotism have mandated that every sect of Christianity insist that their particular doctrinal interpretation is the exclusive and only correct understanding of the will of God. How can this be true? Within the confines of this doctrinal inflexibility lie the seeds of religious disputes and, ultimately, the root causes of endless wars that have been fought, not for God (although in the name of God,) but for dominance of one religious belief system over another.

The Old Testament contains numerous examples of God empowering His "chosen" to destroy those unwilling to submit to His dominance. Historically, nearly all religions have followed suit, providing their own justifications for the slaughter of those who refuse to conform to their divinely inspired 'truths.' I do not believe that the use of religion as a justification for war is divinely inspired. The conflicts that arise between zealots of different religious persuasions are essentially political and territorial issues. In reality, the prophets and leaders of the "chosen" are partisan participants in the politics of religion, *not impartial arbiters of spiritual truth.* The institution of religion has a great deal invested in the perpetuation of the myth of Divine sanction of one religious belief system over another. At present, the myth of Divine sanction under pins the cognitive and social authority of religions worldwide, and legitimizes powerful vested interests, not only in religion, but in society at large.

One of the central and most painful lessons of history is that human beings are incapable of impartiality, especially when it comes to religious belief. The fact that the sacred teachings of Christianity have been repeatedly edited and redefined to suit the purposes of secular rulers raises very important questions. What *is* the real message of the bible? What *did* Jesus believe? Did God really send his Son to earth as a sacrifice to appease his own anger? An anger that arose from God's unwillingness to forgive the mistakes of *his own* creation as they climbed the learning curve from ignorance to knowledge? Until I studied with the Christian Spiritists, I, like many others, couldn't begin to unravel the centuries of doctrinal manipulation that the sacred teachings of Christianity have been subjected to.

Christian History According to The Blessed Spirit

The Filipino Christian Spiritists were the first people I encountered who could explain the mysteries of Christianity in a way that made sense. During my visit to a Christian Spiritist church in the Philippines, I was shown boxes that contained transcripts from hundreds of bible study classes received directly from the Holy Spirit through their mediums. I attended several of the bible study sessions myself, and was deeply impressed by what I learned. With their ability to "speak" to the Blessed Spirit, Christian Spiritists gained access to an *impeccable* source of information that revealed mysteries of the past, present, and future with equal ease.

In cooperating with the Blessed Spirit, Christian Spiritists appear to have entered into synchrony with the progressive revelation of Divine purpose. In the decades that the Christian Spiritists have been studying with the Blessed Spirit, they have been told a very different version of religious history from the one I learned as a youth. It is history from the perspective of the most essential part of ourselves, a part of ourselves that survives death. I do not profess to be an expert in Christian history, nor am I a theologian, but I will try my best to explain in English what was revealed to me in the homes and churches of spirit-directed Filipinos. In order to understand the context of the belief-system of the Christian Spiritists, I found that I needed to study the fundaments of Christian theology. I will now review these fundaments in the order I studied them.

Dispensationalism

Christian Spiritists believe in the Divine ordering of worldly affairs, known in Christian theology as dispensationalism. Dispensationalism is a philosophy of history in which historical events are interpreted according to a specific revelatory system. In the case of Christian Spiritists, these are the prophesies of the Bible as elucidated by the Holy Spirit. The term *progressive revelation* describes the inner mechanism of dispensational theology. Dispensationalists see, in the events of history, distinguishable stages of prophetic fulfillment. This historical process is seen as the stage on which worldly events bring about situations through which the great purposes of God are brought to light. Because the Divine revelations progress in stages, the possibility always remains that new revelations may completely change the context, or meaning, of something previously revealed.

The developing relationship between humanity and the Divine requires that God be regarded as capable of operating in contemporary culture. In present-day Christian theology, the Crucifixion, Resurrection, and Second Coming of Jesus are emphasized as the pivotal events that He incarnated to fulfill. Though the Second Coming is taught as a cornerstone of biblical prophesy, it is not commonly known that, within

The Coming of the Holy Spirit

Western Fundamentalist Christian theology, there are two very different theories regarding the Second Coming. These theories are known as pre-millennial dispensationalism and post-millennial dispensationalism. The millennium is the theological term for the thousand-year reign of peace foretold in the Bible. The dispute among the pre-millennial and post-millennial dispensationalists revolves around whether the Second Coming will take place *before* or *during* the millennium.

In pre-millennial theory, God's purpose for humanity is expressed in a single act: the crucifixion and resurrection of Jesus as a sacrificial offering, in behalf of humanity, to an unforgiving God the Father. Jesus' sacrifice is believed to be the crux of our salvation as human beings. Only those who accept Jesus as their personal Lord and Savior will be saved. All others will be destroyed by God. Pre-millennial theorists profess a predetermined future in which earthly conditions will grow increasingly dangerous and corrupt. Because of the failure of human nature, a terrible war is predicted... one that will begin and rage until the Second Coming. They believe that upon His return, Jesus will initiate the Rapture during which saved Christians will be taken off the earth to dwell in the sky with Him. Following the Rapture, the period termed the Tribulation will begin. During the Tribulation, the Antichrist will rule over a one-world government and turn the earth into a living hell to punish non-Christians. Following the Tribulation, we are told that most of the human race will be annihilated, Jesus will conquer Satan in a terrible conflict and reign for a thousand years of peace with the small band of remaining Christians. In this scenario, Jesus returns *before* the millennium begins. This scenario, however, is *not* the one the Blessed Spirit has revealed to the Christian Spiritists.

Post-millennial Christians believe that human beings will experience a collective spiritual awakening that will usher in God's kingdom on earth. They see a future in which the millennium will be established as the human race awakens to the imminent presence of God's Spirit. In post-millennial theology, God's message to humanity is *not* expressed in a single act. It is expressed through ongoing stages of revelation. As the Divine plan unfolds, spiritual mysteries are revealed that bring issues to light that are relevant to the degree of our spiritual progress. In the process of this great awakening, there *will* be upheavals and reformation of the social and political organization of the human race. The existing status quo, both religious and political, will be replaced by another...one directed by the Holy Spirit.

This awakening is the reason for the Coming of the Holy Spirit. Rather than a final war waged by God, war will cease to exist. The human race will reorganize to heal the planet and each other. False prophesies of mean-spirited Gods and their earthly instruments will be exposed. The cornerstone of post-millennial dispensationalism is the belief that as the *progressive revelation of God's will unfolds, humanity will become increasingly spiritual, work out its problems and, ultimately, establish a*

Divine civilization here on earth. In post-millennial theory, Christ will return *during the millennium* to lead an enlightened humanity into higher realms of perfection and grace. Furthermore, in post-millennial theory, Christ is expected *during* the millennium.

Post-millennial thought is deeply rooted in American history. Throughout the entire Colonial period of American history, post-millennial thought predominated in Christian America. This country was thought of as the place where the millennium would begin. Christians saw themselves as chosen by God to establish heaven on earth. To help bring about the spiritualization of humanity, post-millennial Christians have spearheaded social reform throughout American history. Post-millennial activists were among the first to preach against slavery, to initiate social reform, prison reform, and to lead the temperance movement.

In contrast to the optimism and social involvement of the post-millennial Christians, pre-millennial Christians *condemn* social reform as being inspired by the devil. Because pre-millennial dispensationalism teaches that social conditions will steadily worsen as the apocalypse approaches, any efforts to improve society are seen as being in opposition to the will of God. In their interpretation of biblical prophecy, the world must remain increasingly evil, and degenerate, lest we mortals begin to enjoy ourselves and, thus, lose sight of our impending doom in an imminent apocalypse. The hope, apparently, is that this message of impending doom will motivate us to seek salvation and avoid the coming destruction of everyone but Christians. Let us all pray that the fundamentalists are wrong. In addition to the nihilistic Western interpretations of biblical dispensationalism, I learned that Christian Spiritists had their own unique dispensational beliefs. Reverend Pajarillo provided me with the dispensational teachings they learned directly from the Blessed Spirit.

Christian Spiritist Dispensationalism

In the dispensational system of Christian Spiritism, the bible is believed to be the record of three distinct dispensations; respectively, of the Father, the Son, and the Holy Spirit. During each of these three dispensations, one of the persons of the Holy Trinity intervenes *in history* as the primary tutelary deity. In each of the three parts of the bible, a great purpose of God is declared. The Old Testament is believed to be the record of the dispensation of the First Person of the Trinity, commonly known as Jehovah or Yahweh, the Father aspect of the Holy Trinity. From Genesis through Malachi, the Father intervenes in human history as the advocate and champion of the *Jewish* race. The revelation of Yahweh to the descendants of Abraham is the central theme throughout the biblical narrative of the Old Testament. It is Yahweh who delivers the Law to Moses and establishes the Jews as his chosen people. The

The Coming of the Holy Spirit

dispensation of the *Father* is the first dispensation recorded in the bible.

In the dispensation of the *Son*, Jesus *supersedes* the Father as the preeminent source of the progressive revelation of the will of God. The second dispensation is recorded in the biblical narrative from Matthew through the first chapter of Acts in the New Testament. Though the teachings of Jesus are derived, in part from the biblical narrative in the Old Testament, Jesus' teachings are substantially different from those of Yahweh. As Yahweh is central to the biblical narrative in the Old Testament, Jesus' life and teachings are central to the biblical narrative of the New Testament through Acts. In the second dispensation, Jesus teaches that he has come to establish a new form of worship which he calls "Worship in Spirit and in Truth." He declares a New Covenant.

In the third dispensation, the *Holy Spirit supersedes* both the Father and the Son as the Revelator of the will of God. The third dispensation commences with the Pentecost in the second chapter of Acts and continues to this day. In each of these three dispensations, definitive and often paranormal events have occurred, in which Divine intelligence intervenes directly into the lives of human beings. Throughout the biblical narrative, definitive events have all been brought about in ways that demonstrate the ability of God to operate *within* the historical process. From the plagues called down by Moses upon the Egyptians, to the raising of Lazarus from the dead, the biblical role of the Spirit included the ability, not only to intervene in the physical world, but also to manipulate matter in ways that transcend the physical laws of nature.

As I concentrated my research on comparative religious studies between Christian Spiritism and Western Christianity, I learned that Christian Spiritism was post-millennial and possessed a unique dispensational theory. Impressed with the sophistication of their beliefs, I asked Reverend Pajarillo how and when he first learned dispensational theory. He assured me that their beliefs were not theory; that they had been revealed, like all their teachings had been, by the Holy Spirit. As for the origin of the Christian Spiritist dispensational system, Benjamin said that he didn't know when those beliefs were first introduced in the Philippines, but that they were already present before he was born.

Though he knew nothing of formal theological terminology, he fully understood the essential meanings. The dispensational system of the Christian Spiritists heralded a significant departure from the Christ-centered theology of orthodox Christianity. The centrality of Christ in orthodox theology inferred that the work of salvation had been completed by the crucifixion and resurrection of Jesus. The only thing that remained to bring the salvation history of Christianity to completion was the Second Coming. The dispensational system of the Christian Spiritists inferred, however, that the work of salvation had *not* been completed, and that Jesus *was not alone* in the work of the spiritualization of humanity.

The Mystery of the Holy Trinity

Before I met Benjamin Pajarillo, neither he nor I had ever heard of dispensationalism. I accepted the Christian Spiritist belief that the third dispensation was in progress because the *Doctrina*, the Minutes, and my own experience with the healers all confirmed that something very powerful and spiritual was indeed in progress. When I commenced my study of Christian theology, I did so for one reason: to learn how to explain what I had been taught in the correct terminology. I studied the history of dispensationalism in books written by Christian fundamentalists and found nothing that resembled the Christian Spiritist dispensational system. I concluded that the system was unique to Filipino Christian Spiritists. I learned later that one of the most influential dispensational theories in Christian history had come from the early Catholic Church. I learned of it in an historical reference to an abbot of the Medieval Catholic Church, named Joachim of Fiore (1135-1202 A.D.). The abbot's work is detailed in the book, *The Calabrian Abbot-Joachim of Fiore in the History of Western Thought*, by Bernard McGinn, a professor of Divinity at the University of Chicago.

The basis of the teachings of Joachim of Fiore were revealed to him in a series of visions. One vision, in particular, was the basis for his dispensational teachings. It involved the mystery of the Holy Trinity. Joachim received this vision on the day of Pentecost, in 1183 A.D., while visiting Casamari, one of the most important Cistercian monasteries in Italy. The abbot writes, "I had entered the church to pray to Almighty God before the Holy altar, there came upon me an uncertainty concerning belief in the Trinity, as though it were hard to understand or to hold that all the Persons (Father, Son, and Holy Spirit) were one God and one God all the Persons. When that happened, I prayed with all my might. I was very frightened and was moved to call on the Holy Spirit, whose feast day it was, to deign to show me the holy mystery of the Trinity. The Lord has promised us that the whole understanding of truth is to be found in the Trinity. I repeated this and I began to pray the psalms to complete the number I had intended. At this moment without delay, the shape of a ten stringed psaltery (musical instrument) appeared in my mind. The mystery of the Holy Trinity shone so brightly and clearly in it that I was at once impelled to cry out, What God is as Great as our God!"

The teachings of the Holy Trinity that Joachim received in his vision was radically different from any other theological system before or during his time. Had Joachim been any less formidable a member of the Catholic hierarchy, or possessed any less influence, his theology would never have found acceptance during his time or survived into our own. Joachim summed up the fundamental understanding that was revealed to him during his vision with these words, "Therefore, because there are two divine persons of whom one is ungenerated (unmanifest,) the other generated (sent,) two testaments have been set up, the first of which, as we have said above, pertains especially to the Father, the second to the Son, because the latter is from the former. In addition, *the spiritual understanding, proceeding from both testaments, is one that pertains especially to the Holy Spirit."* In Joachim's vision, the Holy Spirit, as a distinct Divine Person, enters the formal theological world for the first time.

The Holy Spirit revealed to Joachim that the Resurrection was the first stage of the *spiritual understanding* (intellectus spiritualis) meant to be conveyed by both the Old and New Testaments. While the resurrection conveyed the idea of Jesus' victory over death, it alone did not communicate the fullness of its spiritual understanding. Joachim learned that the revelation of the spiritual understanding conveyed through both the Father and the Son was to be fully divulged by the *Holy Spirit in a coming age* which he called the "third status."

I was amazed to find that the mystery of the Holy Trinity, revealed to Joachim, taught that the bible was divided into three status or dispensations, *exactly* like those of the Christian Spiritists. He called the first status the status of Law (Father,) the second status of Grace (Son,) and the third status of Spirit (Holy Spirit,) whom he believed would come in the future. Like the Christian Spiritists, Joachim believed that when the age of the Spirit arrived, the Holy Spirit would communicate Divine knowledge directly to human beings.

In Joachim's vision he saw the coming of what he called the Viri Spirituales (spiritual men) who would possess great spiritual understanding and power. Joachim believed the angel described in the tenth chapter of Revelations to be the Viri Spirituales. In the angel's hand is an open book which Joachim believed contained the revelation of all that has been previously hidden in the Scriptures. The angel is described as having "his right foot upon the sea, and his left foot on the land" which Joachim interprets as meaning that the Viri Spirituales will be grounded in both the Old and New Testaments. In speaking of the spiritualized human beings of the third dispensation, Joachim says, "All those wonderful things written about Solomon and Christ will be completed in them in the Spirit, *because in this people Christ will reign more powerfully."*

As the agents of the Holy Spirit, the Viri Spirituales would serve to prepare the way for the emergence of what Joachim calls the "*Ordo Novus*" or "*New People of God*" in the third status/dispensation. Joachim saw that the Viri Spirituales would be divided into two groups, one of preachers and the other of pure contemplatives. Joachim foresaw that they would engage in conflict with evil and emerge triumphant. In their triumph, they would usher in an age in which the Holy Spirit would do his own work, distinct from that of the Father and the Son. Joachim tells us that, "He (the Holy Spirit) has reserved his own time for himself in which he will do his work, not like some divine powers which are called gifts of the Holy Spirit, but like true Lord and God just as the

Father and Son." Joachim saw that the third dispensation would bring peace, harmony, and spiritual understanding.

The Work of the Holy Spirit

In the Calabrian abbot's vision, he saw that in the Coming of the Holy Spirit, the deeper meaning of the scriptures would be revealed. A spiritual, as opposed to literal, interpretation of the Scriptures would result from a new relationship between the Holy Spirit and humanity. This new relationship was to begin with the bestowal of a special gift of the Holy Spirit that Joachim called intelligentia spiritualis. Professor McGinn states that, "The predominant characteristic of the third status of history, the fundamental dynamic behind all its manifestations, is the fullness of the intelligentia spiritualis (spiritual intelligence) that will be given by the Holy Spirit." According to Professor McGinn, Joachim interpreted the miracle in which Jesus changes water into wine as an analogy of the manner in which the gospel as interpreted by the spiritual intelligence sent by the Holy Spirit would be changed into the intoxicating wine of spiritual understanding and Divine contemplation.

Joachim openly criticized those who were guilty of what McGinn describes as "the intellectual error of the persistence of the literal interpretations of the Scriptures." In his writings Joachim says, "And if the preachers of the Gospel according to the letter were preferred to the Jewish doctors who preached Moses' law, they are still far below those who have spiritual knowledge of that Gospel and who walk in no way according to the flesh, but according to the Spirit." The abbot prophesied that as the third dispensation approached, the conflict between spirit-directed and literalist Christian theologians and churches would become more intense and, ultimately, the "pagans and heretics will outlaw the dissemination of the spiritual understanding."

Reading between the lines, the inferences of the abbot suggests that a conspiracy based on the intentional misinterpretation of the Scriptures originated early in the history of the Church. The abbot describes the nature of the conspiracy by saying, "The external evil they did was a sign of the greater evil they conceived within, that is, to snuff out the spiritual understanding and bury it in the belly of the *letter* so that its voice might be heard no more in their streets nor have any further place in their possessions."

Theologians, past and present, have accused Abbot Joachim of abandoning the centrality of Jesus in salvation history. Joachim believed Jesus to be central to the progressive revelation of the will of God. But the abbot's revelatory experiences had brought him to an understanding of Jesus' role in history that was unique. For Joachim, the Christ-centered interpretation of the bible fails to take into account Jesus' extensive references to the Holy Spirit. When Jesus articulates the coming of the Holy Spirit as an extension of his own work, the inference is that the

The Coming of the Holy Spirit

Holy Spirit is to complete what he began. Joachim was the first in history to assign to Jesus five great works, where other theologians saw only four. In addition to the Nativity, Passion, Resurrection, and Ascension, Joachim added the Sending of the Holy Spirit.

This fifth great work of Jesus, the Sending of the Holy Spirit was thought of as having two separate phases in history. The first was the Pentecost, and the second would take place at the beginning of the third dispensation/status. The second outpouring of the Holy Spirit would culminate in the perfect spiritualization of the saved. Professor McGinn says that, "Joachim had no intention of creating a new theology of history: such a notion would have been abhorrent to him. He was convinced that everything he had to say was clearly revealed in the Scriptures to those who had been granted the *intelligentia spiritualis* and that he was doing nothing more than pointing to something already under our noses." Those who failed to grasp the message, failed simply because they lacked the spirit-directed understanding that revealed the inner significance of the letter.

In placing the coming age of the Holy Spirit at the center of his theology, Joachim reversed the conventional wisdom that all perfection was found in the past, in some golden age such as the time of the primitive Church, which later ages could only hope to revive in imperfect fashion. The Holy Spirit revealed that the age of perfection *lay ahead*. Joachim prophesied the coming of a new stage of history, established by a group of powerful spiritual beings, in which human beings would consciously participate in the revelation of the Divine numen described as "that which leaves the flesh completely behind and passes over into the spirit."

In this revelation of the Holy Spirit's interpretation of the Scriptures, Joachim inferred that fresh, even contemporary meaning would be imparted through texts whose meaning, theologians insisted, were already complete. By placing the magnet of reform in the future rather than the past, the abbot broke with previous theologies of history in a manner that has continued to be a source of inspiration for many, and a bone of contention for others. In the third status, or dispensation, Joachim describes a future event in which a full understanding of the Scriptures will introduce true peace and ecstatic prayer on earth. An event which will usher in an age in which harmony and spiritual insight will bring to completion all that is spiritual in human history...the Age of the Holy Spirit.

Joachim's visionary revelation, however, contradicted Augustine's theology. In 1215 A.D., the fourth Lateran Council of the Catholic Church repudiated Joachim's view of the Trinity. Joachim's theology, however, generated great interest in the religious order founded by Saint Francis of Assisi. The Franciscan Order was deeply inspired by the revelation of the age of the Spirit. One branch of the Order even named themselves the Spiritual Franciscans. Many of the Franciscans saw Francis as the messiah of the Age of the Spirit. They believed its dawning to be imminent, and took liberties in assigning their own interpretations to Joachim's prophesies. The Spiritual Franciscans adherence to the vow of poverty ordered in the Testament of Saint Francis, brought them into direct opposition with the Church and members of the Franciscan Order that didn't share their beliefs.

The Spiritual Franciscans were pronounced heretics and were executed for rebelling against the Pope who ruled that Saint Francis' Testament not be binding. In the revelations of Joachim of Fiore, those who criticized the papacy, the corrupt clergy, and the conspicuous rich found their voice. Widely circulated throughout late medieval Europe and England, Joachim's texts articulated the opposition to the abuses of organized religion, and provided the terminology necessary to indict the notoriously corrupt bureaucracy of the medieval Catholic Church. The spiritually revealed dispensational system of Joachim of Fiore is the grandfather of modern dispensationalism.

With my discovery of the vision and prophesies of Joachim of Fiore, I found the historical precedent of Christian Spiritist dispensational theory. I was astounded at the exact parallels between the Coming of the Holy Spirit, as *foretold* by Joachim of Fiore, and the Coming of the Holy Spirit *described* by Juan Alvear. While Joachim describes the Coming of the Holy Spirit as a *future* event, Juan Alvear announced its *arrival*, how they acquired the knowledge and conversation of the Holy Spirit, and the means imparted to them by the Holy Spirit to proceed with the establishment of the third status/dispensation. I have found no reason to doubt that the Spiritual Messengers of Christ and the *intelligentia spiritualis* described by Joachim, are one.

The boxes of transcribed bible classes, revealed by the Blessed Spirit to the Filipinos, prove conclusively that the Christian Spiritists have incorporated the *intelligentia spiritualis* that Joachim prophesied. Though the Filipino Christian Spiritists clearly possessed the spiritual understanding that Joachim foretold, and applied that revelatory understanding to the study of the scriptures, they were completely unaware of Joachim's prophesies. Having access to the inner teachings and religious practices of the Christian Spiritists, as well as the prophesies of Joachim of Fiore, I began to compare the two in depth.

The beliefs and practices of the Christian Spiritists fulfilled the prophesies of the Calabrian abbot almost to the letter. After reviewing the material, I felt it was reasonable to assume that the Union Espiritista, which had developed under the direct governance of the Spiritual Messengers of Christ, could well be the first dawning of the Ordo Novus (New People of God) that had been revealed to Joachim of Fiore in a vision 800 years earlier. The convergence of the prophesies of Joachim of Fiore and the advent of Christian Spiritism added yet another date to the historical chronology of the Coming of the Holy Spirit.

The Holy Spirit in the Old Testament

Though the term Holy Spirit is found in the Old Testament only three times (Psalm 51:11-Isaiah 63:10&14,) there are other terms used to refer to the Holy Spirit. In particular, the terms 'Spirit of the Lord' and 'Spirit of God' are used throughout the Old Testament. The first reference to the Spirit of God is found in Genesis 1:2, where we are told, "the earth was formless and empty, darkness was over the surface of the deep, and the spirit of God was hovering over the waters."

Reverend Pajarillo emphasized that in order to understand the mission of Jesus in the New Testament, I first had to understand the *prophetic* tradition of archaic Judaism. He began by saying that the role of the Holy Spirit in the Old Testament, consisted of communicating Divine revelations from God to the prophets. As the instruments of the Holy Spirit, the Old Testament prophets were the central source of Divine authority among the Jewish people. Early Judaism was essentially an *intradimensional theocracy*, governed by God, and administered through the oversight and leadership of the prophets. Both the common people and the kings of Israel were accountable to the prophets. In the Old Testament, the blessing of the prophets was essential to the acquisition of kingly authority. The prophet Samuel had sufficient authority to remove Saul from power and declare David the king of Israel. In the Old Testament, the prophets could make or break a king. Eventually, the oversight of the prophets came to be seen as a hindrance and a threat.

The truth sometimes hurts and the people found the constant vigilance and scrutiny of the prophets of God to be a source of embarassment and finally insisted that the prophets stop exposing their shortcomings. This was especially true of the Royals and the aristocrats. Isaiah described the situation in saying that "this is a rebellious people, lying children, children who will not hear the law of the Lord; who have said to the seers, see not; and to the prophets, prophesy not to us reproof (criticism); speak to us deception, prophesy lies; get you out of the way, turn aside out of the path, cause the Holy One of Israel to cease from before us." (Isaiah 30:9) The priesthood succumbed to the pressure of their constituents and Jeremiah tells us, "The prophets prophesy falsely and the priests have supported them; and my people love to have it so." (Jeremiah 5:31) No one wanted to hear the truth. Surrounded by prophets and priests who told them only what they wanted to hear, the people fell under the spell of widespread self-delusion and were blinded to the inevitable consequences of their actions.

In desperation, Jeremiah turned to God and said "Hear me, I beseech thee, O Lord God! Behold, the prophets say to the people, You shall not see the sword, neither shall you have famine, but I will give you assured peace and justice in this country. Then the Lord said to me, The prophets prophesy lies in my name; for I did not send them, neither have I commanded them nor spoken to them; they prophesy to you false visions oracles and divinations and the deceit of their hearts, by sword and famine shall these prophets be consumed." (Jeremiah 14:13) It was inevitable that the revelations of the true prophets would contradict the false prophets and lead to conflict. In Jeremiah 20:1, we are told "Pashur the son of Amariah the priest, who was governor in charge of the house of the Lord, heard Jeremiah the prophet prophesying these things. Then Pashur smote Jeremiah, and put him in the stocks that were in the upper gate of Benjamin."

Unafraid, Jeremiah proceeded to condemn the false prophet saying "And as for you Pashur, you and all the members of your household shall go into captivity; and you shall go to Babylon, and there you shall die, and there you shall be buried, you, and all your friends, to whom you have prophesied lies." (Jeremiah 20:6) With the corrupt priesthood and prophets in direct opposition to the will of God, Jeremiah is told by God to "stand in the court of the Lord's house and speak to all the cities of Judah which come to worship in the house of the Lord all the words I have commanded you to speak, omit not a word. When Jeremiah finished speaking, the priests, false prophets, and people seized him saying, He shall surely be put to death. When the princes of Judah heard these things, they came up from the King's house to the house of the Lord. The priests and the false prophets spoke to the princes and the people saying, This man is guilty of death; for he has prophesied against this city and its inhabitants. Then Jeremiah spoke to all the princes and people saying, "I am in your hands; do with me as it seems right and proper to you. But you must know for certain that if you put me to death, you shall surely bring innocent blood upon yourselves, this city and its inhabitants, for the Lord has truly sent me to speak these words. Then the princes and all the people said to the priests and false prophets, this man is not guilty of death; for he has spoken to us in the name of the Lord our God." (Jeremiah 26:2)

Although public opinion saved Jeremiah, the priesthood and false prophets spared no efforts in enlisting allies in their conspiracy to usurp the rightful position of the true prophets of God. God tells Jeremiah, "I have seen also in the prophets of Jerusalem folly; they commit adultery and walk in lies; they strengthen also the hands of their friends, so that no one turns from their evil way." (Jeremiah 23:13) With the support of the rich and powerful, the priesthood succeeded in gaining the broad public support they needed to destroy the true prophets of God and establish their false teachings as the Word of God. God tells Jeremiah, "I have not sent these prophets, yet they have gone forth; I have not spoken to them, yet they prophesied. How long shall there be in the mouth of the false prophets, prophesies of lies? Prophesies of the deceit of their own hearts? Therefore, behold, I am against the prophets, says the Lord, who pervert their tongues, and say, Thus says the Lord, I am against the prophets who see false dreams, tell them, and lead my people

The Coming of the Holy Spirit

astray by their lies, I did not command them nor send them; you pervert the words of the Living God, the Lord of Hosts, our God." (Jeremiah 23:21,26,30,32,36)

I think that it is safe to say that these scriptures all describe a definitive event in archaic Judaism, an event that has cast a shadow down through the ages. In this rebellion against the oversight of God through the prophets, religion became merely an empty shell, a priviledged social organization for people whose goals and purposes were more political than religious. There can be no doubt that these scriptures describe nothing less than the destruction of God's kingdom on earth for the benefit of a religious bureaucracy. Before the final destruction of the true prophets takes place, the usurper priesthood is exposed and warned. God tells Ezekiel, "Woe to the foolish prophets, who follow their own pride, for they have not seen any vision. They say Thus says the Lord; and the Lord has not sent them; and they persist in confirming a false word. Indeed you have seen a vain vision, and you have spoken a lying divination, and yet you say, The Lord said it; although I have not spoken. Because you have seen false visions and spoken lies, I am against you says the Lord God. And my hand shall be against you says the Lord God. And my hand shall be against the prophets who see false visions and utter lying divinations; they shall not remain in the midst of my people, neither shall they be written in the book of the house of Israel." (Ezekiel 13:4)

Reverend Pajarillo emphasized to me that these verses describe the first battles fought in a war against God, the Holy Spirit, and those who possess the ability to communicate with the Holy Spirit; a war that still rages. In the wake of the successful conspiracy to destroy the intradimensional theocracy that began with Abraham, we are told that the new false priesthood "turned their backs, and stopped up their ears. They made their hearts as hard as flint and would not listen to the words that the Lord Almighty had sent by his Spirit through the earlier prophets." (Zechariah 7:11-12) *This abandonment of the prophetic tradition characterized not only early Judaism, it also defined what was to become the Judaeo-Christian religion.* In the place of the prophets, books were placed at the center of religious life and the so-called 'correct interpretation' of these became the new 'word of God.'

Having abandoned the direct revelation of the Word of God through the prophets, the priesthood insisted that the word of God existed only in their sacred writings. Reverend Pajarillo told me that the Blessed Spirit had revealed that the reference to the Word that existed in the beginning, the Word that was God and was with God (John 1:1,) was a statement regarding the origins of archaic Judaism and the prophetic tradition from which Judaism had evolved; *the prophetic utterances of God through the prophets*. The Word is the true substance of the covenant between God and humanity. The Jewish religion was established by

Abraham. The origin of archaic Judaism is recorded in Genesis 12:1-4. We are told that "the Lord *spoke* to Abram, Depart from your country, and from the place of your nativity, and from your Father's house, to a land I will show you and I will make of you a great people, and I will bless you, and make your name great; and you shall be a blessing. I will bless those who bless you and curse those who curse you; and in you shall all the families of the earth be blessed. *So Abram did as the Lord had spoken to him.*"

Abraham apparently possessed the ability to communicate with God through the Holy Spirit. It was this ability to communicate directly with God that bestowed true spiritual authority. The scriptural spinmeisters that preside over modern seminaries have convinced themselves that they and they alone are authorized to provide us with a 'correct interpretation' of the scriptures. Too bad for us that their 'correct interpretation' is a doom and gloom scenario. The false prophets of Old Testament Judaism erred in painting a rosy picture of a bad situation. The false prophets of modern Christianity err in painting a dismal picture of imminent destruction in the midst of the Coming of the Holy Spirit.

The Mission of Jesus According to the Blessed Spirit

Reverend Pajarillo emphasized to me that the doctrine that teaches that Jesus offered himself as a living sacrifice to atone for the sins of humanity was misunderstood. God tells Jeremiah, "Your prophets have seen false and deceptive visions for you; *and have not revealed anything of your sins, that you might repent* and I should bring you back from captivity." The prophets of God presided over the trials and tribulations of the Old Testament Jews in the same way that the Blessed Spirit presides over the trials and tribulations of the Christian Spiritists. The Holy Spirit, speaking through the prophets, counseled the people in matters that dealt with sin and repentance, offering them specific advice on how to resolve their shortcomings. Why would Jesus need to die for a problem that the Holy Spirit was perfectly capable of dealing with? What was necessary was that the Holy Spirit be restored to its original prominence. In order for that to happen, the intradimensional dialogue that had began with Abraham had to be reestablished. Jesus came to reestablish that dialogue.

That Jesus' mission involved the restoration of the prophetic tradition is articulated by John the Apostle when he tells us, "The Word became flesh and dwelt among us, and we saw his glory, a glory like that of firstborn of the Father, full of grace and truth." (John 1:14) The reference to Jesus being the "Word made flesh" directly connects him to the prophetic lineage that began with Abraham; a lineage that had been overthrown. By the time of Jesus, the prophets of the Spirit of God had been murdered, and the link between God and the people had long been broken. In their place, he found the Temple of God dominated by a politicized priesthood that had arrived at an interpretation of the sacred writings that portrayed God as easily angered and vindictive. A God that needed to be soothed and appeased by offerings. The false priesthood emphasized the ritual sacrifice of animals as the preferred means of currying favor with and avoiding the wrath of God the Father. Jesus was appalled at the marketplace atmosphere of the Temple where the selling of sacrificial animals had become a lucrative business. He was well aware that God had told Jeremiah that "My heart is broken within me because of the prophets; for both the prophets and priests have become pagans; yea, even in my house I found their wickedness, says the Lord." (Jeremiah 23:9) Outraged by the pagan sacrificial practices "Jesus entered into the Temple of God, and began to cast out those who were buying and selling in the Temple; and he overturned the trays of the money changers and the stands of those who sold doves; and he would not allow any man to bring goods into the Temple." (Mark 11:15-16)

As the *inheritor and champion* of the prophetic tradition of Judaism, Jesus drew upon the revelations of his forebears to criticize what he saw as a false priesthood and a corrupt religion. Jesus confronts the spiritually bankrupt priesthood in Jerusalem and tells them, "Woe unto you, Scribes and Pharisees, hypocrites! For you have shut off the kingdom of heaven against men; for you do not enter into it yourselves, and do not permit those who would to enter." (Matthew 23:14) Jesus describes the false priesthood as "children of those who killed the prophets." (Matthew 23:31) "The 'kingdom of heaven' that the Pharisees had 'shut off' is the intradimensional theocracy that Jesus had come to restore. In shutting off this 'kingdom of heaven' Jesus tells the Scribes and Pharisees that "you have taken away the keys of knowledge; you did not enter, and those who were entering you hindered." Jesus is essentially saying that the false priesthood had not only chosen to reject the oversight of God themselves, but actively suppressed any attempts of others to communicate with God directly. Jesus also clearly infers that within this 'kingdom of heaven' we would find the 'keys of knowledge.'

Jesus then exposes the failings of the high priests in the words of their own prophets Jeremiah and Isaiah by saying, "Is it not written, My house shall be called the house of prayer for all the peoples? But you have made it a bandits' cave. And the high priests and the scribes heard it, and they sought how to do away with him; *for they were afraid of him,* because all the people were amazed at his teaching." (Mark 11:17-18) Jesus was well aware that the religious hierarchy was using its authority mainly to enrich themselves and consolidate their secular power and, as such, were guilty of the spiritual equivalent of treason. The doctrine that Jesus died as a sacrifice to appease God's anger against the sins of humanity is merely an attempt to reconcile the pagan sacrificial practices of a false priesthood with the fact that Jesus was hunted down, tortured, and killed. It is the ultimate sacrilege that Jesus' murder was recast in an attempt to lend credence to the pagan sacrificial practices of a priesthood that lived in open defiance against the Holy Spirit. Jesus didn't die for the sins of humanity. It was the sins of an entrenched religious bureaucracy that led to his death.

A Short History of Blasphemy against the Holy Spirit

Reverend Pajarillo told me that in Jesus' efforts to reestablish the kingdom of heaven, he realized that the Pharisaic priesthood who controlled the synagogue would never acknowledge their misdeeds, and he increasingly found himself in opposition to them. As a result of the perversion of the Judaic doctrines that had been intentionally misinterpreted by the Pharisees to justify their actions and preserve their autonomy, Jesus openly disputed the law of Moses. The Pharisees, who had transformed the sacred writings into a law library, presided over the people of Israel in much the same way as lawyers do in the modern world. If they wanted to discredit and destroy anyone, they did so legally. Since they defined the law, they were in a position to bring charges against anyone they chose and find them guilty. Jesus countered the perversion of Judaic law by introducing a new law. The Pharisees, in an attempt to entrap Jesus in a violation of their legal system questioned him often. In one conversation a Pharisee asked Jesus, "Teacher, what is the greatest commandment in the law? Jesus said to him, Love the Lord your God with all your heart and with all your soul and with all your might and with all your mind. This is the greatest and the first commandment. And the second is like to it, Love your neighbor as yourself. On these two commandments hang the law and the prophets." (Matthew 22:36-40)

These two commandments superseded the intricate legal arguments of the Pharisees and established the affirmative rules of human interaction. In the place of all the previous 'thou shall nots' that the Pharisees used to exert their authority, Jesus had only one. In pitting one legalism against another, Jesus mocked the law of the Pharisees in telling them that "he who blasphemes against the Holy Spirit will not be forgiven." (Luke 12:10) This law was, of course, one that all the Pharisees had broken. Having arrived at this point, I will summarize what it is that constitutes blasphemy against the Holy Spirit. 1) Conspiring against and causing harm to those who have prophetic gifts, 2) Pretending that the human interpretation of sacred writings is equivalent to the knowledge and conversation of the Holy Spirit of Truth, 3) Misleading innocent people with false prophesy, 4) Standing in opposition to those who speak

Words of Wisdom, 5) Standing in opposition to those who speak Words of Knowledge, 6) Standing in opposition to those able to Discern the True Spirit, 7) Standing in opposition to those who possess the Gift of Faith, 8) Standing in opposition to those who possess the Gift of Healing, 9) Standing in opposition to those who possess the Gift of the Working of Miracles, 10) Standing in opposition to those who possess the Gift of Prophesy, 11) Standing in opposition to those who possess the Gift of Diversity of Tongues, and 12) Standing in opposition to those who possess the Gift of Interpretation of Tongues.

The great majority of modern Christian theologians teach the doctrine of cessationism. Cessationists teach that the gifts of the Holy Spirit ceased in the 1st century A.D. According to these learned seminarians, the gifts of the Holy Spirit just died out because they were no longer needed. Why would God need the Holy Spirit when he has human beings who possess the 'correct interpretation' of the bible? The history of the Western Church is the history of the opposition to the work of the Holy Spirit. From the time of the Edict of Milan (313 A.D.,) the miraculous work of the Holy Spirit has been ruthlessly suppressed in one wave of terror after the next. If blasphemy against the Holy Spirit is in fact the worst sin one can commit, as Jesus has said, then how are we to characterize Christian Churches that believe in cessationism? I found a wealth of information on cessationism and the history of the opposition of the Church to the work of the Holy Spirit on the Internet under the topic of cessationism. I also found William DeArteaga's book *Quenching the Spirit* to be a good resource. As for the current debate regarding the 'correct interpretation' of the bible, search the Internet for the topic of millennialism and read *House Divided-The Break-Up of Dispensational Theology* by Greg L. Bahnsen and Kenneth L. Gentry.

It is well established that the Western Church has stood in opposition to the work of the Holy Spirit since its inception. With that being the case, the Western Christian Churches that espouse cessationism cannot possibly be the true Church referred to in the bible as the Body of Christ. If the orthodox Church is not the Body of Christ, then where is it? In a conversation Jesus had with a Samaritan woman at a well, he said, "Believe me, the time is coming, when neither on this mountain nor in Jerusalem will they worship the Father. You worship what you do not know; but we worship what we do know; for salvation is from the Jews. But the time is coming, and it is here when the *true worshipers shall worship the Father in spirit and in truth*; for the Father also desires worshipers such as these. *For God is Spirit*; and those who worship him must worship him *in spirit and in truth*." (John 4:21-24) In these three short verses, Jesus defines the identity of God, foretells a new form of worship, and defines the true worshipers as those who practice the new form of worship. It is reasonable to assume that those who practice the form of worship prophesied by Jesus would constitute the true Body of Christ.

Worship In Spirit and In Truth

Having been born in the 20th century, both I and Reverend Pajarillo could research over 800 years of church history and draw conclusions that had not been available to Joachim of Fiore. While the abbot regarded literal interpretation of the Scriptures as the root of all evil, Reverend Pajarillo felt that a larger pattern, an abuse of spiritual authority, described the problem more clearly. Benjamin explained to me that Jesus was constantly at odds with the religious authority figures of his day because his stated purpose in life was to reestablish a spiritual source of authority.....one that directly challenged the authority of the existing priesthood.

Jesus was committed to religious reform. His proposed return to the prophetic tradition of his ancestors, in which the Spirit of God played a central role, would have effectively removed the corrupt, materialistic priesthood from power. Restoring the Holy Spirit as the interpreter of spiritual matters would have ended the human domination of religion. Having the Holy Spirit as the sole authority on spiritual matters was the last thing that the priesthood wanted. Jesus taught that, rather than himself or the Father, it was the Spirit of God that would eventually be regarded as the universal object of worship. It was clearly Jesus' intention to lay the groundwork for the dispensation of the Holy Spirit. Jesus foretold not only the Coming of the Holy Spirit, but a new form of worship that would emerge in conjunction with the coming of the Holy Spirit. This form of worship would be appropriate in an environment in which a *revealed spiritual presence communicated openly with the Church.*

Placing the Holy Spirit at the center of religious life called for a new priesthood, one capable of presiding over the new form of worship. The new priesthood, like the prophets of the Old Testament, required the ability to communicate with the messengers of the Holy Spirit. The Apostles were the first priests of the new form of worship that Jesus introduced. It was explained in depth by the Apostle Paul in his letters to the Corinthians. Paul gives sermon after sermon defining the Holy Spirit as a *subjective presence*, a dynamic revelatory presence that was capable of operating through the members of the "Body of Christ" in powerful, and decidedly paranormal, ways. Paul says that, "The spirit has demonstrated its power and wisdom through me so that your faith might not rest in the *wisdom of men,* but in the power of God." (1 Corinthians 2:5) In this new form of worship, "in Spirit and in Truth," spiritual authority would no longer reside in the "wisdom of men." Spiritual authority would become the exclusive possession of a living presence that could only be communicated with "in Spirit and in Truth."

Under the tutelage of Christian Spiritists, I began to understand the role Jesus had played in a new light. From the Christian Spiritist perspective, Jesus had spent his life laying the foundation for what is currently known as a *spiritual paradigm shift.* With the arrival of the Holy Spirit during the Pentecost, the worship of the "Father" ended, and

The Coming of the Holy Spirit

worship "In Spirit and in Truth" began. The prophetic traditions of early Judaism paralleled Christian Spiritism in many ways. The word "prophet" is derived from the Greek "prophetes," and describes individuals who, at certain times, become dissociated from their own words and thoughts.

There are many references to these dissociative states in the Old Testament. Saul is told, "The Spirit of the Lord will come upon you in power, and you will prophesy with them; and you will be changed into a different person." (I Samuel 10:6-7) God tells Jacob, "My Spirit, who is on you, and my words that I have put in your mouth will not depart from your mouth..." (Isaiah 59:21) During these times of dissociation, the prophet's faculties of speech and thought are assumed by external independent personas who express views and information via the bodies of their hosts. Among the Hebrew prophets, these personas included angels such as Gabriel, the Holy Spirit, and whomever God chose to reveal his message through. The term commonly used by Christian Spiritists to describe this dissociative behavior is *mediumship*.

In describing God as Spirit, and the true worshipers as those who worshipped in Spirit and in Truth, Jesus described a form of worship that had not yet emerged in any formal sense. Prior to the Pentecost, the inner workings of the Jewish prophetic tradition was the closely guarded secret of a select group of men who were naturally predisposed to function as prophets. Though the Apostles make explicit references to their firsthand experiences as instruments of the Holy Spirit, there is nothing in the biblical narrative that describes any specific religious practices involved in 'worship in Spirit and in Truth.'

The Subversion of Worship in Spirit and in Truth

The insight I have gained from the prophesies of Joachim of Fiore and from contemporary Christian Spiritism, have brought into question all that I have been taught about Christianity. Is Christian Spiritism the first dawning of Ordo Novus, as predicted by Joachim? The preponderance of confirming evidence I have found in the exact parallels between the work of the Christian Spiritists and the prophesies of the Holy Spirit as revealed through Joachim of Fiore, strongly suggest that Christian Spiritism, as it is practiced in the Philippines, *is* precisely the form of worship Jesus prophesied. Through Worship in Spirit and in Truth, a new intradimensional order...a spiritual government...is emerging here on earth.

The contemporary emergence of the form of worship that Jesus prophesied apparently took place in the Christian Spiritist communities of the Philippines and Brazil. I believe that 'true, or Christian spiritism' as it is practiced in the Philippines, is Worship in Spirit and in Truth for several reasons. The Minutes reveal the degree of authority the Blessed Spirit exercised in even the most mundane matters of the Union. The Union has always been under the direct oversight of the Holy Spirit. The testing of spirits who spoke through the mediums of the Union is a matter of record. The 'Keys' that I described in chapter five insured that only the forces of Christ in the spirit world could communicate through the mediums of the Union. Having excluded the lower spirits, the Blessed Spirit trained the members of the Union, teaching them to become masters of intradimensional communication. The form of worship practiced by the Christian Spiritists *reestablished* the intradimensional theocracy that characterized early Judaism. Once again, the Holy Spirit is communicating Divine wisdom directly to human beings.

Reverend Pajarillo emphasized that the exact analogies between the healing ministry of Jesus and that of Christian Spiritism, existed because both worshipped in Spirit and in Truth. Worship in Spirit and in Truth had predisposed Jesus' followers to receive the Holy Spirit, and has done the same for Christian Spiritists. Reverend Pajarillo demonstrated that the practice of Worship in Spirit and in Truth empowered human beings, enabling them to link up to the Holy Spirit and learn to function as instruments of the power of God.

Constantine merged Church and State into a theocratic war machine.

In the centuries following Jesus' ascension, this new form of worship that Jesus had prophesied, disappeared from history. I asked Benjamin why Jesus' prophesied form of worship had taken nearly two thousand years to establish itself. He told me that the Blessed Spirit revealed that it had been suppressed by the military dictators, kings, emperors, and clergy, who ruled the ancient world, because it compromised their imperial autonomy. These glorified tyrants strived for total domination of their subjects and saw in religion an obvious way to expand their control. Secular rulers were jealous of the reverence and unquestioning obedience that their subjects reserved for God and the clergy. They also recognized that religious converts became fierce warriors when they believed they were fighting for God.

While the Roman emperors found the willing martyrdom of early Christians to be unsettling, Constantine saw, in the great courage of the Christians, the makings of an invincible army. Through his conversion to Christianity, Constantine positioned himself as a latter-day Joshua who saw an opportunity to unite the religious and secular communities into a war machine sanctioned by "God the Father." With Constantine's conversion to Christianity and his establishment of Christianity as the 'state' religion of the Byzantine empire, Church and state were merged into a theocratic war machine. This drew heavily on the Jewish war mythology of the Old Testament to justify and encourage military adventurism. Beginning in the fourth century A.D., armies of *non-Jewish* soldiers, marched off to fulfill the imperial ambitions of the Byzantine empire, with the Divine sanction of Yahweh.

The Holy Trinity of State sponsored Christianity

With the entire biblical justification of their regimes resting on the theological position of the military sanction of "God the Father," they saw that Christianity had to reflect that position, and no other. They proceeded to define the state-controlled Church as the only valid Christian institution, and the worship of "God the Father" and "Jesus the Son" as the only valid form of Christian worship. In doing so, they expanded the role of the "Father" from that of the protector and champion of the Jews, to the supreme deity of the Christians as well. It was in this original heresy, carried out by the State disguised as the Church, that the henchmen of Constantine succeeded in "snuffing out the spiritual understanding, and burying it in the belly of the letter," and reducing the role of the Holy Spirit to a national security issue for a civilization built on a lie.

The long chain of military dictators who followed Constantine in their role as God's 'chosen,' were well aware that there were those who possessed true spirituality and were, in truth, what they and their clergymen only pretended to be. In order to establish a form of Christianity that excluded the oversight of the Holy Spirit, the Church proceeded, with the full cooperation of the state, to eliminate any trace of Christianity that had preserved the resurgence of the prophetic tradition embodied in Jesus' teachings. Anyone who held opposing religious views became both enemies of the state and *enemies of God*. Thus, those who possessed true spirituality, spirituality as it was defined by Jesus, were falsely portrayed as enemies of God. Using everything in their power to block the spiritual paradigm shift that Jesus had prophesied, these founding fathers of Western civilization demonized, tortured, and murdered anyone who disagreed with them, or expressed dissenting views. Establishing victory in war and military dominion as definitive 'proof' of God's approval, Constantine succeeded in replacing the 'Golden Rule' with the 'law of the jungle.' This unholy alliance between Church and State set the stage for all out war against those possessing spiritual gifts of any kind.

From the "Golden Rule" to the "Law of the Jungle"

The Oversight of the Holy Spirit

To summarize, the early prophets maintained an ongoing intradimensional dialogue with the Spirit of God. Maintaining a dialogue with the Spirit of God enabled the priesthood to receive knowledge, and act, in accordance with the will of God. In attempting to reestablish the prophetic tradition and restore the oversight of the Holy Spirit to Judaism, Jesus openly exposed a priesthood whose words, thoughts, and deeds no longer reflected the will of God. In laying the foundation for a spiritual paradigm shift from human-directed to spirit-directed religion, Jesus posed a significant threat to the priesthood in Jerusalem and inevitably suffered humiliation and death at their hands.

Reverend Pajarillo told me that it wasn't the Jews as a race that Jesus condemned. It was the abuses of false religions *defined and controlled* solely by human beings, who, in the biblical narrative, happened to be Jewish. History has proven that every religious bureaucracy since Constantine has recreated the sins of the Pharisees. The Luciferian failing of spiritual pride, of wanting to be greater than God, combined with the very real economic and political advantages of wielding godlike power, has been too great a temptation for mere humans to resist. When compared to the war the Western Catholic and Protestant Churches fought against the Holy Spirit, the Pharisaic resistance against the Holy Spirit was mere child's play. Reverend Pajarillo also emphasized that it was important to remember that the actual leaders of this conspiracy against the Holy Spirit were very few in number. The great majority of both Jews and Christians who aided and abetted the religious bureaucracies were as much victims as those they victimized.

When I finally grasped the practical consequences of the paradigm shift to Worship in Spirit and in Truth, I understood why those who have possessed the 'gifts,' described in the bible as gifts of the Holy Spirit, have suffered one disaster after the next. The history of organized religion is clearly the history of human beings usurping the prerogatives of God. Then, as now, those who control the spiritual lives of their fellow human beings revel in their pretense to divinity, and more often than not, will lend their support and official blessings to any secular government that allows them to maintain their privileged status. It is not difficult to imagine the reaction of any religious bureaucracy to the emergence of a new spiritual paradigm that would strip them of the Divine prerogatives they have come to enjoy.

During Jesus' life, his attempts to prepare the world for the emergence of the Holy Spirit, as *the source* of spiritual revelation and authority in religious matters, posed a threat not only to the Jewish priesthood in Jerusalem, but to *all religious bureaucracies to come*. After Jesus exits the biblical narrative, the Holy Spirit, and the spiritually gifted human beings through which it operates, replaced Jesus as the prevailing threat to false religions and those who derive their sustenance from them.

Among the most horrible atrocities ever committed by Christians were those committed against the unfortunate human beings who possess the miraculous gifts of the Holy Spirit. In the process of subverting the revelation of the Holy Spirit, state-sponsored Christianity has long since been deformed into that which it preaches against. Throughout history, the great masses of humanity have drifted along in the iron grip of dysfunctional state-sanctioned religious leaders who have consistently sought religious conversion through coercion, and intimidated millions of innocent people into the *denial* of the Holy Spirit in the name of Christ.

As this extreme persecution of spiritually sensitive individuals has unfolded in Western culture, the possibility of the Holy Spirit establishing Worship in Spirit and in Truth has become increasingly difficult. Traumatized by its own history, mainstream Western culture lacks a positive understanding of the Spirit and, as such, is not properly predisposed to participate in, or even understand, spirit-directed activities. The Christian suppression of the paranormal function is part of an historical conspiracy. Throughout history, the leaders of Western Christianity have conspired to prevent the Spirit of Truth from ever having the opportunity to critique their doctrines in any way. Underlying this suppression of paranormal function has been the determined effort to prevent the Holy Spirit from ever seeing the light of day.

Christian religion has been dominated by the "wisdom of men" for far too long. The vast discrepancies between the spirit-directed ministry of the New Testament, and the human domination of all aspects of the modern Church are no longer questioned. Human domination of religion is seen as a 'tradition,' our cultural heritage. Priests and clergy, whatever their beliefs, are automatically assumed to represent God. Their sermons are presumed to reflect the 'Will of God' based on the 'correct interpretation' of the bible. Reverend Pajarillo made it very clear to me that religious authority doesn't come from books. It comes from knowing God and understanding the ways of the Holy Spirit. The prophets of old relayed the revelations of the Holy Spirit directly from God. It was the ability to communicate with God that qualified the prophet to represent God's will.

On January 20th 1994, the Pentecost-like events that Reverend Pajarillo predicted would take place, began in Toronto, Canada. At the Toronto Airport Vineyard Fellowship, senior pastor John Arnott ended the first of four scheduled meetings. Following Reverend Arnotts' address, he invited those who wanted to receive prayer to come forward. Much to his astonishment, the entire congregation came forward. As the congregation stood there, the Holy Spirit descended upon them and physical manifestations of the movement of the Holy Spirit began. These physical manifestations included falling to the ground and 'resting in the Spirit,' laughter, weeping, shaking, trembling, receiving and sharing prophetic insights, visions, and a range of other spiritual experiences. This outpouring of the Holy Spirit came to be known as the "Toronto

Blessing." The 'spiritual domino 'effect that I witnessed in regard to the healing work of the Holy Spirit in the Philippines is apparently at work in the Toronto Blessing as well. The Airport Vineyard Fellowship has become a major destination of spiritual pilgrims. More than 300,000 people have made the trip to Toronto since 1994. Upon returning to their home congregations, similar physical manifestations have begun.

The cessationists, as one might imagine, are falling all over themselves in their attempts to discredit the phenomenon. Despite their efforts, the "Blessing" has circled the globe. The United Kingdom has been particularly affected. The Church of England Newspaper estimates that more than 2,000 congregations in the United Kingdom have experienced the "Blessing." And that is considered to be a conservative estimate. Countries where the "Blessing" has manifested include Argentina, South Africa, India, Mainland China, and Siberia, Russia. In the wake of this new outpouring, the issues that Jesus faced are being raised once again. There is a great deal of opposition to the "Blessing" from the orthodox Church. The manifestation of the Holy Spirit is a terrible threat to a consensus religious orthodoxy that depends upon our separation from and ignorance of the Holy Spirit for a living. The scholars of mainstream Christian theological seminaries are feverishly looking for 'sound doctrine' that definitively discredit the ecstatic, emotional experiences of charismatics. I will now summarize some of their arguments against the work of the Holy Spirit.

Cessationist Arguments Against the Charismatics

For the most part, the debate going on between cessationists and charismatics is a battle of scriptures. For every scripture that cessationists quote to support their position, charismatics have three that invalidate cessationism. I am not going to get into the scriptural debate. You will find the whole argument on the Internet. The ideological basis of fundamentalist theology is undergoing an intense internal debate. There is a great deal at stake. Fundamentalist Christianity is a formidable cultural, economic, and increasingly political force. In any argument against charismata, fundamentalists generally try to cast the spiritual phenomenon in question as being evil. One cessationist theologian's argument against charismata went something like this: 1) The indigenous Pentecostal churches of the third world, which he describes as 'nonwhite,' will overwhelmingly outnumber Protestants in the very near future, laying claim to what the writer calls the "spiritual center of Christianity." 2) The members of the charismatic Church emphasize subjective experience of God and the outer manifestations of these experiences as the core religious experience. 3) In order for the fundamentalists to accept that a spiritual 'gift' is 'from God,' an exact scriptural precedent must exist. If one cannot be found, the subjective experiences and outer manifestations of the charismatics are automatically thought to be 'from the devil.' Thus, the burden of proof is on the charismatics to prove scripturally that everything they are experiencing are identical to those that took place in the New Testament.

The fundamentalist professor then says that the fact that the number of charismatic worshippers is growing; their followers are enthusiastic, and alleged miracles are happening, is no reason to assume that the phenomena is from the Holy Spirit. He then tells us that we shouldn't trust the veracity of modern charismata because the gifts of the Holy Spirit ceased 1,900 years ago in the Church. The fact that they ceased, forces the conclusion that the new outpouring cannot be from God. The professor then gives his ridiculous summary of how the work of the Holy Spirit ceased in Church history. I think the cessationists have conveniently overlooked the fact that the Gifts of the Holy Spirit didn't 'cease' at all. They were viciously 'suppressed.' As I have said, the history of the Church *is the history of the war against the Holy Spirit*. I find it ironic that ministers live in total denial of the immediate power and presence of the Holy Spirit and condemn the movement of the Holy Spirit as the work of the devil. This is especially ironic when we consider that, according to Jesus himself, the very worst sin you can commit is to work against, and speak badly of, the Holy Spirit.

This outpouring is now in its infancy. The Toronto Blessing sounds very similar to the Pentecost-like event described in the Doctrina that took place in the Philippines ninety years ago. I predict that the repeated immersion of large numbers of spiritually inclined people in the "Blessing" and other similar events will soon lead to the *emergence of a natural leadership* within the ranks of the spiritually inclined. As these anointings continue, those individuals who are naturally predisposed to cooperate in and facilitate the work of the Holy Spirit will be recognized by their congregations and find themselves called to service for the greater glory of God. As the *real* Body of Christ awakens, the members will recognize those in their midst whom God has chosen as the new prophets, healers, and ministers. Eventually, the 'awakened' Church will receive revelation and instruction directly from the Holy Spirit concerning the work that it is to undertake. It has truly been an astounding turn of events to realize that the crumbling book of Minutes contained not only the history of Filipino Christian Spiritism, but the blueprints of the future of Western Charismatic Christianity as well.

It is difficult to imagine a Christian church through which authority is mediated from the Holy Spirit directly to church members. At first glance, the idea seems so farfetched that it's easy to dismiss as impossible. How would responsibility be delegated in a tax-exempt corporation where the Holy Spirit is the CEO? Even after translating the Minutes of the Union Espiritista, and knowing for certain that the contents were genuine, I still wasn't able to connect with the incredible truth staring me in the face. The Minutes proved something far more amazing than psychic surgery, it *proved* the existence of a form of Christianity governed by the

Holy Spirit. In the documents I have translated, are the specific details of a corporate structure through which the direct governance of the Holy Spirit has been achieved.

Within this organization, individuals possessing natural aptitudes for trance-possession, mediumship, high ethical standards, and proper predisposition, have made it possible for Christian Spiritists to *communicate* with the Holy Spirit for 90 years. In addition to natural mediums, Christian Spiritists encourage the development of Christian mediumship in *all* their members. Christian mediumship training teaches Christian ethics and mediumship *simultaneously* with the goal of awakening one to the work of the Holy Spirit. As the Minutes illustrate, the common denominator of all activities presided over by the Holy Spirit is the spiritual development of the individual members.

The Holy Spirit is not far away in heaven, removed from the affairs of human beings. The Holy Spirit *is* God, as it exists *in* the members of the Body of Christ here on earth! The Christian Spiritists accept as literal truth that the Holy Spirit entered into the bodies of the Apostles during the Pentecost and bestowed nine spiritual gifts, in order that the power of God could be brought forth into *this* world. The central role of the Holy Spirit in Christian Spiritist worship certainly contradicts the insistence of cessationist Christians that trance-possession and mediumship must be condemned, feared, and strictly avoided. The defining event that led to the formation of the early Christian Church, was nothing less than the mass '*spiritual possession*' of the Apostles by the Holy Spirit. Shortly after the Pentecost, the 'spiritual domino effect' begins and the Holy Spirit possesses the Gentiles as well. In this state of Divine possession, ordinary human beings received the power to awaken others through healing and teaching.

The Holy Spirit is not bound by religious doctrines or affiliation. Though it is universally available to all, Christian Spiritists teach that the Blessed Spirit will not manifest itself either *through or in the presence of* people who lack the necessary reverence and deference. Depending upon the Holy Spirit as their source of spiritual revelation motivates Christian Spiritists to maintain a high degree of spiritual integrity. In spirit-directed religion, righteousness is an essential requirement in maintaining an ongoing dialogue with the Holy Spirit. As the writings of the Old Testament prophets make abundantly clear, any deviation from righteousness strains the link between the Revelator and the Spirit Protector.

The Secret Tradition of Christian Spiritism

I have been asked many times, why the Holy Spirit would have chosen to manifest in a place as destitute and deprived as the Philippines? Benjamin explained that just as Jesus had been forced to establish his ministry outside the organized religious community in Israel, the Holy Spirit has been working outside the confines of organized religion for centuries. Cessationists haven't given the Holy Spirit any other options. The emergence of new forms of Catholic Christianity that Pope Paul VI acknowledged at Vatican II is well underway. The Pope's admission that "a certain theological pluralism finds its roots in the mystery of Christ" is an understatement. The indigenization of Protestant charismatic religion is now taking place throughout the world as well, minus the cessationist error.

Reverend Pajarillo explained that the emergence of Christian Spiritist communities in Brazil and the Philippines are historical examples of how the Holy Spirit operates in history. With the arrival of Magellan in the Philippines, the strategy of the Holy Spirit begins to unfold. In order to finally accomplish the paradigm shift into 'Worship in Spirit and in Truth,' the Holy Spirit intervened in a culture where *spirit-directed, organized religion was already well established*. Far from the centers of Western culture, and a Christian religion dominated by men, the Holy Spirit sent the Spiritual Messengers of Christ into a culture where they were certain to be properly understood and received. I have no doubt that there are a number of other events similar to the one that took place in the Philippines that I am not personally aware of.

Like a Divine chess master, the Holy Spirit has been planning one strategy after the next for centuries, planting a seed here and a seed there. The prophesies and healing work of Edgar Cayce, the transpersonal spirituality that emerged in the sixties, the Toronto Blessing, the spirit-directed miracles of Arigo, psychic surgery, and the emergence of Christian Spiritism in the Philippines and Brazil, have all been characterized by the progressive revelation of the Holy Spirit through *Divine spiritual possession*. This dispensational post-millennialist understanding, discerned by the members of a minority religious sect in the Philippines, and based on the work of the Holy Spirit, has, until now, been a secret tradition of the Christian Spiritists.

Central to the secret tradition of the Christian Spiritists is the knowledge that we are presently in the dispensation of the Holy Spirit. Christian Spiritists believe that there will be a Second Coming of Christ. This will take place after the spiritualization of humanity is brought about by the Second Coming of the Holy Spirit. Juan Alvear questioned the Blessed Spirit at length about the spiritual events that led to Christian Spiritism. In the first chapter of the Doctrina, Alvear asks the Spirit, "How do we classify the periods pertaining to the emergence of modern (Christian) Spiritism?"

<u>Spirit</u>: Three phases, First, the appearance of various phenomenon in America since 1848. Secondly, the development of the science and moral philosophy derived from the wise based on the phenomenon in Europe and America. Thirdly, the founding of schools of moral evangelism which arose from the knowledge of the Holy Spirit. From this came the true *spiritism* in formal mediums, followed by the emergence of conferences and evangelical sessions."

According to the Spirit, the three contemporary events that led to Filipino Christian Spiritism are: 1) The Spiritualism movement that began with the Fox sisters in 1848 in upstate New York, 2) The Spiritist Doctrine that Allan Kardec received from the Blessed Spirit, and 3) The formal inception of worship in Spirit and in Truth based on the revelation of the Holy Spirit. Since the spiritualist phenomena bore little resemblance to the paranormal activities of the Holy Spirit described in the biblical narrative, Alvear questioned the Spirit about the differences:

Alvear: How do you explain why spiritualistic phenomenon like knocking sounds, levitation of tables and other objects in mid-air, the appearance of hands writing from nowhere, and other related phenomenon were the first occurrences of modern Spiritism?

Spirit: Because these events were intended by God to be the beginning, or introduction, of big things that heaven has in store in the end, which is the revelation or appearance of the Holy Spirit.

Continuing to question the Blessed Spirit, Alvear asks:

Alvear: What spirits are responsible for the spiritualistic phenomenon?

Spirit: The elemental and raw spirits.

Alvear: Why should the raw spirits first begin this?

Spirit: It did not come from their own desire. They are under the direction of brilliant spirits who are called the Spiritual Messengers of Christ. The manifestations of the raw spirits are used to call the attention of the masses of innocent people and of the curious and onlookers. There are still a majority of curious individuals and they marvel and delight in flocking to these occasions. In this manner, the people learn of the aforesaid rough phenomena and gather to witness, thus opening the door for yet greater manifestations. The phenomena brought about by the raw spirits and elementals will also come to the attention of wise men, compelling them to research the origins of such occurrences. The priests and pastors will also be compelled to make studies so that they will know how to explain the phenomena.

Alvear: Are these rough phenomena made by the higher spirits who guide the lesser or rough spirits? Are they the ones who lift tables, benches, and other household articles? Do they make the noises that come from things and objects?

Spirit: No, because they (the brilliant spirits) will lose their dignity and besides, it is not becoming for them to do unrefined performances on earth. People who are not used to hard work cannot perform the work of laborers; likewise, the finest spirits cannot perform vulgar deeds. The brilliant spirits can be compared to master architects, professors, heads of state, and heads of organizations or foundations. They are in charge of planning, to direct and govern the unrefined spirits. They are chosen to fulfil God's will. (Alvear 1909)

The Restoration of the Sanctuary

After learning that Christian Spiritists believed that the Spiritualism movement, which began in with the Fox sisters in 1848, was the work of the Holy Spirit, I questioned Reverend Pajarillo about spiritualism. The Spiritualism movement, according to Benjamin, was an elementary lesson in the reality of another dimension. He said that there was much that had to be *unlearned* in preparation for the Coming of the Holy Spirit. Overcoming the irrational fear of all spirits was fundamental to restoring a dialogue with the elevated spirits. After having been characterized for centuries by the Church as evil demons, the spirits freely offered advice and entertained their hosts with amazing, yet posivitively benign, displays of spiritual power. The Spirits quickly dispelled the idea that they were evil, or of the devil, and initiated the first of the spiritual interventions that was to lead to Christian Spiritism.

The Christian Spiritist belief that the year 1848 marked the first stage of the Coming of the Holy Spirit intrigued me, and prompted me to study the 1800's for anything that would lend credibility to their assertions. I discovered that a number of new Christian sects were established during the same time period as the Spiritualism movement. One in particular supported the assertions of the Christian Spiritists, the sect formed by William Miller. Believing that Jesus was due to return, Miller became obsessed with determining when this great event would occur. He researched the scriptures for a specific chronology of the Second Coming in the prophesies of both the Old and New testaments. Finally, he found a prophesy in Daniel that seemed to describe the event in which the entire salvation history of the bible culminated. The biblical reference which seemed to elucidate the event was Daniel 8:14 which stated, "Unto two thousand and three hundred days; then shall the sanctuary be cleansed." (King James Version) "And he said to him, for two thousand and three hundred days; then righteousness shall prevail." (Lamsa Version from Aramaic,) and finally "For two thousand three hundred evenings and mornings; then shall the rights of the sanctuary be restored." (Revised Berkeley Edition)

Through extensive biblical research Miller learned that, in prophetic terminology, one day equaled one year. He came to this conclusion after cross referencing Numbers 14:34 and Ezekiel 4:6. Miller recognized that the period of 2,300 years extended far beyond the Jewish Dispensation; and therefore, could not refer to the "sanctuary" of that dispensation. Knowing the number of years that were prophesied, he had only to find the starting point of the prophetic cycle before he could accurately predict the time of the Second Coming. He continued his analysis of the prophesies with great resolve. In analyzing the prophesies of Daniel, Miller found the reference that he had been looking for. The beginning of the 2,300 years' period coincided with the original decree to rebuild Jerusalem following the Babylonian captivity. Miller found the decree in

The Coming of the Holy Spirit

the seventh chapter of the book of Ezra. (Ezra 7:12-26)

The original commandment had come from three kings of Persia, Cyrus, Darius, and Ataxerxes. These three kings completed the decree in 456 B.C.. To determine the year of the Second Coming, Miller simply subtracted 456 from 2300. According to the revelation of this biblical prophesy, Miller and his associates were convinced that the "cleansing of the sanctuary" which they believed would take place in conjunction with the Second Coming of Jesus in the flesh would occur in the *Fall of 1844*! Convinced that the return of Jesus was imminent, Miller stopped farming and became a preacher. With his chronology of the cycle of biblical prophesy as the basis of his ministry, he was very successful and, in 1833, received a license to preach from the Baptist church of which he was a member.

Miller converted thousands with his prediction of the Second Coming of Jesus. The orthodox churches were disturbed by his success as many members of their churches were converted to the doctrine of Millerism which taught the advent or Second Coming of Jesus with a captivating urgency. Many Millerites were gleaned from pre-existing churches. As the ministers of other churches watched their congregations shrink, they became alarmed and began to see Miller as a threat. Miller's doctrinal bearings were closely examined by the orthodox churches. To their dismay, they were unable to find any flaws in his teachings. In desperation, Miller's opponents declared that the prophesies of Daniel and Revelation were incomprehensible prophetic mysteries which were sealed and could not be understood. Needless to say, this reasoning didn't convince many of Miller's followers to return to the churches they had abandoned. As is often the case, the more vicious the attacks against Miller became, the more convinced his followers became that he was right.

The prophesies which seemed to point to the coming of Jesus in the fall of 1844 took deep hold in the minds of the Millerites. Farmers began to abandon their fields, mechanics their tools, and traders their merchandise, to prepare for the imminent coming of the Lord. Those who believed Miller watched with great anticipation for the coming of their Savior as the expected event drew near. In the weeks preceding the appointed time, Millerites examined their every thought and emotion as if they might be their last. Meanwhile, in fear of possibly missing the boat, Miller's opponents finally conceded that his reckoning of the prophetic periods was correct and even agreed that some great event was about to take place.

According to his detractors, the great event was not the second coming of Jesus, but the conversion of the world. The Fall of 1844 came and went and Jesus did not return in the flesh, nor was the world converted. *In spite of the fact that the prophesies of both Miller and his opponents were false, the second coming of Jesus and the conversion of the world became the preeminent themes of Apostolic as well as Evangelical*

Christianity and remain so to this day. God does indeed work in mysterious ways.

Miller and his followers were stunned and bewildered by the failure of the prophesy. Miller reevaluated the scriptures and concluded that he had made no mistake in his reckoning of the prophetic periods. It was certainly simple enough to subtract 456 from 2300. Miller decided that the mistake had been made in his understanding of the term "sanctuary." Adhering to pre-millennial thought, Miller believed that the term "sanctuary" referred to the earth and that the cleansing of the sanctuary referred to the apocalyptic destruction that was to precede the Second Coming of Jesus. To make a long story short, Miller never managed to solve the mystery of the sanctuary, whose cleansing and restoration would characterize the culmination of the work of the Holy Trinity.

I asked Reverend Pajarillo what he thought the 'sanctuary' was, and he said that it was the *perispirit*. He then said that the information Allan Kardec had received, detailing the means through which the Spirit communicated with the material world, was as true for the Old Testament prophets as it was for Christian Spiritists. Reverend Pajarillo had apparently questioned the Blessed Spirit about the prophesies of Daniel. The Second Coming of the Holy Spirit began in 1848, only four years after Miller had predicted. After three thousand years of obscurity, the Holy Spirit decided to reestablish contact. The Spirit of God had always communed with the prophets via the *perispirit.* The receptor site on the subtle body that enabled human beings to communicate with God had indeed atrophied from neglect. After centuries of cessationist lies and spiritual persecution, the perispirit was definitely due to be both 'restored' and 'cleansed.'

True Spiritism is Born

The belief that spiritualism and Christianity had anything in common was never taken seriously in America. The orthodox religious community eventually triumphed over the spiritualists and spiritualism. Christian Spiritists, as I have pointed out, saw the American Spiritualism Movement as only the first of *three* events that led to true Spiritism. Not only was the spiritualist phenomenon the first stage in the progressive revelation of modern Spiritism, it was produced by lower spirits and elementals in order to get the attention of the public. The two final stages in the progressive revelation of the Holy Spirit required a sophisticated understanding of the spiritual realm possessed by only a small number of Westerners.

Spiritualism was dismissed as a fraud in the conventional wisdom of most Westerners. Those like Allan Kardec, however, who continued to communicate with the spirits were amazed to find that the intervention of the spirits was moving into another phase, one which Kardec called 'true' or 'Christian Spiritism.' The leading luminary of the Christian Spiritism movement in the Philippines, Juan Alvear, speaks of the transition from Spiritualism to Christian Spiritism when he states: "The presence of spirits, voice pulsations, music, lights, etc., and occurrences in other nations, have been widespread, but today's events are different because spoken words and writing are being received through sanctified Christians, who, through their sanctification, have become vehicles of the Holy Spirit of Truth as prophesied by Christ. Is this not what happened to the prophets who received the word of God which they wrote? Now, spread all over the world are the new prophets called mediums who receive the word of God through his spirits. Thus is fulfilled the words of God which said, "On the last day my spirit shall pervade all mankind, your sons and your daughters shall be prophets, the young men shall see visions, and the old men and women shall dream new dreams."

Alvear believed that there was a direct connection between Spiritism and the teachings of Jesus. He also believed that the Holy Spirit was using spiritualism to bring human beings into a new and positive relationship with the spiritual world. In regard to this work of the Holy Spirit, Alvear asks the Blessed Spirit:

<u>Alvear</u>: But what is the purpose of these manifestations of the spirit?
<u>Spirit</u>: It is God's will that the concept of mankind be changed with regard to the dead, and to the spirits so that they can be understood, and in order to understand that the spiritual world is a source of strength on earth, amidst the turmoil and darkness, and that the spiritual world guides men on earth to their destiny which is the will of Christ. (Alvear 1909)

Alvear elaborates on his understanding of the advent of Christian Spiritism by saying, "Spiritism is the work of the spirit of God, and because of heavenly assistance, the activity of the spirit is greatly increasing as we have witnessed throughout the world. The prophesy stated by God through the prophet Joel (2:28-31) that his spirit will be poured upon all flesh (humanity) is being fulfilled. What Christ has foretold about the arrival of the Spirit of Truth in John (14:16-26 and 16:7-13) is also being fulfilled. In the Church, the coming of the Spirit of Truth has been ignored or condemned. Yet through Spiritism, the Spirit of Truth will elucidate the *true meaning of Christ's teachings* and they will be interpreted in real spirit and in truth which is known only in spirit."

The Filipinos first made contact with the Messengers of Christ through individuals who possessed natural mediumistic ability. They succeeded in opening up an intradimensional dialogue with the Spiritual Messengers of Christ through a traditional ceremony they used to "speak" with the indigenous spirits of the Philippines. Using their traditional ceremonies in the Christian context of establishing communication with the Holy Spirit, the Filipinos received the *intelligentia spiritualis* that Joachim of Fiore predicted. *It was in this, the third stage, that the 'true' or 'Christian Spiritism' began.*

The Return of the Holy Spirit

In "speaking" with the Blessed Spirit, the Filipino Christian Spiritists received profound insights into the true meaning of biblical Scriptures. In addition to scriptural insight, the Blessed Spirit gave the Filipinos accurate advice concerning their day to day struggles while establishing the Union Espiritista. This included advice on how to deal with problems arising from improperly predisposed mediums, rebellious spiritist centers, obsessed mediums, fanatical mediums, and ultimately, the means to maintain order and confirm that the mediums were the instruments of the Messengers of Christ, and *only* of Christ.

The Christian Spiritists came to know the Holy Spirit as the central intelligence of a living, benevolent, and powerful composite spiritual being. In their intimate work with the Holy Spirit, the Filipinos received an in-depth knowledge of the skills needed to train mediums to perpetuate the mission of the Holy Spirit. This Christian mediumship training facilitated the development of a plurality of spiritual gifts among the members of the Union. The most prominent and well known of these are the healing gifts. Among these is the ability to open the human body with bare hands, remove various obstructions, and then close the body without a scar, the ability to materialize and dematerialize cotton wool, the ability to make incisions at a distance, and the ability to give "spiritual injections" (using a non-physical "needle" that often leaves visible puncture holes in the patient's arms,) to name a few. The paranormal abilities of the psychic surgeons may represent, as parapsychologists believe, the physical dimension of some unknown law of physics. They may also represent, as psychologists believe, an unknown potential of the human mind. Frankly however, my research, which I have detailed, indicates that the paranormal abilities of the Christian Spiritists are the *atavistic resurgence* of potent spiritual forces, demonstrated first by the Old Testament prophets, then by Jesus and his Apostles two thousand years ago, and finally through the Christian Spiritist communities in Brazil and the Philippines. As unlikely and unbelievable as this may sound, the previous chapters document the reasons why I believe this to be fact.

While pre-millennial Christians loudly insist that the Holy Spirit stopped operating 1,900 years ago, a genuine spiritual awakening is taking place both inside and outside the confines of their churches. Joachim of Fiore predicted, and Juan Alvear professes, a new age that is now *in progress*. It is a new age first foretold in the *prophesies of Jesus.* If the teachings of Jesus had been followed to the letter, this new age would have dawned a long time ago. In 1848, the Holy Spirit apparently had no choice but to initiate this new age *outside* the confines of orthodox Christianity. Millions of people around the world have received the knowledge and conversation of the Holy Spirit within the context of their own individual understanding and spiritual predisposition and are cooperating with it. Millions more will soon.

A Final Thought

The belief in life after death is among the most ancient of human beliefs. The great majority of religions teach that the human soul survives death. If the soul does indeed survive death, then there must be a dimension in which it lives. The Mazatec shaman, Maria Sabina, describes this dimension as: "*a world beyond ours, a world that is far away, nearby, and invisible, and that is where God lives, where the dead live, the spirits and the saints. A world where everything has already happened and everything is known. That world talks. It has a language of its own. I report what it says.*"

Similar descriptions of this spiritual dimension are reported throughout the world. The Taoists of ancient China tell us that, "*It manifests itself as kindness, but conceals its workings. It gives life to all things, but does not share the anxieties of the Holy Sage. Its glorious power, its great field of action, are of all things the most sublime.*" The position advanced by the Christian Spiritists is that the spiritual dimension is under the governance of a central Divine intelligence. In a dimension inhabited by countless spirits of every degree and predisposition, the Holy Spirit sent by Jesus is *in control*. Christian Spiritism emphasizes that the spirit world empowers and helps those who empower and help others. The Taoists articulate the same understanding when they tell us, "*The kind man discovers it and calls it kind. The wise man discovers it and calls it wise. The people use it day by day and are not aware of it, for the way of the superior man is rare.*" The Holy Spirit is universally available. Like the sun, it provides life unconditionally for everyone, regardless of their beliefs.

Before Reverend Pajarillo passed away, I promised him that I would do my best to present the complex and extraordinarily enlightening information that he had conveyed to me, to the world at large. As anyone who has been to the Philippines will tell you, much of traditional Filipino culture is fast disappearing. Christian Spiritist culture still survives, but only on the impoverished fringes of a society in turmoil. I sincerely hope that this information will enlighten human understanding, stem the tide of negativism and fatalism inherent in modern Christianity, and clear the way for the progressive revelation of the will of God.

In the remote provinces of the rural Philippines, far removed from the scrutiny of the punishing God of the pre-millennialists, Christian Spiritists, working under the aegis of the Holy Spirit, have brought to light a very special form of worship... one that enables ordinary human beings to function in paranormal capacities for the greater glory of God. I believe, as the Spiritist Doctrine teaches, that a component of our consciousness not only survives death, but resides in the after-death state even while we are *living*. This component of our consciousness links us to a subtle realm inhabited by all who have gone before us. I am convinced that within this subtle realm a wonderful power exists, a power that has influenced historical events toward a coming spiritual awakening.

Regarding the opposition of organized religion, Juan Alvear predicted that: "Through the revelation of the Holy Spirit, the resistance of the church and other opposing groups to the advent of the Holy Spirit, will slowly disintegrate because all will come together in the teachings of the Spirit of Truth which will reign at the Second Coming of Christ to fulfill a mission no longer guided by the minds of men, but received from the spirit directly in the fulfillment of the Holy Spirit."

We must learn to love and trust this spiritual power that resides within each of us and links us to the eternal. Christ is indeed returning in the flesh, but it is in and through the flesh of those who are motivated by kindness, goodness, and compassion. In the gnostic Gospel of Thomas, Jesus said, "I have thrown fire on the world and, behold, I am guarding it until it is ablaze." Perhaps some day, the fire of the spirit *will* establish itself here on earth and that which is 'wholly other' will come and bask in its warmth with us.

Glossary

A Memorial: A petition brought before Congress in April of 1854 asking that Congress appoint a scientific commission to investigate the phenomenon of spiritualism.

Alvear, Juan: A founding member of the Christian Spiritist Union of the Philippines and author of the first textbook of the Union entitled *The Doctrina Espiritista (Short Spiritist Doctrine.)*

Angina Pectoris: A syndrome characterized by paroxysmal constricting pain below the sternum, most easily precipitated by exertion or excitement and caused by ischemia of the heart muscle, usually due to heart disease such as arteriosclerosis.

Animism: 1.The attribution of conscious life to natural objects or to nature itself. 2. The belief in the existence of spiritual beings that are separable or separate from bodies. 3. The hypothesis holding that an immaterial force animates the universe.

Apparatus: A wooden tripod upon which sits a movable circular table top. The letters of the alphabet and numbers one through ten is drawn on the surface of the table top. A device used by mediums to receive messages from the spirit world.

Automatic Writing: Scripts produced without the control of the conscious self. In its highest form, it is an excellent channel for teachings from the spirit world. Usually the hand writes rapidly, often in an unfamiliar handwriting.

Bathala: The Supreme God of the pre-Christian Filipinos.

Belk, Henry: Parapsychological researcher and founder of the Belk Research Foundation. Henry Belk participated in and funded the research done on Arigo in Brazil as well as Antonio Agpaoa in the Philippines. He commissioned Harold Sherman to write the book *Wonder Healers of the Philippines.*

Bisa: A Filipino term for the different types of supernatural power through which healing is accomplished.

Blanche, Juan: A Christian Spiritist psychic surgeon renowned for his ability to make incisions in patients from a distance without touching them.

Blessed Spirit: One of the terms used by the Christian Spiritists to describe the elevated spiritual entity that carries out the work of the Holy Spirit.

Body Of Christ: The church.

Channeling: The modern term for spiritualist communication through mediums.

Chirino, Father Pedro: A Spanish Catholic priest and historian of pre-Christian Filipino society during the early colonial period.

Christian Mediumship Training: A specialized training used by Christian Spiritists to teach mediums to become instruments of the Holy Spirit.

Christian Spiritism: An interpretation of Christian doctrine that emphasizes the role of the Holy Spirit as one of primary importance. Originally derived from the indigenization of Christianity into the pre-existing shamanic and animistic beliefs of the Filipinos. Later Christian Spiritism was reformulated by the Filipinos along the lines of the spiritualist philosophy of the French spiritualist Allan Kardec. Kardec referred to Christian Spiritism as true spiritism.

Christian Spiritists of the Philippines Inc.: The religious organization founded by Eleuterio Terte following the scism with the Union Espiritista.

Clairaudience: The psychic ability to hear sounds beyond the normal range of the senses.

Clairvoyance: The psychic ability to see objects or actions beyond the natural range of the senses.

Combined Fluid: A term used by spiritualists to describe the process by which spirits communicate through mediums. The spirit is believed to condense the universal fluid and combine it with the terrestrial fluid of the medium. Once the fluids combine properly, the spirit can communicate or even manipulate matter through the medium.

Comforter: One of the terms used by Jesus to describe the Holy Spirit.

Conversion Experience: An experience that leads one to adopt a new religion, faith, or belief.

Cupping: An Asian medical technique devised to create a primitive vacuum by placing a cup over a source of heat normally placed on the patient's skin. As the source of heat exhausts itself, the oxygen within the cup is consumed and a vacuum is formed.

Demetrio, Father Francisco: A Jesuit priest and professor at the University of Santo Tomas in Manila and the Ateneo in Cagayan de Oro City in Mindanao. Father Demetrio is a prolific writer on the subject of Filipino Folk religion both ancient and modern.

Deontological: The philosophical argument that proposes that deception of any sort is immoral and not to be used. This belief is held by many doctors in regard to the use of placebos in medical practice.

Dispensationalism: A theological philosophy that teaches that there is a divine ordering of worldly affairs.

Distant Healing: Healing that takes place without the physical presence of the patient.

Doctrina Espiritista: The first textbook of the Christian Spiritist Union of the Philippines. Written in 1909 by Juan Alvear under the pen name of J. Obdell Alexis.

Dossey, Dr. Larry: Author of *Space, Time, and Medicine, Beyond Illness,*

Glossary

Recovering the Soul, Meaning and Medicine, and *Healing Words*. Former Chief of Staff of Humana Medical City Dallas and current co-chairman of the Panel on Mind/Body Interventions, Office of Alternative Medicine, National Institutes of Health.

Double Blind: A research protocol in which experimental subjects and experimenters are unaware of the roles they play in the experiment.

EDSA, Miracle at: The term coined to describe the overthrow of the Marcos administration by the massing of civilians at the prompting of Cardinal Jaime Sin at the site of the rebel headquarters at Camp Crame in Quezon City.

Enrile, Juan Ponce: The Minister of Defense of the Marcos administration whose defection sparked the rebellion that led to the overthrow of the Marcos Regime.

Espiritistas: A colloquial term used by Filipinos to describe Christian Spiritists.

Espiritu Santo: The Spanish term for the Holy Spirit.

Fox Sisters: The sisters, Margaretta and Kate Fox who started the Spiritualism Movement in New York in 1848.

Freitas, Jose de: The given name of the famous Brazilian psychic surgeon who is commonly known as Arigo.

Gahoy: A Tagalog term for witchcraft or the harm inflicted by a witch. The negative effect of air wafted from a sweating person just arrived from a distant journey.

Gifts of the Spirit: The gifts of the Holy Spirit referred to in the Bible in I Corinthians 12: 1-10.

Hahnemann, Samuel: The German doctor who founded homeopathy.

Healing Waters: The name given to the subterranean cave in the province of Pangasinan in the northern Philippines that is sacred to the Christian Spiritists.

Holy Spirit: The third person of the Christian Trinity.

Homeopathy: The method of treating disease by drugs, given in minute doses which would produce in a healthy person symptoms similar to those of the disease.

Hooponopono: A Hawaiian healing practice that utilizes forgiveness processes to restore harmony to both individual and groups.

Hypnosis: A condition or state allied to normal sleep which can be artificially produced and is characterized by marked susceptibility to suggestion, loss of will power, and more or less loss of sensation.

Indigenization: Is a term used to describe the assimilation of foreign concepts and beliefs within the contexts of other indigenous cultures.

Influencing: A Christian Spiritist term for the induction of trance in mediums by the mediumship trainers or Director of Mediums.

Ingkanto: Filipino term for dangerous spirits invoked by evil sorcerers. Ingkanto are said to appear as handsome men or beautiful women.

Injections, Spiritual: A metaphor of an injection with a hypodermic needle. When giving a spiritual injection, the healer will hold his or her hand in the same position that would be used if they were holding an actual hypodermic needle. The "needle" is then plunged into the arm of the patient and the "contents" are injected.

Interfaith Spiritual Church: The religious organization founded by Marcos Orbito and located in the province of Tarlac, in the town of San Manuel.

Joachim of Fiore: An Abbot of the medieval Catholic Church who received a series of visions from the Holy Spirit foretelling the coming age of the Holy Spirit.

Kardec, Allan: The pen name of the French spiritualist Denizard Rivail. Kardec wrote *The Book of Spirits*, *The Book of Mediums*, and *The Gospels as Interpreted by Spiritism*.

Kardecist: Of or referring to the writings or philosophy of Allan Kardec.

Keys of Jesus: The Christian Spiritist term for the documents received from the Spiritual Protector of the Union Espiritista by the President and the Director of Mediums that insured that the spirits that spoke through the mediums were elevated and genuine.

Kulam: The Tagalog term for witchcraft or the harm inflicted by a witch.

Magnetic Fluid (Terrestrial): A term borrowed from Allan Kardec and used by Christian Spiritists to describe a vaporous magnetic component found in human beings that is believed to be derived from the magnetism of the earth, animals, vegetables, and minerals. The terrestrial fluid is considered to be the simplest form of the universal fluid. Human beings possessing an abundance of terrestrial fluids are believed to be capable of healing others.

Magnetic Fluid (Universal): A term described by Allan Kardec as the pervasive universal element, the elementary principle of all things. Kardec taught that the spirits were able to condense the universal fluid into a semi-material envelope Kardec called the perispirit. The perispirit was the means by which the spirits were able to connect with, penetrate, and operate through mediums.

Magnetic Healing: Healing believed to be brought about through the transference of magnetic fluid from the healer into the patient.

Magnetic Massage: Magnetic healing in which the magnetic fluid is transferred into the patient through massaging the afflicted part.

Mananambal: A Filipino term for a shamanistic folk healer.

Mangkukulam: A Tagolag term for a practitioner of witchcraft.

Materialization: To cause to become real or actual. To assume material form. To take physical form or shape.

Medium: A person serving or conceived as serving as an instrument for the manifestation of another personality or for some sort of supernatural agency. A person thought to have the power to communicate with agents of another world or dimension.

Nabuksan: The Tagalog term for the opening to the spirit that takes place in mediums in training.

Nagcoralan: A small village in rural Nueva Ecija that was the birthplace of Alex Orbito.

Nocebo: A term used to describe the negative potential of the placebo.

Orbito, Alex: World renowned Filipino psychic surgeon and founder and Director of the Philippine Healer's Circle and the Philippine Spiritual Help Foundation.

Pajarillo, Benjamin: General Director of Mediums of the Christian Spiritists of the Philippines, psychic surgeon, and Christian mediumship trainer.

Pentecost: The seventh Sunday after Easter. The descent of the Holy Spirit upon the Apostles as recorded in the second chapter of Acts in the New Testament.

Perispirit: A Kardecist term that describes the semi-material envelope of a spirit. The perispirit is believed to be the means through which a spirit connects itself to the bodies of living mediums prior to the intervention of the spirit.

Philippine Healer's Circle: An organization founded by Alex Orbito to consolidate the efforts of the Filipino healers and psychic surgeons towards the common goal of international recognition and acceptance of spiritual healing.

Placebo, Active: A placebo that has both characteristic physiological effects attributed to the drug and effects resulting from nonspecific or incidental factors unrelated to the proven effects of the active drug.

Placebo, Effect: a mysterious process in which psychological factors such as belief and expectation trigger a healing response that can be as powerful as any conventional therapy. This includes therapies involving drugs, surgery, or psychotherapy.

Placebo, Passive: A substance containing no medication and prescribed or given to reinforce a patient's expectation to get well.

Placebo Surgery: A placebo effect that takes place as a result of patient's belief that a surgical operation has taken place.

Protector: A term used by Allan Kardec to describe a wise trustworthy spirit of high degree. The Protector is also regarded as being sufficiently elevated and powerful to ensure protection against unevolved spirits within the context of mediumistic activities.

Psychographic (Writing) Medium: A medium who produces scripts believed to originate from agents of the world or dimension where spirits reside.

Psychokinesis: A direct influence exerted on a physical system by a person without the use of any known physical instruments or intermediating forms of physical energy.

Psychoneuroimmunology: A field of scientific inquiry that researches the pathways by which mind, brain, and immune system interact in producing disease or well being.

Rapping, Spirit: A spiritualist term used to describe the mysterious noises made by the spirits to communicate with the living.

Seance: A meeting of spiritualists seeking to receive communication from spirits.

Shamanism: The animistic religion of tribal peoples in which mediation between the visible and spirit worlds is effected by shamans. While the term shaman has its roots among the peoples of Northern Asia, it is currently used to describe similar religious practices of tribal peoples throughout the world.

Sherman, Harold: The author commissioned by Henry Belk to write the book, *Wonder Healers of the Philippines*.

Sin, Cardinal Jaime: The Cardinal of the Roman Catholic Church of the Philippines.

Sison, Josephine: A famous Filipino Christian Spiritist healer renowned for her ability to heal with a unique form of psychic surgery. In her healing work, Sison used cotton wool which she apparently materialized and dematerialize into and out of the bodies of her patients to absorb and remove the health related problems of her patients.

Sleight-of-Hand: A trick or set of tricks performed by a magician so quickly that the manner of execution cannot be observed or detected.

Sleight-of-Hand Psychic Surgery: A form of psychic surgery that utilizes the techniques of sleight-of-hand to produce a metaphor of a surgical operation.

Spirit Directed Chemotherapy: A term I use to describe the ability of the Brazilian psychic surgeon Arigo to prescribe specific pharmaceutical drugs for the treatment of cancer while under the mediumistic direction of the spirit he referred to as Dr. Fritz.

Spirit Directed Healing: Healing that takes place as a result of the intervention of elevated spiritual forces through spiritually evolved human beings possessing the will to help others and mediumistic abilities.

Spirit-Directed Psychic Surgery: A paranormal intervention in which the body is opened with bare hands and diseased objects removed by mediumistic spiritual healers while under the influence of highly evolved benevolent spirits.

Spirit of Truth: A term used by Jesus to describe the Holy Spirit.

Spiritual Messengers of Christ: A Christian Spiritist term for the elevated spirits who are the ministers of Jesus Christ. They are also believed to be the spirits who direct and govern the unrefined spirits. The administrative spirits in charge of planning who are chosen to fulfill the will of God. The group of spirits who contacted the Filipino Christian

Glossary

Spiritists in middle of the nineteenth century and directed the evolution of the Filipino Christian Spiritist community from its inception on into the present day.

Spiritualism: The belief or doctrine that the spirits of the dead, surviving after the mortal life, can and do communicate with the living through a person (a medium) particularly susceptible to their influence. A philosophy, doctrine, or religion emphasizing the spiritual aspect of being.

Split/Level Theology: A term used by Filipino anthropologists to describe a theology in which monotheism and animism are not seen as being in conflict. This split/level theology is common among Filipinos.

Suggestive Therapeutics: The term for any form of therapeutic intervention that directly or indirectly involves the power of suggestion.

Tallmadge, Nathaniel: Former senator and Governor of Wisconsin who delivered the spiritualist petition to the U.S. Congress in April of 1854.

Terte, Eleuterio: Reputed to be the first of the modern Christian Spiritists to practice psychic surgery. Terte founded the Christian Spiritists of the Philippines to preserve the original intent of the Christian Spiritist community.

Therapeutic Touch: A healing technique developed by Dolores Kreiger Ph.d.. In this technique which is an innovation on healing by laying on of hands, the healing energy is directed into the patient's body through the hands which are held a short distance from the patient's body.

Third Dispensation: The dispensation of the Holy Spirit which is believed to have commenced at the Pentecost and is now in progress. A divinely revealed religious system that expresses the particular form of worship and spiritual communion most beneficial to the work of the Holy Spirit.

Trance: A sleep like condition which enables the subject's body to be used by a discarnate spirit. It is a state which is best achieved in collaboration with a teacher. The depth of unconsciousness reached, and the degree of control varies greatly in individual mediums.

Union Espiritista: The original and oldest Christian Spiritist organization in the Philippines. The Christian Spiritist Union of the Philippines was founded on February 19, 1905 and incorporated January 21, 1909.

Universal Fluid: A term used by spiritualists to describe the pervasive universal element, the elementary principle of all things.

Utilitarian: Pertaining to or consisting in utility. Having regard to utility or usefulness rather than beauty or ornamentality. The utilitarian

INDEX

A

A Memorial,71
Achterberg, Jeanne,176
Acupuncture,5,6,7
Acupuncture, International College of, 7
Alexis, J. Obdell,68
Aloha Aina,3
Alvear, Juan,67,76
American Medical Assoc.,148,149
Angina Pectoris,165,166
Animism,54
Apparatus,90,124
Aquino, Corazon,118,119,122
Aquino, Benigno,118,119,122
Arigo,191,192,193,195
Automatic Writing,128,129,130,131,132

B

Bathala,54
Beecher, Henry Dr.,166
Belk, Henry,191
Benson, Herbert,148
BioKinesiology,5
Bisa,53,55,56,170,171
Blanche, Juan,32,33,197
Body of Christ,61
Brazilian Psychic Surgery,192,195
Brazilian Spiritism,194,195,196
Bucklew, L.W. Dr.,168

C

Castellano, Lita,127
Capron, Eliab,72
Cessationism,
Chesi, Gert,151
Chi,5,6
Chi Kung,5
Chirino, Pedro,54,59,161
Christi, Froilan,30,38,41
Christian Mediumship Training,79,80,127,128,
129,130,131,132,133,135,136
Christian Spiritism,67,75,76,227,228,232
CSPI,126,190
Clairaudience,114
Clairvoyance,114,132,133,134
Cobb, Leonard Dr.,166
Combined fluid,187,188
Conversion Experience,9,150

Concentration, 18
Cousins, Norman, 165, 167
Crame, Camp, 119
Cupping, 33

D

Debunkers, 148
Dead Sea Scrolls, 110
Demetrio, Francisco, 60
Deontological, 169
Dispensationalism, 208, 209, 210, 211, 213

Distant Healing, 19, 198
Doctrina Espiritista, 68
Dossey, Larry Dr., 178, 184
Double Blind, 177, 178

E

EDSA, Miracle at, 122
Enrile, Juan Ponce, 118, 119
Espiritu Santo, 55
Essenes, 20
Exorcism, 53, 54, 55, 56

F

Fox Sisters, 70, 71, 75
Freitas, Jose De, 191
Fritz, Alphonso Dr. 191, 192

G

Gahoy, 52, 53
Gandhi, Mahatma, 121
Gifts of the Spirit, 62
Goodheart, Joseph Dr., 5
Goodwin, James & Jean Drs., 168
Group Confucius, 193
Grunbaum, Adolph, 167
Guinsad, Lino, 85, 86, 113

H

Hahnemann, Samuel, 193, 194
Healing Waters, 39, 41
Healing Missions, 137, 138, 139, 140, 141, 142, 143, 144
Hendrix, Jimi, 3
Holy Spirit, 13, 18, 56, 61, 74, 199, 211, 215, 217, 226, 227, 233
Homeopathy, 193, 194
Hooponopono, 5
Hypnosis, 162

I

Ilocano, 37
Indigenization, 57
Induction of Trance (Influencing) 89, 97, 129
Ingkanto, 53
Injections, Spiritual, 196

Interfaith Spiritual Church,34,35,36,37

J

Jayasuriya, Anton,7
Jesuit,60
Joachim of Fiore,212,213,214,215,216
Jocano, Lando,53

K

Kahunas,5
Kapaahu,6
Kardec, Allan,70,72,73,74,75,185,186,187,188
Kardecist,194
Ke Ola Hou,10,14
Keys of Jesus,103,104,105,106
Kreiger, Dolores,148
Krippner, Stanley,165
Kulam,52,53

L

Living Truth, The Church of,6
Lomi Lomi,5
Lourdes
Lugar, Richard Sen.,118
Lupao, Nueva Ecija,123

M

Magellan,54,55
Magnetic Fluid,30,187
Magnetic Healing, 23
Magnetic Massage,23
Magno, Gary and Terry,147
Mananambal,53,56,57,161
Mangkukulam,53
Marcos, Ferdinand,118,119,120,123
Maria, Brazilian Psychic surgeon,192,195
Maui,44,45,46
Materialization & Dematerialization,197,198
McGill, Ormond
Meditation,16,34
Medium,75,76,113,114,232
Mediums, The Book of,73
Milan, Edict of
Meek, George,165,167
Minutes of Union,81,86,87,88,89,110
Monotheism,54

N

Nabuksan,128
Nagcoralan,42,43
Nag Hammadi Texts,110
Neuropeptide T,172
New Covenant,117
New Jerusalem,133,136

Index

New Testament,115
Nocebo,167,171
Noetic Sciences, Institute of,165
Nonlocal,257,258,259

O

O'Regan, Brendan,165,166,168,169
Ohana,3
Old Testament,217
Olmstead, Mark,7,8,9,10,11,12,14,15,16,17,
18,19,23,29,31,37,39,41,44,150
Orbito, Alex,9-26,34,37,41-46,151
Orbito, Marcos,34
Ordo Novus,213,216
Ormond, Ron

P

Pajarillo, Benjamin,113,114,115,123-141,144,157,158,160
Pangasinan,37
Parapsychology,151,152,153
Paul, Apostle,63,64
Pentecost,62,117,187
Pentecostals,51
People Power Revolution,118,119,120,121,122,123
Perispirit,186,188
Pert, Candace,172
Pharisee
Philippine Healer's Circle,26,31
Photovoltaics,4
Placebo, Active,170
Placebo Effect,162,167,171,173
Placebo Surgery,165,166
Plainemason, Madame,72
Pope Paul VI,58
Prayer,16,34
Premillennial 209, 210, 241
Postmillennial 209, 210, 241
Psychic Surgery,7,8,16,17,18,19,153,156,157,158
Psychographic (Writing) medium,132
Psychokinesis,176,177
Psychoneuroimmunology,172
Puharich, Andrija,191,192
Pulos, Lee Dr.,192

Q

Quezon City,77

R

Rainbow Bridge,3
Ramos, Cypriano,79,80,81,85
Ramos, Fidel,118,119
RAM (Reform Army Movement),119
Randi, James,148,149,193
Rapping, Spirit,70

Revolution of 1896,67,68
Rivail,70,72,73,74,75,185,186,187,188
Ross, Sherman, Dr., 168
Rossi, Earnest L.,172,174,175

S

Sacred Caves of Espiritistas,34,38,39,40,41,42
Scripps Research Foundation,171
Sanctuary,229,230,231
Seance,70
Sepulveda, Siegfreid,86,87,88
Shamanism,52,53,54,55,56,57,59,60,62,63
Sherman, Harold,183
Shiatsu,5
Shields, Sen.James,72
Simeona, Moornah,11
Simon Peter,117
Sin, Cardinal Jaime,119,122
Sison, Josephine,197,198
Sleight-of-hand, Therapeutic,160,161,162
Sleight-of-hand psychic surgery,157,158,159,160,162
Solfvin, Jerry,178
Spirit Directed Chemotherapy,192
Spirit directed healing,186,187
Spirit Directed Psychic Surgery,188
Spirit of Truth,61,72,116
Spiritism, Gospel As Interpreted by,73
Spiritist Banners,30,41,91,119
Spirits of Light,78
Spirits, The Book of,73
Spiritual Messengers of Christ,87,88,90
Spiritualism,70,71,74,75
Split/Level Theology,54
Suggestive Therapeutics,162

T

Tai Chi Chuan,5
Tallmadge, Nathaniel,72
Terrestrial Fluid,187
Terte, Eleuterio,126,189,190
Therapeutic Touch,148
Third Dispensation,210,211,213,214,215,216
Toronto Blessing
Touch for Health,5
Trance,59

U

Union Espiritista,68,77,78,80
Unsolved Mysteries,147
Universal Fluid,186
Utilitarian,169

V

Ver, Fabian,120

Index

Veritas, Radio,119
Viri Spirituales,213
Vogel, Dr. Albert,168

W

Witchcraft,53,54,55
Worship In Spirit and Truth,61,219,220,221,222,225,233

X
Y
Z

Permissions Page

I want to thank the following for allowing me to use excerpts from their published works:

1) George Meek-Healers and the Healing Process

2) Earnest L. Rossi-The Psychobiology of Mind/Body Healing-WW Norton & Co. New York

3) Shirley Maclaine-Going Within-Bantam Doubleday Dell-New York

4) Institute of Noetic Sciences-Investigations-Brendan O'Regan & Thomas J. Hurley-

5) Marvin W. Meyer-The Secret Teachings of Jesus-Four Gnostic Gospels-Random House-New York

6) Larry Dossey-Healing Words-The Power of Prayer and the Practice of Medicine-Harper San Francisco

7) Richard Wilhelm-I Ching-Princeton University Press

8) Bernard McGinn-The Calabrian Abbot-Joachim of Fiore in the History of Western Thought-MacMillan-New York

Bibliography

1. Achterberg, Jeanne-Imagery in Healing, Shamanism & Modern Medicine-Shambala Publications-Boston-1985

2. Ader, R (Ed.)-Psychoneuroimmunology-Academic Press,New York-1981

3. Alvear, Juan (pen name J. Obdell Alexis)- A Short Spiritist Doctrine-Privately Published-San Fabian, Pangasinan,Philippines-1909

4. American Medical Association News (article)-Psychic Surgeon Branded a Quack by Cure-Seekers-11/6/67

5. American Medical Association News- (article) Psychic Surgeon Flees to Philippines-2/10/69

6. Anima, Nid-Witchcraft Filipino Style-OMAR Publications-1978

7. Beltran, Benigno P.SVD-The Christology of the Inarticulate-Divine Word Publications-Manila, Philippines-1987

8. Blonston, Gary- Healer Treats first Patients Secretly (article)-Detroit Free Press- 10/8/67

9. Blonston, Gary- Healer's Pilgrims Show Gain (article)- Detroit Free Press- 10/10/67

10. Borkan, Lois- Dr. Tony, Manila's Psychic Surgeon(article)- Fate Magazine- pp. 42-12/66

11. Boyer, Paul-When Time Shall Be No More,Prophesy Belief in Modern American Culture- Harvard University Press- 1995

12. Brennan, Barbara Ann- Hands of Light,A Guide to Healing Through the Human Energy Field- Bantam-New York-1988

13. Brenneman,R.J.-Psychic Surgeon 'Brother Joe' Jailed by California Judge after State Investigation (article)- Skeptical Inquirer- 1989

14. Brown, Slater- The Heyday of Spiritualism-Pocket Book Edition-Simon and Schuster-1972

15. Bulatao, Jaime C. SJ- Organismic Involvement in an Image World and Folklore- Chapter 19 in Dialogue for Development-Francisco R. Demetrio SJ (Editor)- Xavier University- Cagayan de Oro City, Philippines- 1975

16. Bulatao, Jaime C. SJ- When Roman Theology Meets an Animistic

Culture(article)- Kinaadman,A Journal of the Southern Philippines- Volume VI, no.1- 1984

17. Bulatao, Jaime C. SJ- Phenomenon and Their Interpretation- Ateneo de Manila University Press-Manila, Philippines-1992

18. Carollo, R- Psychic Surgery, Defended by Some, Scorned by Doctors (article)-Spokane Chronicle-2/5/89

19. Casalinda-The Philippine Chronicles of Fray San Antonio-published jointly by-The Historical Conservation Society of the Philippines/ Casalinda/The Franciscan Fathers-1977

20. Chesi, Gert- Faith Healers in the Philippines- Perlinger-Austria- 1981

21. Collage Magazine- Psychic Surgery, Fraud or Phenomenon (article)- San Jose,CA-8/79

22. Cousins, Norman- The Mysterious Placebo (article)- Saturday Review- pp.9-16- Oct. 1977

23. Cousins, Norman- Anatomy of an Illness,As Perceived by the Patient- W.W. Norton- New York-1979

24. Cousins, Norman-The Healing Heart- W.W. Norton-New York-1983

25. Demetrio, Francisco R. SJ- On Orasyones, or Magical Prayers and Living Christianity- Department of Philippine Studies- Xavier University- Cagayan de Oro City, Philippines- 12/72

26. Demetrio, Francisco R. SJ- Librito sa Orasyones- Department of Philippine Studies- Xavier University- Cagayan de Oro City, Philippines- 12/72-(A special issue of the MUSAR News for the Philippine Folk Congress)

27. Demetrio, Francisco R. SJ- Towards an Understanding of Philippine Myths (article)- Asian Folklore Studies- Nanzan Institute for Religion and Culture Vol.XXXVII-1-Nagoya, Japan-1978

28. Demetrio, Francisco R. SJ- The Shaman as Psychologist (article)- Asian Folklore Studies- Nanzan Institute for Religion and Culture Vol.XXXVII-1-Nagoya, Japan-1978

29. Demetrio, Francisco R. SJ- Philippine Shamanism and Southeast Asian Parallels (Chapter 19)-Dialogue for Development- Xavier University- Cagayan de Oro City,Philippines-1975

30. Dooley, Anne- Spirit Surgery in Operation, 70 Patients treated in Six Hour Trance Session (article)- Psychic News-London-1/29/66

Bibliography

31. Dooley, Anne-Every Wall a Door: Exploring Psychic Surgery and Healing- Abelard/Schumann-London- 1972

32. Dossey, Larry M.D.- Healing Words, The Power of Prayer and the Practice of Medicine- Harper San Francisco- 1993

33. Dossey, Larry M.D.- Prayer is Good Medicine- Harper San Francisco- 1996

34. Ellerbe, Helen- Dark Side of Christian History- Morningstar Books- 1995

35. Estrada, Honorato A.- Mystic Healing In Pangasinan (article)- Manila Bulletin- 12/2/64

36. Fuller, John G.- Arigo, Surgeon of the Rusty Knife- Thomas J. Crowell Co.-1974

37. Gardner, M- Cruel Deception in the Philippines (article)- Discover Magazine- 8/84

38. Gould, Merle- 1st Rare Pictures of Psychic Surgeons at Work (article)- Cosmic Star, Hollywood CA- 8/65

39. Hoeller, Stephen A.- The Gnostic Jung and the Seven Sermons to the Dead- Theosophical Publishing House-1989

40. Hudson, Thomson J.- Physical Manifestations and the Philosophy of Christ- Hudson-Conan Publishing Co.- 1978

41. Jocano, F. Landa- Folk Medicine in a Philippine Municipality- published by National Museum of the Philippines, Manila- 1973

42. Joy, H. Wendey- Espiritista- New Day Publishers, Quezon City, Philippines- 1982

43. Kardec, Allan- The Spirit's Book- Livraria Allan Kardec Editora (LAKE)- Sao Paulo, Brazil- 1968

44. Kardec, Allan- The Medium's Book- Psychic Press Limited- London- 1971

45. Kardec, Allan- The Gospel According to Allan Kardec-translated from the Spanish edition of the Gospel According to Spiritism by Dr. Francis Harber- Original Publications div. Jamil Products Corporation- New York-1980

46. Kardec, Allan- Spiritualist Initiation- Livraria Allan Kardec Editora (LAKE)- Sao Paolo, Brazil- 1950

47. Karnow, Stanley- In Our Image, America's Empire in the

Philippines- Ballantine Books- New York- 1989

48. Krippner, Stanley Ph.d- Psychic Healing in the Philippines (article)- Journal of Humanistic Psychology, Vol.16 No. 4- Fall 1976

49. Krippner, Stanley and Villoldo, Alberto- The Realms of Healing- Celestial Arts- Berkeley- 1976

50. Lamsa, George M.- The Holy Bible from Ancient Eastern Manuscripts- A.J. Holman Co.- Philadelphia- 1957

51. Licauco, Jaime T.- The Magicians of God, The Amazing Stories of Philippine Faith Healers-National Book Store Inc., Manila, Philippines- 1981

52. Lieban, Richard W.- Cebuano Sorcery, Malign Magic in the Philippines- University of California Press-Berkeley and Los Angeles- 1967

53. Lincoln, P.J. & Wood, N.J.-Psychic Surgery, A Serological Investigation (letter)- Lancet-1979

54. MacLaine, Shirley- Going Within- Bantam Books- 5/89

55. Manila Daily Mirror-Healers, Prophets, or Fakes (article)- Manila, Philippines- 1/12/57

56. Manila Daily Mirror-Boy 4, Turns Faith Healer (article)- Manila, Philippines- 8/5/58

57. Manila Daily Mirror-Philippine Medical Association Poises Ax on Faith Healing (article)-Manila, Philippines- 10/9/59

58. Manila Daily Mirror-Medical Examiners Poise Raps against Faith Healers (article)- Manila, Philippines- 2/19/61

59. Manila Daily Mirror- Faith Healer Denounced (article)- Manila, Philippines- 10/15/63

60. Manila Times- Baclaran Faith Healer Observed (article)- Manila, Philippines- 8/1/56

61. Manila Times- Strange Occurrences Defy Scientific Explanations (article)- Manila, Philip-pines- 12/2/60

62. Manila Times- Faith Healers Display Work (article)- Manila, Philippines- 2/20/61

63. Marasigan, Vicente SJ- A Banahaw Guru,Symbolic Deeds of Agapito Illustrisimo- Ateneo de Manila University Press- Quezon City, Philippines- 1985

64. Maynard, Nettie Colburn- Was Abraham Lincoln a Spiritualist?- Psychic Book Club- London- 1956

65. McGinn, Bernard- The Calabrian Abbot-Joachim of Fiore in the History of Western Thought-Macmillan-New York-1985

66. McGregor, Pedro & Smith, T. Stratton- Jesus of the Spirits- Stein and Day- 1966

67. McLenon, J.- Firewalking and Psychic Surgery: Defining the Paranormal by investigating its Boundaries- Journal of Indian Psychology- 1985

68. Meek, George W.- Healers and the Healing Process- Theosophical Publishing House- 1977

69. Meek, George W.- A Guide to Spiritual and Magnetic Healing and Psychic Surgery in the Philippines- privately printed by Author, 1412 Jackson St. Fort Myers, FL 33901

70. Mercado, Leonardo N. SVD-Elements of Filipino Philosophy- Divine Word University Publications- Tacloban City, Philippines- 1973

71. Mercado, Leonardo N. SVD- Elements of Filipino Theology- Divine Word University Publications- Tacloban City, Philippines-1975

72. Meyer, Marvin W.- The Secret Teachings of Jesus, Four Gnostic Gospels-translated by Author- Random House- New York- 1984

73. National Inquirer- He Operates on Patients without Instruments or Anesthetic (article)- Vol. 41, No.9- 11/6/66

74. National Council Against Health Fraud- NCAHF Statement on Faith Healing and Psychic Surgery (article 2/6/87)- NCAHF Newsletter- 7/8/87

75. Needleman, Jacob- Lost Christianity, A Journey of Rediscovery- Harper and Row- 1985

76. Nolan, Albert OP- Jesus Before Christianity- Claretian Publications- Quezon City, Philippines- 1976

77. Ormond, Ron & McGill, Ormond- Into the Strange Unknown- Esoteric Foundation-1958

78. Ormond, Ron & McGill, Ormond- Amazing Seances in the Philippines (article)- Psychic News-2/17/62

79. O'Regan, Brendan & Hurley, Thomas J. Psychoneuroimmunology: The Birth of a New Field- Investigations- Vol.1 no.2- The Institute of

Noetic Sciences- 1983

80. O'Regan, Brendan & Hurley, Thomas J.- Placebo, The Hidden Asset in Healing- Investigations- The Institute of Noetic Sciences- 1985

81. Patterson, Major T.E.- Spiritual Healing In the Philippines- Chimes Magazine-5/65

82. Philippine Society for Psychical Research Foundation- Faith Healing In the Philippines, Part I Faith Healing and Psychic Surgery, Part II Faith Healing and Psychic Surgery, An Esoteric Version, and Part III Politics and the Paranormal- 1985

83. Psychic News- Camera Records Amazing Spirit Operations (article)- London-10/31/64

84. Psychic News- I Saw Psychic Surgeon remove Tumors without a Knife in painless Spirit Operation says Famous Researcher (article)- London-8/14/65

85. Psychic News- Most Astounding Spirit Pictures (article)- London-9/4/65

86. Psychic News- British Actor Sees Astounding Operations in Philippines (article)- London-4/23/66

87. Psychic News- I Saw Psychic Surgeon use Sleight-of-Hand (article)- London-1/13/68

88. Randi, James- Faith Healers- Prometheus Books- Buffalo, New York- 1987

89. Rogo, D.S. & Bayless, R.-Psychic Surgery- Journal for The Society for Psychical Research- 1968

90. Rossi, Earnest L.- The Psychobiology of Mind/Body Healing:New Concepts of Therapeutic Hypnosis- W.W. Norton and Co. Inc.- New York/London- 1986

91. Ryrie, Charles C.- Dispensationalism- Moody Bible Institute- 1995

92. Sacramento Union- Woman Sentenced for Illegal Practice of Medicine (article)- 9/19/88

93. Scheiber,B- Psychic Surgery Comes to Denver (article)- Rocky Mountain Skeptic-pp.9-10-1986

94. Shorter, Aylward- Jesus and the Witchdoctor- Orbis Books- 1985

95. Silliman, Robert B.- Religious Beliefs and Life at the Beginning of the Spanish Regime in the Philippines- College of Theology, Silliman

University- Dumaguete City, Philippines- 1964

96. Sitter, A.J.- Bleeding them Dry (article)- Arizona Republic- 8/13/86

97. Sherman, Harold- Wonder Healers of the Philippines- DeVorss- Los Angeles- 1967

98. Slate, B. Ann- My Daughter's Surgery by Filipino Spiritism (article)- Fate Magazine- 3/66

99. Star, The- Andy Kaufman's Final Bizarre Bid to Beat Cancer with Psychic Surgery (article)- 6/5/84

100. Steinecke, Joyce- Filipino Hand Surgeon Startles Audience (article)- Palm Beach Post- 3/11/67

101. St. Clair, David- Psychic Healers- Doubleday- 1974

102. Tao Video Productions- Psychic Surgeon of the Philippines, Reverend Alex L. Orbito- videotape- 1985

103. Taylor, Eldon Phd- Wellness: Just a State of Mind? Publisher's Press- Salt Lake City, Utah- 1992

104. Valentine, Tom- Psychic Surgeon is Real! Philippine's famed Dr. Tony Performs some Remarkable Feats (Part 1)-National Tattler- 8/20/72

105. Valentine, Tom- Healers Inconsistent Methods Spark Controversy Over Psychic Surgery (Part 2)- National Tattler- 8/27/72

106. Valentine, Tom- Psychic Surgery- Henry Regnery- Chicago- 1973

107. Vesme, Caesar de-Experimental Spiritualism, Vol.2 of Peoples of Antiquity- Rider and Co.-1931

108. Watson, Lyall- The Romeo Error- Anchor/Doubleday- New York-

Illustrations Credits

1) Alex Orbito operates on Mark's shoulder in the Philippines.- page.12

2) Alex Orbito arrives in Hawai'i.- page 15

3) The front gate at Alex Orbito's Healing Center.- page 22

4) Alex prays, and concentrates to God.- page 24

5) Japanese patients prepare for healing.- page 25

6) Interfaith Church- page 34

7) Healer gives spiritual injection to young girl.- page 35

8) Charging water with magnetic fluid.- page 36

9) The rock formation at the entrance to the cave called "the cave of the elephant" by the Espiritistas.

10) Alex Orbito meditates shortly after we enter the cave.- page 39

11) Alex Orbito prays, asking for protection and guidance before we proceed deeper into the cave.- page 40

12) I receive a blessing from Alex Orbito in a subterranean pool called "the healing waters"- page 41

13) Cultivating rice in Nueva Ecija.-page 42

14) Water buffaloes rest after a hard days work.- page 43

15) Planting rice in the terraced paddies of the Cordillera mountains.- page 52

16) The Spanish dealt harshly with those who disagreed with them.- (The Execution of the Inca)-(LIBRARY OF CONGRESS) page 56

17) Jesus confronts demon possessed man at Gadara.- page 57

18) Jesus exorcizes demons into a herd of pigs.- page 58

19) The Bishop of Barcelona ordered that Spiritist books be confiscated and burned. (Book Burning)- (LIBRARY OF CONGRESS) page 67

20) The first textbook of the Union Espiritista.- page 69

21) Margaretta and Kate Fox.- (LIBRARY OF CONGRESS) page 71

22) Allan Kardec- (LIBRARY OF CONGRESS) page 73

23) The Constitution of the Union Espiritista.- page 78

24) The Corporate Minutes of the Union Espiritista (1919-1933)- page 84

25) The Cross at EDSA. page 121

26) Director of Mediums opens Spiritual Service.- page 123

27) Director of Mediums induces trance in young medium.- page 128

28) Induction of trance is complete,- page 129

29) The Blessed Spirit delivers sermon through medium.- page 130

30) Blessed Spirit delivers sermon through Reverend Pajarillo.- page 131

31) Scribes record the revelations received from the Holy Spirit.- page 132

32) Healers concentrate to God in preparation for Healing Session.- page 133

33) The Holy Spirit descends upon the Healers.- page 134

34) Young healers prepare to dispense Magnetic Fluid.- page 135

35) Young healers proceed to heal elderly woman.- page 136

36) Healer gives spiritual injection.- page 137

37) Young couple come to spiritual service for marital counseling and healers hold an open Bible over them as minister asks God to resolve their dilemma.- page 138

38) Couple receives magnetic healing from spirit-filled healers.- page 139

39) Reverend Pajarillo prepares to baptise new converts the morning after the spiritual service.- page 140

40) New converts are baptised in the Pacific ocean.- page 142

41) Reverend Pajarillo and Reverend Esther Bacani bid me farewell.- page 143

42) Constantine merged Church and State into a theocratic war machine. (Constantine I on horse)-(BETTMAN ARCHIVE) (SF1355)- page 226

43) The Holy Trinity of State sponsered Christianity. (Trinity)-(LIBRARY OF CONGRESS)- page 227

44) From the "Golden Rule" to the "Law of the Jungle" (Auto-da-fe)-(LIBRARY OF CONGRESS)- page 228

Unless otherwise indicated, all illustrations in this book are the property of Harvey J. Martin.

Order Form

Postal orders: Metamind Enterprises, POB 15548, Savannah, GA 31416 USA

Fax orders: (912) 598-4900

Credit Card orders: Order *ONLINE* from Metamind Publications!
www.Metamind.net or www.AramaicBibleCenter.com
(Have your Visa or MasterCard Handy)
ready) Email Comments to: metamind@bellsouth.net
Special Services: 912.598.9650

Please send _____ copy/copies of:

The Secret Teachings of the Espiritistas
By Harvey Martin

$24.95 each _____
Ga. residents add 6.5% ($1.62 ea.) _____
Book Rate: $2.25 for 1st book, $1.00 each add'l _____
Air Mail: $3.95 per book _____
(Surface shipping may take three to five weeks)

TOTAL _____

Send to:
Company name:_____
Name: _____
Address: _____
City:_____ State:___ Zip: _____-_____
Fax number: _____
E-mail _____

Payment:
Cheque__ , Money order__
Credit Card: VISA__ , Master Card__ ,

Card Number_____
Name on card:_____ Exp. date:____ /____

Please send the *Healer's Internet Resources* report to me FREE with my order: yes____ no____

Order Form

Postal orders: Metamind Enterprises, POB 15548, Savannah, GA 31416 USA

Fax orders: (912) 598-4900

Credit Card orders: (ready)

Order *ONLINE* from Metamind Publications!
www.Metamind.net or www.AramaicBibleCenter.com
(Have your Visa or MasterCard Handy)
Email Comments to: metamind@bellsouth.net
Special Services: 912.598.9650

Please send _____ copy/copies of:

THE SECRET TEACHINGS OF THE ESPIRITISTAS
By Harvey Martin

$24.95 each   _____
Ga. residents add 6.5% ($1.62 ea.)   _____
Book Rate: $2.25 for 1st book, $1.00 each add'l   _____
Air Mail: $3.95 per book   _____
(Surface shipping may take three to five weeks)

                                                        TOTAL _____

Send to:
Company name:_____
Name: _____
Address: _____
City:_____ State:___ Zip: _____-_____
Fax number: _____
E-mail _____

Payment:
Cheque__ , Money order__
Credit Card: VISA__ , Master Card__ ,

Card Number_____
Name on card:_____Exp. date:____/____

Please send the *Healer's Internet Resources* report to me FREE with my order: yes____ no____

Centro General
Octava

Presidente P. Andrade   No. 7   Medium Ma Crespo
Secret. J. Andrade   M. Canosito y J. Canosito(?)

En Manila en el Centro La Constancia á 9 de Noviembre de 1919 siendo á las 11 a.m. reunido los presentes y despues de la invocacion de costumbre, ~~se comunicó~~

Esp. Tienes consultas?
Pres. Si querido protector, por orden recibida del protector en la noche del Jueves ultimo estando en sesion obligó á la medium vidente Telesfora que acudiese á este Centro General hoy.
Esp. Que ha dicho tus instrucciones?
Pres. No señor solamente dijo que se presente, si quereis vos esta afuera esperan
Esp. Que entre.
Pres. Presenta esta la hermana.
Esp. Si ella ve los espiritus.
Telas. Si señor.
Esp. Como te presenta?
Telas. Veo á ver al Maestro con una tunica blanca muy clara.
Esp. Y los otros espiritus?
Telas. Veo á Maria con traje color ceniza á Miguel con traje de guerrero y á Rafael con un rayado muy largo y con ella un pescado.
Esp. ¿ Y á la Luz ?
Telas. Y á la luz veo señor un rayo brillante que viene sobre el aparato
Esp. Bien ¿ cuando veis espiritus inferiores que haceis?
Telas. Ruego a Dios que les de la luz necesaria ó enseño tambien á nuestro capitan San Miguel para que nos alige y mande á correspondientes sitio
Esp. Bien, ahora para alejarles?
Telas. Señor primero pido perdon de mis faltas y despues pedir luz de Dios para todos aquellos pobres hermanos, y yo asi comprendo señor.
Esp. Bien, cuando celebrais sesiones en tu casa por consultas procura hacerlo mas recogimiento, dentro en una habitacion y no en un sitio donde pasan todos.
Telas. Si señor asi lo haré, puedo marcharme ya Señor.
Esp. Si. Y tu tambien Andrade en las consultas familiares, no es propio

Centro General
Octava

Presidente P. Andrade   No. 1   Medium Mn. Crespo
Secret. J. Andrade   M. Candito y J. Gonzalez.

En Manila en el Centro La Constancia á 9 de Noviembre de 1919 siendo á las 11. a.m. reunido los presentes y después de la invocación de costumbre, se comunicó

Esp. Tienes compañeros?
Pres. Si querido protector, por orden recibida del protector en la noche del Jueves último estando en sesión obligó á la medium vidente Telesfora que acudiese á este Centro General hoy.
Esp. Que ha dicho tus instrucciones?
Pres. No señor, solamente dijo que se presente, si quereis vos estar afuera esperar
Esp. Que entre.
Pres. Presenta está la hermana.
Esp. Si ella ve los espíritus.
Teles. Si señor.
Esp. Como te presentas?
Teles. Veo á vos al Maestro con una túnica blanca muy clara.
Esp. Y los otros espíritus?
Teles. Veo á Maria con traje color ceniza, á Miguel en traje de guerrero y á Rafael con un rayado muy largo y con ella un pescado.
Esp. ¿ Y á la Luz ?
Teles. Y á la luz veo señor un rayo brillante que viene sobre el aparato
Esp. Bien ¿ cuando ves espiritus inferiores que haces?
Teles. Ruego á Dios que les dé la luz necesaria é invoco también á nuestro capitan San Miguel para que nos alije y mande á correspondiente sitio
Esp. Bien, ahora para alejarte?
Teles. Señor primero pido perdón de mis faltas y después pedir luz al Padre para todos aquellos pobres hermanos, y yo así comprendo señor.
Esp. Bien, cuando celebres sesiones en tu casa por consultas procura hacerlo mas recogimiento hasta en una habitación y no en un sitio donde sean todos.
Teles. Si señor así lo haré. puedo marcharme ya Señor.
Esp. Si. Y tu también Andrade en las consultas familiares, no es propio